Developing Nonprofit Human Service Leaders

Developing Nonprofit and Human Service Leaders

Essential Knowledge and Skills

Larry D. Watson
The University of Texas at Arlington

Richard A. Hoefer
The University of Texas at Arlington

Los Angeles | London | New Delhi
Singapore | Washington DC

Los Angeles | London | New Delhi
Singapore | Washington DC

FOR INFORMATION:

SAGE Publications, Inc.
2455 Teller Road
Thousand Oaks, California 91320
E-mail: order@sagepub.com

SAGE Publications Ltd.
1 Oliver's Yard
55 City Road
London EC1Y 1SP
United Kingdom

SAGE Publications India Pvt. Ltd.
B 1/I 1 Mohan Cooperative Industrial Area
Mathura Road, New Delhi 110 044
India

SAGE Publications Asia-Pacific Pte. Ltd.
3 Church Street
#10-04 Samsung Hub
Singapore 049483

Acquisitions Editor: Kassie Graves
Managing Editor: Catherine Forrest
Editorial Assistant: Elizabeth Luizzi
Production Editor: David C. Felts
Copy Editor: Matt Sullivan
Typesetter: C&M Digitals (P) Ltd.
Proofreader: Sally Jaskold
Indexer: Judy Hunt
Cover Designer: Michael Dubowe
Marketing Manager: Shari Countryman

Printed in the United States of America.

Library of Congress Cataloging-in-Publication Data

Watson, Larry D. (Larry Dan)

Developing nonprofit and human service leaders : essential knowledge and skills / Larry D. Watson, Richard Hoefer.

pages cm
Includes index.

ISBN 978-1-4522-9152-9

1. Nonprofit organizations—Management. 2. Social work administration. 3. Leadership. I. Hoefer, Richard. II. Title.

HD62.6.W37 2014
658.4'092—dc23   2013027425

This book is printed on acid-free paper.

13 14 15 16 17 10 9 8 7 6 5 4 3 2 1

Contents

Preface

Austin and Kruzich (2004) noted a number of shortcomings when they reviewed 11 human services administration textbooks a decade ago. They stated that emphasizing content over application or skill building was done in almost all texts; learning through case-based and problem-centered exercises was minimal; transmitting content was seen as more important than providing learning strategies for content integration; describing managerial practice was done in the absence of social environment theory; and developing textbooks was done without reviewing empirical research on what managerial practice is. This set of five interpretations represents a powerful indictment of the texts available at the time, most of which still exist in updated editions that have not been radically revised to meet the challenge of contemporary human service and nonprofit leadership. Other texts have been developed, but they have not heeded the lessons that Austin and Kruzich described, nor the similar issues found by Au (1994) a decade earlier.

We have built this book from the ground up, making three decisions that we believe make this text particularly compelling for contemporary nonprofit and human services administration and leadership courses, generalist macro practice courses desiring a concise book to cover essential topics in administration and leadership within human services, as well as practitioners looking for an accessible overview of essential knowledge combined with exercises that can be done on their own or in groups at the office.

DECISION 1: FOCUS ON DEVELOPING PRACTICE SKILLS AS MUCH AS SUBSTANTIVE CONTENT

Our first decision to develop a "better book" was to focus as much on the development of practice skills as on substantive content. Each chapter contains at least three hands-on experiential exercises (including a substantial in-basket case exercise) and three additional assignments. The exercises are designed to provide opportunities for readers to apply the substantive information in the chapter and to better internalize what the ideas mean in practice.

Most other administration texts in nonprofit studies and human services programs have discussion questions in them. We do not. Students and readers generate *their own* discussion questions when they are faced with *applying* concepts in addition to *reading* about them. The addition of these exercises (which include activities, small-group or paired discussion, responding to YouTube videos, and other approaches to application) marks this book as substantially different from other texts in the field. It places students in the center of learning, allowing the instructor to "flip the classroom," if that is desired. Students are more likely to come to class prepared to interact with each other and the concepts, rather than waiting to be told what is in the chapter when they know that they will be called on to apply the ideas in class. Having exercises ready to use encourages students to come prepared.

In our book, both substantive content and skill development are central.

DECISION 2: CONNECT *ALL* CHAPTERS TO SKILL DEVELOPMENT

Almost all textbooks about nonprofit and human services leadership recognize the importance of context. These other books tend to take an expository view of the topics of sector history, values and ethics, and administrative and organizational theories. Our second major decision as we wrote this book was to see these topics as areas ripe for skill development, just as much as the more traditional "skills" areas such as planning, evaluation, fund development, and so on. We believe, for example, that administrators must be able to look outside of their organization to discover the larger picture of the contemporary political, economic, and social environment whenever needed. While we describe our ideas on key current trends, others (including students and practitioners reading this book) will have access to different pockets of information and will perhaps focus on entirely different trends that make a difference to them. Thus, learning to find their own context is important to nonprofit and human service leaders.

We also emphasize applying values and ethics in practice situations and the importance of understanding administrative and organizational theory *in situ*. Too often, the obligatory chapters on "ethics" and "theory" are merely skimmed and forgotten, instead of being seen as unique sets of tools to help lead to understanding and action. Ethics must underlie administrators' behavior, or else the scandals that have harmed the reputations of many organizations will continue to erode public trust in the nonprofit sector as a whole. Theory points the way, in many cases, to solutions to dilemmas about how leaders in nonprofits should act. But if none of these foundational topics are seen as skill related, their worth is left untapped.

In our book, everything is connected to knowledge and skills that can be improved.

DECISION 3: USE A COMPREHENSIVE CONCEPTUAL OVERVIEW

Our third decision in designing this book that separates it from many others is to use a comprehensive conceptual overview of human service administration. This overview is based on original work by Schmid, but was expanded and linked with skills and theories by Hoefer (2010). Described in Chapter 4, the conceptual overview places administrative skills into four quadrants derived from two continua: task vs. people orientation and internal vs. external orientation. While ethics surrounds and underlies the use of all administrative skills, other skills that are in the literature can be placed (more or less) neatly into one of the four resulting quadrants: internal and task orientation (Quadrant I); internal and people orientation (Quadrant II); external and task orientation (Quadrant III); or external and people orientation (Quadrant IV).

We believe the use of a conceptual approach such as this is quite beneficial. First, as the model is empirically tested as having validity, it comports with the reality seen by nonprofit managers, administrators, and leaders. Giving readers a peek at the overall field in this way provides scaffolding for their learning specific knowledge and skills. What they learn from this text, its exercises, and its assignments can be put into a framework to be filled in with additional knowledge and experiences they claim from other sources.

The four quadrants based on two continua are ideal for mapping administrative skills to the different quadrants. While there is perhaps some debate over which list of skills for nonprofit leaders is most useful (Hoefer, 2003; Menefee, 2000; Wimpfheimer, 2004), Hoefer (2010) has used three skills lists and mapped the skills to this four-quadrant conceptual overview. In this book, we have chosen skills from each of the quadrants to provide coverage of essential skills from all aspects of the nonprofit administrator's world.

In our book, all the pieces (skills) can be linked into a conceptual framework.

WHO IS THIS BOOK FOR?

This book is not for everyone. It has two primary audiences that we feel will be well served by the approach we take and the elements we have included.

The first audience we see comprises instructors (and their students) who want a nonprofit leadership or human services administration text that provides essential information in a concise format. Not everyone needs or wants a full-scale, comprehensive, all-in-one text. This may be because some are teaching on a quarter system, have only a portion of a semester to devote to administration and leadership, or have other materials that cover other topics in a longer course. We know that other highly targeted books have found a home in nonprofit education circles and believe this book will fill a similar gap for similar reasons.

The second audience is anyone seeking a text that connects experiential learning exercises, case studies, and carefully crafted assignments with essential substantive information. This second audience may overlap considerably with the first but also expands beyond it. We know that adult learners seek to learn from experience and practice as well as from reading. We also know that one of the main issues in human services administration is that good clinicians are promoted to supervisory (and higher) positions without having the opportunity to receive training or education in management or leadership skills. With both audiences, having a text that combines exercises with substantive information accelerates learning and retention of knowledge.

The exercises in this book, when combined with the essential ideas and facts around each topic, assist readers as they grapple with the ideas and skills needed for nonprofit leadership. If we can help students and current practitioners develop more skills through cases, assignments, and exercises, these ideas and skills will be more quickly integrated into practice, and at a higher level of achievement. Armed with a conceptual view of the roles of nonprofit leaders and a larger repertoire of skills, we may anticipate larger cohorts of new nonprofit leaders sticking within the field for a longer career. Ultimately, this can lead to better outcomes for service recipients.

A NOTE ABOUT EPAS

If you are a social work educator, you already know about the Council on Social Work Education's Educational Policy Accreditation Standards (EPAS) and the need to link coursework to achieving competencies for social work graduates. This book has been designed to assist you in meeting those standards. Each educational policy is listed below, and the sections or elements of this book that apply are described afterward.

Educational Policy 2.1.1—Identify as a professional social worker and conduct oneself accordingly. Social workers serve as representatives of the profession, its mission, and its core values. They know the profession's history. Social workers commit themselves to the profession's enhancement and to their own professional conduct and growth. Social workers

- advocate for client access to the services of social work;
- practice personal reflection and self-correction to assure continual professional development;
- attend to professional roles and boundaries;
- demonstrate professional demeanor in behavior, appearance, and communication;
- engage in career-long learning; and
- use supervision and consultation.

This book provides a thorough grounding in how students may serve as representatives of the profession. Specific topics of the book include social work values and ethics (Chapter 2), advocacy (Chapter 14), and how to work with others to continue learning to be an effective human services administrator (Chapters 5 and 13). The many exercises and assignments throughout the book provide opportunities for readers to practice personal reflection and self-correction as they learn about proper professional roles and boundaries. Material is presented regarding professional behavior, appearance, and communication in the process of communication and persuasion.

Educational Policy 2.1.2—Apply social work ethical principles to guide professional practice. Social workers have an obligation to conduct themselves ethically and to engage in ethical decision making. Social workers are knowledgeable about the value base of the profession, its ethical standards, and relevant law. Social workers

- recognize and manage personal values in a way that allows professional values to guide practice;
- make ethical decisions by applying standards of the National Association of Social Workers Code of Ethics and, as applicable, of the International Federation of Social Workers/International Association of Schools of Social Work Ethics in Social Work, Statement of Principles;
- tolerate ambiguity in resolving ethical conflicts; and
- apply strategies of ethical reasoning to arrive at principled decisions.

Chapter 2 presents a detailed explanation of the values and ethical basis for human services administration and leadership, drawing on the National Association of Social Workers' Code of Ethics. Readers see how to resolve issues and are provided case studies to apply abstract concepts to practice. They learn to tolerate ambiguity as they apply strategies of ethical reasoning to arrive at their decisions.

Educational Policy 2.1.3—Apply critical thinking to inform and communicate professional judgments. Social workers are knowledgeable about the principles of logic, scientific inquiry, and reasoned discernment. They use critical thinking augmented by creativity and curiosity. Critical thinking also requires the synthesis and communication of relevant information. Social workers

- distinguish, appraise, and integrate multiple sources of knowledge, including research-based knowledge and practice wisdom;
- analyze models of assessment, prevention, intervention, and evaluation; and
- demonstrate effective oral and written communication in working with individuals, families, groups, organizations, communities, and colleagues.

The development of critical thinking skills is infused throughout the book by the use of individual assignments and interactive exercises. Some of these outputs are written, while others are oral or even artistic in nature. All aspects of the text are designed to challenge students to read and apply material to encourage their personal growth. Students come away with a greater understanding of professional processes in human services leadership and with the ability to analyze models of program development, evaluation, funding, marketing, and advocacy, among other topics.

Educational Policy 2.1.4—Engage diversity and difference in practice. Social workers understand how diversity characterizes and shapes the human experience and is critical to the formation of identity. The dimensions of diversity are understood as the intersectionality of multiple factors including age, class, color, culture, disability, ethnicity, gender, gender identity and expression, immigration status, political ideology, race, religion, sex, and sexual orientation. Social workers appreciate that, as a consequence of difference, a person's life experiences may include oppression, poverty, marginalization, and alienation as well as privilege, power, and acclaim. Social workers

- recognize the extent to which a culture's structures and values may oppress, marginalize, alienate, or create or enhance privilege and power;
- gain sufficient self-awareness to eliminate the influence of personal biases and values in working with diverse groups;
- recognize and communicate their understanding of the importance of difference in shaping life experiences; and
- view themselves as learners and engage those with whom they work as informants.

The underpinnings of this book are planted in understanding diversity and difference and the ways that leaders and managers must address them in ways that maximize their positive impact. Leaders should strive to be the leaders of everyone in the organization, and the book provides skills to do so, regardless of age, class, color, culture, disability status, ethnicity, gender, gender identity and expressions, immigration status, political ideology, race, religion, sex, or sexual orientation.

Educational Policy 2.1.5—Advance human rights and social and economic justice. Each person, regardless of position in society, has basic human rights, such as freedom, safety, privacy, an adequate standard of living, health care, and education. Social workers recognize the global interconnections of oppression and are knowledgeable about theories of justice and strategies to promote human and civil rights. Social work incorporates social justice practices in organizations, institutions, and society to ensure that these basic human rights are distributed equitably and without prejudice. Social workers

- understand the forms and mechanisms of oppression and discrimination;
- advocate for human rights and social and economic justice; and
- engage in practices that advance social and economic justice.

We believe one of the primary directives of human service and nonprofit leaders is the advancement of human rights and social and economic justice. This is carried out by having knowledge and skills relating to effective administrative practice, which can then be applied to promote services that seek to end oppression and discrimination and to improve the life chances of marginalized populations. The material in Chapter 14 directly relating to advocacy is key to becoming effective in these tasks.

Educational Policy 2.1.6—Engage in research-informed practice and practice-informed research. Social workers use practice experience to inform research, employ evidence-based interventions, evaluate their own practice, and use research findings to improve practice, policy, and social service delivery. Social workers comprehend quantitative and qualitative research and understand scientific and ethical approaches to building knowledge. Social workers

- use practice experience to inform scientific inquiry, and
- use research evidence to inform practice.

Chapter 7 addresses this educational standard directly. It describes the use of logic models and program evaluation to ascertain the effectiveness of programs, interventions, and policies. Linking process and outcome evaluation together with an overview of methods, readers will be able to run programs using research and apply their practice to inform the evaluation questions they ask. Additional information is provided to assist students in evaluating the impact and process of their advocacy efforts (Chapter 14).

Educational Policy 2.1.7—Apply knowledge of human behavior and the social environment. Social workers are knowledgeable about human behavior across the life course, the range of social systems in which people live, and the ways social systems promote or deter people in maintaining or achieving health and well-being. Social workers apply theories and knowledge from the liberal arts to understand biological, social, cultural, psychological, and spiritual development. Social workers

- use conceptual frameworks to guide the processes of assessment, intervention, and evaluation; and
- critique and apply knowledge to understand person and environment.

Leadership and administration are, ultimately, processes designed to change the behavior and thinking of humans. Social workers should understand theories and conceptual frameworks as they look at improving the world at all levels of intervention. Assessment for, intervention by, and evaluation of programs, interventions, and policies requires the ability to understand, critique, and apply knowledge of decision making and other administrative tasks, all of which take place in a dynamic social, economic, and political context. This book provides readers with considerable information, coming from many academic disciplines, relating to human behavior in an organizational and social milieu.

Educational Policy 2.1.8—Engage in policy practice to advance social and economic well-being and to deliver effective social work services. Social work practitioners understand that policy affects service delivery, and they actively engage in policy practice. Social workers know the history and current structures of social policies and services, the role of policy in service delivery, and the role of practice in policy development. Social workers

- analyze, formulate, and advocate for policies that advance social well-being; and
- collaborate with colleagues and clients for effective policy action.

This text combines in one book much of the essential knowledge needed to be effective in effective advocacy and service work service delivery. Leadership, advocacy, personal communication, planning, program evaluation, budgeting, fund development, marketing, and more—all vital topics of nonprofit leaders in the 21st century—are covered.

Educational Policy 2.1.9—Respond to contexts that shape practice. Social workers are informed, resourceful, and proactive in responding to evolving organizational, community, and societal contexts at all levels of practice. Social workers recognize that the context of practice is dynamic, and use knowledge and skill to respond proactively. Social workers

- continuously discover, appraise, and attend to changing locales, populations, scientific and technological developments, and emerging societal trends to provide relevant services; and
- provide leadership in promoting sustainable changes in service delivery and practice to improve the quality of social services.

By providing information related to the context of human services leadership linked to values and ethics of social work, this book is able to show readers how to assess new trends and developments, and to provide leadership across the gamut of human services issues that stand in the way of improving the quality of social services across the United States and internationally.

Educational Policy 2.1.10(a)–(d)—Engage, assess, intervene, and evaluate with individuals, families, groups, organizations, and communities. Professional practice involves the dynamic and interactive processes of engagement, assessment, intervention, and evaluation at multiple levels. Social workers have the knowledge and skills to practice with individuals, families, groups, organizations, and communities. Practice knowledge includes identifying, analyzing, and implementing evidence-based interventions designed to achieve client goals; using research and technological advances; evaluating program outcomes and practice effectiveness; developing, analyzing, advocating, and providing leadership for policies and services; and promoting social and economic justice.

Educational Policy 2.1.10(a)—Engagement

Social workers

- substantively and affectively prepare for action with individuals, families, groups, organizations, and communities;
- use empathy and other interpersonal skills; and
- develop a mutually agreed-on focus of work and desired outcomes.

Educational Policy 2.1.10(b)—Assessment

Social workers

- collect, organize, and interpret client data;
- assess client strengths and limitations;
- develop mutually agreed-on intervention goals and objectives; and
- select appropriate intervention strategies.

Educational Policy 2.1.10(c)—Intervention

Social workers

- initiate actions to achieve organizational goals;
- implement prevention interventions that enhance client capacities;
- help clients resolve problems;
- negotiate, mediate, and advocate for clients; and
- facilitate transitions and endings.

Educational Policy 2.1.10(d)—Evaluation

Social workers critically analyze, monitor, and evaluate interventions.

All of these topics and subtopics are addressed in this book for the specialty area of administrative practice. Readers learn how to engage others, assess agency- and community-level concerns, intervene when problems occur, and evaluate the impacts of programs, interventions, and policies.

The student who completes this book will have an excellent grounding in the 10 competencies required by the Council on Social Work Education, within the context of administration and leadership of human services organizations. An instructor who adopts this book will have a clearly enunciated connection with all of the 10 core competencies of social work administrative practice. The program or school of social work that endorses this book may find the reaffirmation process a bit easier.

BEFORE WE BEGIN

We believe that leadership, administration, and management in the nonprofit and human services arenas depends a great deal on the ability to begin, cultivate, and maintain meaningful personal relationships with those around you. While it may at times be difficult and full of challenges, we know that the satisfactions and joys of the work are abundant as well. We present this book to all of our students—past, present, and future—and to those dedicated nonprofit leaders we have had the pleasure of working with over the years.

REFERENCES

Au, C. (1994). The status of theory and knowledge development in social welfare administration. *Administration in Social Work, 18*(3), 127–157.

Austin, M., & Kruzich, J. (2004). Assessing recent textbooks and casebooks in human services administration. *Administration in Social Work, 28*(1), 115–137.

Hoefer, R. (2003). Administrative skills and degrees: The "best place" debate rages on. *Administration in Social Work, 27*(1), 25–46.

Hoefer, R. (2010). Basic skills of nonprofit leadership. In Agard, K. (Ed.), *Leadership in nonprofit organizations* (pp. 321–328). Thousand Oaks, CA: Sage.

Menefee, D. (2000). What managers do and why they do it. In R. Patti (Ed.), *The handbook of social welfare management* (pp. 247–266). Thousand Oaks, CA: Sage.

Wimpfheimer, S. (2004). Leadership and management competencies defined by practicing social work managers. *Administration in Social Work, 28*(1), 45–56.

Part I

Context

The Context of Nonprofit Administration

INTRODUCTION

The larger context of human services nonprofit administration must be considered before you read chapters on any other topics. By understanding the "big picture," you will be able to fit the individual skills and ideas into a larger framework so that their importance is clearer. Nonprofit agencies of course operate as part of society, and the nature of the broader culture and trends have considerable impact on what individual nonprofit managers and leaders can accomplish and how they go about their work.

The literature is full of information about how nonprofit managers must be aware of, and deal with, changes in their agencies' worlds. Managed care (Jones, 2006; McBeath & Meezan, 2006), an uncertain political and economic climate (Golensky & Mulder, 2006; Hopkins & Hyde, 2002; Schmid, 2004), policy reform (Regehr, Chau, Leslie & Howe, 2002; Reisch & Sommerfeld, 2003), requirements for outcome budgeting (Martin, 2000), and the introduction of performance measurement systems (Zimmermann & Stevens, 2006) are just a few topics affecting human service administrators today.

Although many trends are important, six are described here as having a significant impact on nonprofit administrators. After reading about these trends, you will understand better why specific preparation for being an administrator is important, and working through practical exercises and assignments like those in this book is valuable for your learning process.

COMPETITION FOR RESOURCES IS GREATER

Put simply, nonprofit administrators operate in an environment of increasingly scarce resources and increased competition for those resources. Funding from government at local, state, and federal levels is strained due to political pressure to lower tax rates (or at least keep them steady). Many states and localities have delayed contracted payments to nonprofit organizations for months, causing those nonprofits to face cash-flow problems and undermining the service providers' fiscal health. Some nonprofits have found that getting a government contract causes more harm than benefit because the amount they are paid is lower than the cost of providing the services required to fulfill the terms of the contract.

Getting a contract or grant is more difficult. While numbers fluctuate depending on the source chosen and years of comparison, there is no dispute that the number of nonprofits has grown. According to the prestigious Urban Institute (2012), the number of nonprofits grew by about 25% between 2001 and 2011, from 1,259,764 to 1,574,674. More nonprofits have turned to foundations and government grants for support even as funding from those sources decreased.

Foundation funding has had ups and downs in the past decade, but, even in its good years, increases in this type of philanthropy cannot equal the amount of funding lost at the governmental level. Even individual-level giving has decreased for many non-disaster related human service nonprofits (although some types of nonprofits have seen individual donations increase in recent years). The ability of middle-class, middle-aged donors to give has been impacted by uncertainty over their home's value, their employment situation, and the value of their retirement nest eggs. Increasingly, these families have had increased financial responsibilities toward young adult children and parents with medical and other issues. This "sandwich generation" has been hard-pressed to keep their giving to charity at the same level as in prior years.

MORE SKILLS ARE REQUIRED FOR NONPROFIT ADMINISTRATORS

Challenges are greater now for human service agencies than ever before (Hopkins & Hyde, 2002; Perlmutter, 2006). The range of skills needed to cope with this difficult environment is also greater than what was needed previously (Golensky & Mulder, 2006). Administrators need to be competent not only at internally oriented activities such as budgeting, supervision, and human resources, but also at externally oriented capacities such as advocacy, community collaboration, and fundraising (Alexander, 2000; Golensky & Mulder, 2006; Hoefer, 2003; Hopkins & Hyde, 2002; Menefee, 2000; Menefee & Thompson, 1993). Increasingly, cross-sector partnerships involving the government, business, and nonprofit sectors are used to achieve progress on social issues (Selsky & Parker, 2005). The term *social enterprise* has popped up as a way to incorporate for-profit principles into nonprofit operations. Nonprofit managers must respect and understand how to collaborate with counterparts in other sectors who have different perspectives. The most important skill of all, given the rapidly evolving landscapes of human services, may be the ability to manage change.

WHAT IS SOCIAL ENTERPRISE?

Social enterprises are businesses whose primary purpose is the common good. They use the methods and disciplines of business and the power of the marketplace to advance their social, environmental, and human justice agendas.

Three characteristics distinguish a social enterprise from other types of businesses, nonprofits, and government agencies:

It directly addresses an intractable social need and serves the common good, either through its products and services or through the number of disadvantaged people it employs.

Its commercial activity is a strong revenue driver, whether a significant earned income stream within a nonprofit's mixed revenue portfolio, or a for-profit enterprise.

The common good is its *primary* purpose, literally "baked into" the organization's DNA, and trumping all others.

Source: Social Enterprise Alliance (n.d.).

RESEARCH AND EVIDENCE OF PROGRAM EFFECTIVENESS ARE ESSENTIAL

Evidence-based practice and research/program evaluation are becoming more important to funders and other stakeholders. As the need to compete for resources intensifies, human service agencies must become more effective. One way to accomplish this is to use service technologies that have research to support their claims of helping solve client problems. The movement toward evidence-based practice, while compelling theoretically, may require culture change within agencies (Johnson & Austin, 2006). As difficult as this is to accomplish, some grant-providing agencies, such as the federal Substance Abuse and Mental Health Services Administration (SAMHSA), provide strong incentives and greater funding opportunities for agencies willing to use program models that have been tested empirically and have evidence of effectiveness. Interventions that have received research validation are listed on the National Registry of Evidence-based Programs and Practices (available online at www.nrepp .samhsa.gov). Additional reviews of evidence-based social work practice are located on the website for the Campbell Collaboration (www.campbellcollaboration.org) and elsewhere.

Similarly, research and program evaluation within agencies is usually required as a condition of receiving a grant. Agencies struggle with how to cope with such demands, having neither the staff time nor the knowledge base to analyze data they collect (Stoecker, 2007). Performance measurement, within the context of program evaluation and accountability, is a salient example of the need for additional research skills for nonprofit managers (Zimmermann & Stevens, 2006). Salipante and Aram (2003) argue that nonprofit managers must move beyond being *users* of knowledge to becoming *generators* of knowledge. Education for nonprofit administration should stress the ability to collect, manage, and analyze data to make management decisions.

A CRISIS IN HUMAN SERVICE LEADERSHIP HAS EMERGED

One source of leadership for nonprofit human service administrators has been social workers. Social work education, however, is currently producing fewer administrative practice students (Ezell, Chernesky, & Healy, 2004) than in the past. At the same time, the number of business schools, schools of public administration, and programs in nonprofit management producing graduates, who compete with social workers for administrative jobs, has increased rapidly (Mirabella, 2007; Packard, 2004). Research shows that experienced leaders in nonprofit institutions (whether social workers or not) are leaving the field (Birdsell & Muzzio, 2003; Faffer & Friedland, 2007). Not only are current leaders retiring, but many direct-service human service workers, their supervisors, and even middle-level managers also exhibit little desire to take over top positions within their agencies (Faffer & Friedland, 2007).

Research indicates that social work educators, public administration educators, and current leaders in nonprofit and government organizations agree for the most part on what nonprofit administrators should know how to do (Hoefer, 2003), so the educational background of the administrators may be less important than whether applicants have the actual skills needed to be successful in leading nonprofits. Still, it is unclear whether all of the academic programs put together are graduating sufficient numbers of people (especially people of color and women) with high enough skill levels to fill the leadership gap that is emerging.

DIVERSITY IN THE WORKPLACE IS INCREASING

Considerable attention has been given to the decreasing percentage of people in the United States who are of European ancestry, and to the increasing percentage of people from Hispanic,

African American, and Asian backgrounds. For example, half the growth in the American population from 1990 to 2010 (or 30 million people) was among Hispanics (El Nasser & Overberg, 2011). Hispanics now account for about one in six of all Americans and have had larger numbers than African Americans since 2003. The Asian population doubled between 1990 and 2010 and now makes up nearly 5% of Americans. Of considerable importance over the long term is the increase in the number of people who identify as multi-racial, a category available on the U.S. Census only since 2010 (El Nasser & Overberg, 2011).

This type of diversity, racial and ethnic, is extremely important for the running of nonprofits, particularly in terms of leadership style. But other types of diversity exist as well. Women in 2010 earned more degrees in college and post-graduate work than men (El Nasser & Overberg, 2011), and should be expected to occupy more top leadership positions in the nonprofit sector (and elsewhere). The debates about "male" and "female" styles of leadership have softened over the past few decades, with a consensus emerging that leaders must have a variety of skills, including those skills historically seen as male traits, such as financial savvy, and those traits historically seen as female, such as listening and nurturing.

Human service organization leaders also are challenged to be able to relate to differences between younger workers (Generations X and Y, Millennials, and so on), as well as members of the aging Boomer and Bust generations. This is not only within the organization in terms of supervision and leadership styles, but also among donors. Gay, lesbian, bisexual, and transgendered persons have distinct viewpoints about many human service issues, and their communities often are strong stakeholders of certain types of nonprofits.

This type of discussion often can seem as if diversity were a problem, when in fact, the range of ideas and experiences in the workplace may now be broader than at any other time in history. This is definitely a positive aspect of today's nonprofit workforce! Still, it is an issue that must be addressed and sometimes "managed" so that different stakeholder groups, with their unique perspectives, see value in differences that can sometimes cause misunderstanding or even conflict.

TECHNOLOGY'S IMPACT IS INCREASING

Two or three decades ago, most personal computers in the workplace were in the hands of secretaries so they could more efficiently type correspondence and reports dictated or handwritten by others higher in the hierarchy. Nonprofits rarely had computers, and the most common use in nonprofits was for correspondence or budgeting (Mutschler & Hoefer, 1990). Information was kept in file cabinets on paper records. Client information could be accessed only in person. Information needed for budgeting or financial reports was often meticulously collected shortly after the end of each month.

Currently, nonprofits are highly computerized, with internal networks and high-speed Internet connections. In most agencies, databases keep client records well protected behind significant firewalls. Information is easily accessible to all who have a need to know that information. Administrators can pull up financial information in real time. A great deal more information is available from many sources so that decisions can be made based on current data. Choosing from among hardware options (once easily solved by buying IBM products) has become more challenging as desktops compete with laptops, notebooks, tablets, mini-tablets, and even smartphones. Software may be more standardized with Microsoft Office products, but other options exist as well.

Forms of community outreach have moved from quarterly or annual reports to daily updates on organizational websites. Web 2.0 applications and myriad forms of social media—such as Facebook, blogs, Twitter, and reddit—exist, and nonprofits are often called on to make greater use of them (Edwards & Hoefer, 2010; Kanter & Fine, 2010).

While more information can be beneficial, too little attention has been paid to the potential for information overload and "analysis paralysis" that may occur while waiting for additional data to solve unclear problems. Nonprofit leaders may become less sure of the decisions to make if they cannot learn to change data to information, and information to wisdom.

All of these trends impact the ability of nonprofit leaders to achieve high results. Yet, research tells us it is important for nonprofit administrators to perform well. Poertner's (2006) literature review links higher social administration skills with better client outcomes. Ritchie and Eastwood (2006) show that nonprofits' financial performance is improved if executives have appropriate experience. In short, supervisors, managers, and leaders clearly have tangible and lasting effects on their organizations and, ultimately, clients' lives. A well-led organization will achieve more, and at higher levels, than an organization with poor leadership. It is up to the future leaders themselves to learn and apply the necessary skills to their jobs, but this process can be made easier if supported by well-designed educational programs. We now briefly turn to the purposes of nonprofit management educational programs and their efforts to produce competent professionals.

THE PURPOSES OF NONPROFIT ADMINISTRATION EDUCATION

A process is said to fail when it does not accomplish its purposes. What are (or should be) the goals of an educational program when it comes to human service administration at the master's level? We will consider two of the primary educational routes to becoming a nonprofit leader: the professions of social work and public administration. (While there are schools offering a degree in nonprofit management, these schools do not have a separate accrediting body as do social work and public administration programs.) Interestingly, the accrediting bodies for both these professions have moved toward an educational model of ensuring that students learn professional competencies, so the discussion is similar for both.

The Council on Social Work Education (CSWE, 2007) describes the purposes of social work education as to "prepare competent and effective professionals, to develop social work knowledge, and to provide leadership in the development of service delivery systems." The National Association of Schools of Public Affairs and Administration (NASPPA, 2009) states, "The degree program's primary focus shall be that of preparing students to be leaders, managers, and analysts in the professions of public affairs, public administration, and public policy."

The CSWE and NASPAA formulations are noticeably short on details, befitting organizations moving toward achievements of competencies by students and allowing considerable variation in programmatic and educational approaches, with more emphasis on measuring educational program outcomes than in directing what the specific outcomes should be. Still, more specificity about what nonprofit administration students are supposed to learn is important.

A more precise view regarding the purpose of a professional education is provided by Armitage and Clark (1975), who argue,

1. The ultimate purpose of a profession is practice.

2. The purpose of professional education is to effectively teach practice behaviors.

3. Practice behaviors can be specified as the operational objectives of social work [or other professional] education. (cited in Gingerich, Kaye, & Bailey, 1999, p. 120)

Following this formulation, graduates of nonprofit administration–focused social work and public administration or other educational programs should be able to perform the practice behaviors of nonprofit administrators. This is similar in spirit to Patti's (2000) statement,

If graduate education has not instilled ways of thinking about organizational issues and managerial strategies for addressing them, if it has not socialized graduates to the expectations of managers, if it has not imparted technical skills and language, then potential employers are not likely to perceive graduates as credible candidates for managerial jobs. (p. 18)

If the situation Patti describes is true, then we believe the graduate education experience has failed. We believe that students need to learn from experiential cases and assignments that take them beyond the classroom in addition to learning from lectures, books, videos, discussions, and other means. That is why we put this book together—to provide information (supplemental to other information sources) and also exercises, assignments, and recommendations for additional resources for learning.

SUMMARY

This chapter has highlighted six trends that are shaping the world of nonprofit administrators and leaders. Each is difficult to handle on its own, but in combination, they become extremely challenging. We believe that only skilled practitioners, armed with knowledge and experience, have a chance to overcome them. This book is our effort to bring insight and experiential learning to the classroom by focusing on practical application of concepts and self-learning by students to meet their educational needs and goals.

The trends identified in this chapter (greater competition for resources, greater numbers of skills being required, the need for research and evidence-based programs, the emergence of a leadership crisis, greater levels of diversity in the workplace, and the increasing use of technology) must not be examined in isolation because a nonprofit executive does not face these trends sequentially—rather, they come forward simultaneously, with varying strength, each day. As difficult as the job may be, it is also extremely rewarding. Prepared with commitment to clients, appropriate job competencies, practical experience, and the will to move forward, nonprofit leaders make an important difference in their organizations and communities every day.

REFERENCES

Alexander, J. (2000). Adaptive strategies of nonprofit human service organizations in an era of devolution and new public management. *Nonprofit Management and Leadership, 10*(3), 287–303.

Armitage, A., & Clark, F. W. (1975). Design issues in the performance-based curriculum. *Journal of Education for Social Work, 11*(1), 22–29.

Birdsell, D., & Muzzio, D. (2003). *The next leaders: UWNYC leadership development and succession management needs.* New York: United Way of New York City.

Council on Social Work Education (CSWE). (2007). *Educational policy and accreditation standards,* Draft of September 24, 2007. Retrieved October 28, 2007, from http://www.cswe.org/NR/rdonlyres/450CD3CE-3525-4CE1-9031-59EA4DC77EDA/0/EPASDraftSeptember242007Rev10122007.pdf

Edwards, H., & Hoefer, R. (2010). Are social work groups using Web 2.0 effectively? *The Journal of Policy Practice, 9*(3–4), 1–20.

El Nasser, H., & Overberg, P. (2011, August 10). Census tracks 20 years of sweeping change. *USA Today.* Retrieved from http://usatoday30.usatoday.com/news/nation/census/2011-08-10-census-20-years-change_n.htm

Ezell, M., Chernesky, R., & Healy, L. (2004). The learning climate for administration students. *Administration in Social Work, 28*(1), 57–76.

Faffer, J., & Friedland, S. (2007). Addressing the professional leadership crisis in the Jewish family service field. *Journal of Jewish Communal Service, 82*(1–2), 139–144.

Gingerich, W., Kaye, K., & Bailey, D. (1999). Assessing quality in social work education: Focus on diversity. *Assessment & Evaluation in Higher Education, 24*(2), 119–129.

Golensky, M., & Mulder, C. (2006). Coping in a constrained economy: Survival strategies of nonprofit human service organizations. *Administration in Social Work, 30*(3), 5–24.

Hoefer, R. (2003). Administrative skills and degrees: The "Best Place" debate rages on. *Administration in Social Work, 27*(1), 25–46.

Hopkins, K., & Hyde, C. (2002). The human service managerial dilemma: New expectations, chronic challenges and old solutions. *Administration in Social Work, 26*(3), 1–15.

Johnson, M., & Austin, M. (2006). Evidence-based practice in the social services: Implications for organizational change. *Administration in Social Work, 30*(3), 75–104.

Jones, J. (2006). Understanding environmental influence on human service organizations: A study of the influence of managed care on child caring institutions. *Administration in Social Work, 30*(4), 63–90.

Kanter, B., & Fine, A. (2010). *The networked nonprofit: Connecting with social media to drive change.* San Francisco: Jossey-Bass.

Martin, L. (2000). Budgeting for outcomes in state human agencies. *Administration in Social Work, 24*(3), 71–88.

McBeath, B., & Meezan, W. (2006). Nonprofit adaptation to performance-based, managed care contracting in Michigan's foster care system. *Administration in Social Work, 30*(2), 39–70.

Menefee, D. (2000). What managers do and why they do it. In R. Patti (Ed.), *The handbook of social welfare management* (pp. 247–266). Thousand Oaks, CA: Sage.

Menefee, D., & Thompson, J. (1993). Identifying and comparing competencies for social work management: A practice-driven approach. *Administration in Social Work, 18*(3), 1–25.

Mirabella, R. (2007). University-based educational programs in nonprofit management and philanthropic studies: A 10-year review and projections of future trends. *Nonprofit and Voluntary Sector Quarterly, Supplement, 36*(4), 11S–27S.

Mutschler, E., & Hoefer, R. (1990). Factors affecting the use of computer technology in human service organizations. *Administration in Social Work, 14*(1), 87–101.

National Association of Schools of Public Affairs and Administration (NASPAA). (2009). *NASPAA accreditation standards: Preconditions for accreditation review 3: Primary purpose.* Retrieved from http://naspaa.org/accreditation/NS/naspaastandards.asp

Packard, T. (2004). Issues in designing and adapting an administration concentration. *Administration in Social Work, 28*(1), 5–20.

Patti, R. (2000). The landscape of social welfare management. In R. Patti (Ed.), *The handbook of social welfare management* (pp. 3–25). Thousand Oaks, CA: Sage.

Perlmutter, F. (2006). Ensuring social work administration. *Administration in Social Work, 30*(2), 3–10.

Poertner, J. (2006). Social administration and outcomes for consumers: What do we know? *Administration in Social Work, 30*(2), 11–24.

Regehr, C., Chau, S., Leslie, B., & Howe, P. (2002). An exploration of supervisors' and managers' responses to child welfare reform. *Administration in Social Work, 26*(3), 17–36.

Reisch, M., & Sommerfeld, D. (2003). Welfare reform and the future of nonprofit organizations. *Nonprofit Management and Leadership, 14*(1), 19–46.

Ritchie, W., & Eastwood, K. (2006). Executive functional experience and its relationship to the financial performance of nonprofit organizations. *Nonprofit Management and Leadership, 17*(1), 67–82.

Salipante, P., & Aram, J. (2003). Managers as knowledge generators: The nature of practitioner-scholar research in the nonprofit sector. *Nonprofit Management and Leadership, 14*(2), 129–150.

Schmid, H. (2004). Organization-environment relationships: Theory for management practice in human service organizations. *Administration in Social Work, 28*(1), 97–113.

Selsky, J., & Parker, B. (2005). Cross-sector partnerships to address social issues: Challenges to theory and practice. *Journal of Management, 31*(6), 849–873.

Social Enterprise Alliance. (n.d.). *What's a social enterprise?* Retrieved from https://www.se-alliance.org/what-is-social-enterprise

Stoecker, R. (2007). The research practices and needs of nonprofit organizations in an urban center. *Journal of Sociology and Social Welfare, 34*(4), 97–119.

Urban Institute. (2012). *Nonprofits.* Retrieved from http://www.urban.org/nonprofits

Zimmermann, J., & Stevens, B. (2006). The use of performance measurement in South Carolina nonprofits. *Nonprofit Management and Leadership, 16*(3), 315–327.

HELPFUL TERMS

Competency-based education—an approach to education that emphasizes student outcomes, that is, that graduates should know how to perform tasks well. This approach to education contrasts with focusing on the inputs of the education process, such as number of teachers, amount spent per student, and so on.

Council on Social Work Education (CSWE)—the sole accrediting body for social work programs in the United States, it sets and maintains educational standards at the bachelor's and master's levels.

Diversity in the workplace—workers with a wider variety of ethnicities, races, gender identities, and age groups are now working side-by-side than in the past. This fact has the potential for both increased difficulties and unparalleled opportunities for creative approaches to workplace and social issues.

Evidence-based practice—a (controversial) movement within social work to more closely tie interventions to a scientific research base to ensure that the practices are effective in achieving positive and anticipated client outcomes.

Foundation—a foundation is an organization that has been established according to law to receive donations and to disburse funds in accordance with its founding documents. There are several different types of foundations, such as corporate foundations, family foundations, and community foundations.

Government grant—local, state, and federal government agencies provide funding to nonprofits to achieve certain purposes, such as decreasing homelessness or preventing the transmission of HIV/AIDS. Nonprofits compete to receive these awards.

Individual giving—donations of money to charities by individuals and families. This category does not include donations by corporations or foundations.

National Association of Schools of Public Affairs and Administration (NASPAA)—the accrediting body for master's-level education programs in public service.

Program evaluation—a type of applied research that determines the ability of a program to achieve its stated goals. Program evaluation is often divided into process evaluation, which evaluates how well the program operates and was implemented, and outcome evaluation, which examines the extent to which program goals were achieved.

Social enterprise—an organization whose primary purpose is the common good, accomplished by using the methods and disciplines of business and the marketplace to address social needs.

Stakeholder—any person or group of persons or organization that has an interest in the workings and activities of an organization. Examples of stakeholders for nonprofit organizations include funders, clients, staff members, and the general public.

EXERCISES

1. In-Basket Exercise

Directions

You are Oscar Cervantes, director of planning at the United Way of Metropolitan Gotham. Read the following memo from your boss, the CEO of United Way. She is asking for you to provide her with information so she can be a panelist at a roundtable discussion attended by many of the community's movers and shakers. She wants a page of talking points, a backup memo of three to five pages, and an oral briefing from you on the answers you have developed. Additional details are in the memo.

Memo

Date: August 21, 20XX

To: Oscar Cervantes, Director of Planning

From: Jaylynn Banks, CEO, United Way of Metropolitan Gotham

Subject: Roundtable Presentation

I have been asked to be part of a Roundtable Presentation at Gotham University in two weeks' time. The topic is "Current Context and Future Possibilities for Nonprofits in Gotham."

I am simply too busy to do the necessary preparation for such a roundtable, but all the heavy hitters in the funding, business, and civic sectors of our city will be there, so I need to do this.

But I need your help. Here are the questions that will be asked of each panelist, and I need you and your team to come up with answers.

1. How has the recent (last two to three years) economic situation impacted the nonprofit sector?

2. What does the near-term (five years) future funding picture look like for nonprofits in general in our community?

3. What feasible policy changes would have the most positive or negative impacts on nonprofits?

I know this isn't much time to prepare, but you and your team work with these types of questions all the time, so I know I can count on you for an oral briefing, talking points, and three to five pages of background information so that I can represent the United Way of Metropolitan Gotham well.

2. Become a Nonprofit Futurist

Purpose: In ancient times and up to now, people who claim to know what is going to happen can influence others (and make a very good living at it!). The purpose of this exercise is to make yourself an expert in one aspect of the future context of nonprofits.

Preparation: Examine the history of one aspect of the nonprofit sector in your community. This may be an area of practice, such as child welfare, health, the arts, or any other part of the nonprofit world in your area. Think carefully about the trajectory and possible future of this practice area. Or you may wish to predict the future of something else, such as the effect of global climate change on the nonprofit sector where you live. Those with a political perspective might wish to address a subject such as "Nonprofits in a Tea Party World."

Task: After choosing your topic, prepare three scenarios as to what will happen in the next five years, writing each up in no more than two to three pages. Make one scenario purposely gloomy, another particularly positive, and the third what you think will be the most likely future. Be prepared to present your thoughts to others in your class or at work to get their reaction to your predictions.

3. Host a Roundtable Discussion

Purpose: To connect with nonprofit leaders and learn their views about the current context and future of nonprofits in your community.

Preparation: Invite three or four current or past nonprofit leaders from your community together for a roundtable discussion. They may be from similar or varied parts of the non-profit world, including human services, arts, museums, or other parts, depending on your community. This could be done several times in a semester, with different leaders. You may wish to send them a set of questions that will be asked so they may prepare answers, although you may wish to have a mix of prepared questions and "pop" questions that emerge from student interest.

Task: Have one or more students pose questions to the panel members, with follow-ups allowed. It would be a plus if this panel discussion could be filmed and even posted to the web (only with signed releases from the participants, of course).

ASSIGNMENTS

1. One task of nonprofit managers is to gather additional information on topics important to their organization. This assignment asks you to "curate" information for yourself and others in your class or group. Be willing to post the results of these assignments to a class or group wiki or other method of dissemination.

   A. Find two or three blogs that address topics of interest to the nonprofit sector. Look over their posts for the past few months. What do they discuss that supports, supplements, or contradicts what is discussed in this chapter? What evidence do the blog posters provide?
   B. If possible, post to one of the blogs something you've found interesting from this chapter or from your own thoughts. What type of response do you get from the blog author and others who read it?

2. Search through academic literature databases or other locations to find two to three articles that describe trends affecting the nonprofit sector. Compare the trends you find with those found by others in your class or group. Which are mentioned often, and which are spotted only once or twice? Select one from the most commonly mentioned group and one from the seldom-mentioned group to discuss with your colleagues in class or at work or internship. What thoughts do others have about these trends and their importance?

3. Choose one of the trends you've identified or read about. Prepare a one-minute oral presentation to share this with your class or other group. It is best to be able to present this conversationally and without notes, as if you were in a meeting where it was important for others to know this information because of its impact on your organization.

Values and Ethics in Administration

2

To be a successful human services administrator, you must have knowledge in many different areas of administration. These areas of needed expertise include knowledge of the political and economic dimensions of social services administration, coupled with the leadership skills necessary to move an organization forward. You will also need to know and understand different theories of administration, as well as practical skills such as governance strategies, employee relations, supervision, management strategies, and agency–environment relations. However, all of these areas of skills and expertise are not enough to be a successful administrator. As an administrator, you must also have skills in recognizing and dealing with ethical issues and questions. An administrator must understand the ethical issues and dilemmas of administration and be able to analyze situations using moral reasoning and decision-making strategies. Ethical risk management is a way to avoid complaints and even possible lawsuits.

ETHICAL DILEMMAS

An ethical dilemma "is that situation in which an action is required that reflects only one of two values or principles that are in opposition to one another" (Beckerman, 1997, p. 6). Ethical dilemmas arise when decisions of conflicting ethical responsibility must be made by the administrator. For example, think about decisions that must be made about the use of agency resources. If you are facing budget cutbacks, how do you decide how to use the funds available? Do you use the remaining resources to help as many people as possible before the money runs out, or do you use the limited resources to help those most in need (Reamer, 2000)? Both directions are admirable. It is good to want to help as many people as possible with the resources of the organization, but there is also a strong case to be made that the resources should be directed to those with the most need.

CLASSICAL THEORIES OF ETHICS

For you to develop a framework for ethical decision making, it is important that you have a basic understanding of the theories of ethics. As you will learn in Chapter 3, theories are the lens through which we view the world and, in this case, how we make ethical administrative decisions. Two classic approaches to ethics are the *deontological* theories and the *teleological* theories: "Deontological ethics are ethics of duty or principle, while teleological ethics are ethics of results or consequences" (Chandler, 2001, p. 179).

Deontological Theories

Deontological theories claim that certain actions or behaviors are inherently right or wrong and that actions are good or evil. These theories are based on the idea that there are higher-order principles. From a religious standpoint, this approach is based on the belief that God has determined what is right and what is wrong.

Teleological Theories

Teleological theories are based on the assumption that individuals faced with an ethical dilemma should measure the moral rightness of their actions based on the moral goodness of the consequences. In other words, one should act in a manner that produces the most favorable outcome. Fox (1994) described this set of theories as being based on the idea that the ends justify the means. Teleological theories are based on the belief that decisions should be made that will do the most good and impose the least harm. It is the result that is important, regardless of any inherent right or wrong as proposed in deontological theories.

Utilitarianism

Utilitarianism is a subset of the teleological theories. This approach holds that the proper sets of actions are those that promote the greatest good for the greatest number in society (Solomon, 1992). Two applications of utilitarianism are act utilitarianism and rule utilitarianism (Gorovitz, 1971). In *act utilitarianism*, the rightness of an action is determined by the goodness of its consequences in that individual case. This approach would look only at the individual case at hand and would not be concerned with the impact on other cases. In contrast, *rule utilitarianism* requires one to anticipate the long-term consequences and act accordingly in all similar situations (Grobman, 2011). Think about the implications of these two approaches from the standpoint of a human services administrator. Can you make a decision based only on the situation at hand, or must you consider that you will need to apply the decision to future similar cases that will arise? Will your decision in one instance set a precedent for future cases? More recent theories focus on the core concepts of ethical behavior.

THREE CORE CONCEPTS OF ETHICS

Denhardt (1991) outlines three core concepts of ethical behavior: honor, benevolence, and justice. *Honor* is defined as adherence to the highest standards of responsibility, integrity, and principle, and denotes a quality of character in which the individual exhibits a high sense of duty, pursuing good deeds as ends in themselves, not because of any benefit or recognition that might be accrued because of the deeds. *Benevolence* is the disposition to do good and to promote the welfare of others, and implies not only actions that promote good and the welfare of others, but also motivation to pursue those ends. *Justice* signifies fairness and regard for the rights of others. The rights of others include, most fundamentally, respect for the dignity and worth of each individual. Justice further involves a commitment to developing and preserving rights for individuals that will ensure that their dignity and worth will not be violated by others in society.

CODES OF ETHICS

Codes of ethics are systematic efforts to define acceptable conduct (Plant, 1994). Many professions have codes of ethics that range from being very general to very specific and prescriptive. Human service administrators come from a variety of disciplines and backgrounds, but their different codes of ethics are often very similar. If you think about it, this is not surprising since the codes of ethics are based on many of the theories, concepts, and principles outlined above.

Three of the most common degrees held by administrators are master of social work (MSW), master of business administration (MBA), and master of public administration (MPA). Look at each of the three codes of ethics (or oaths) and see how they are similar and how they are different. In the "Resources" section at the end of this chapter, there are links to each code discussed in the following sections.

MSW Administrators

Social work administrators are guided by the Social Work Code of Ethics. Take a look at the preamble to the social work code and think about how the code can be a guide in social work administration.

Preamble

The primary mission of the social work profession is to enhance human wellbeing and help meet the basic human needs of all people, with particular attention to the needs and empowerment of people who are vulnerable, oppressed, and living in poverty. A historic and defining feature of social work is the profession's focus on individual wellbeing in a social context and the wellbeing of society. Fundamental to social work is attention to the environmental forces that create, contribute to, and address problems in living.

Social workers promote social justice and social change with and on behalf of clients. "Clients" is used inclusively to refer to individuals, families, groups, organizations, and communities. Social workers are sensitive to cultural and ethnic diversity and strive to end discrimination, oppression, poverty, and other forms of social injustice. These activities may be in the form of direct practice, community organizing, supervision, consultation administration, advocacy, social and political action, policy development and implementation, education, and research and evaluation. Social workers seek to enhance the capacity of people to address their own needs. Social workers also seek to promote the responsiveness of organizations, communities, and other social institutions to individuals' needs and social problems.

The mission of the social work profession is rooted in a set of core values. These core values, embraced by social workers throughout the profession's history, are the foundation of social work's unique purpose and perspective:

- service
- social justice
- dignity and worth of the person
- importance of human relationships
- integrity
- competence

This constellation of core values reflects what is unique to the social work profession. Core values, and the principles that flow from them, must be balanced within the context and complexity of the human experience.

MBA Administrators

There is not a standard code of ethics for administrators holding the MBA degree. Even though there is not a formalized code of ethics, there have been attempts to move toward a code of ethics by the development of an "oath." The mission for the oath is to facilitate a widespread movement of MBAs who aim to lead in the interests of the greater good and who have committed to living out the principles articulated in the oath. The oath is a voluntary pledge for graduating and current MBAs to create value responsibly and ethically based practice. Those supporting the oath have formed a coalition of MBA students, graduates, and advisors, representing over 250 schools from around the world (MBA Oath, 2013).

The MBA Oath (short version) states,

As a manager, my purpose is to serve the greater good by bringing people and resources together to create value that no single individual can create alone. Therefore, I will seek a course that enhances the value my enterprise can create for society over the long term. I recognize my decisions can have far-reaching consequences that affect the well-being of individuals inside and outside my enterprise, today and in the future. As I reconcile the interests of different constituencies, I will face choices that are not easy for me and others.

Therefore I promise:

- I will act with utmost integrity and pursue my work in an ethical manner.
- I will safeguard the interests of my shareholders, co-workers, customers and the society in which we operate.
- I will manage my enterprise in good faith, guarding against decisions and behavior that advance my own narrow ambitions but harm the enterprise and the societies it serves.
- I will understand and uphold, both in letter and in spirit, the laws and contracts governing my own conduct and that of my enterprise.
- I will take responsibility for my actions, and I will represent the performance and risks of my enterprise accurately and honestly.
- I will develop both myself and other managers under my supervision so that the profession continues to grow and contribute to the well-being of society.
- I will strive to create sustainable economic, social, and environmental prosperity worldwide.
- I will be accountable to my peers and they will be accountable to me for living by this oath.

This oath I make freely, and upon my honor. (MBA Oath, 2013)

MPA Administrators

The code of ethics for the American Society for Public Administrators calls for administrators to serve the public interest, respect the constitution and the law, demonstrate personal integrity, promote ethical organizations, and strive for professional excellence.

The American Society for Public Administration (ASPA) advances the science, art, and practice of public administration. The Society affirms its responsibility to develop the spirit of responsible professionalism within its membership and to increase awareness and commitment to ethical principles and standards among all those who work in public service in all sectors. To this end, we, the members of the Society, commit ourselves to uphold the following principles:

1. Advance the Public Interest. Promote the interests of the public and put service to the public above service to oneself.

2. Uphold the Constitution and the Law. Respect and support government constitutions and laws, while seeking to improve laws and policies to promote the public good.

3. Promote Democratic Participation. Inform the public and encourage active engagement in governance. Be open, transparent and responsive, and respect and assist all persons in their dealings with public organizations.

4. Strengthen Social Equity. Treat all persons with fairness, justice, and equality and respect individual differences, rights, and freedoms. Promote affirmative action and other initiatives to reduce unfairness, injustice, and inequality in society.

5. Fully Inform and Advise. Provide accurate, honest, comprehensive, and timely information and advice to elected and appointed officials and governing board members, and to staff members in your organization.

6. Demonstrate Personal Integrity. Adhere to the highest standards of conduct to inspire public confidence and trust in public service.

7. Promote Ethical Organizations: Strive to attain the highest standards of ethics, stewardship, and public service in organizations that serve the public.

8. Advance Professional Excellence: Strengthen personal capabilities to act competently and ethically and encourage the professional development of others. (American Society for Public Administrators, 2013)

CODES OF ETHICS IN OTHER DISCIPLINES

Of course, there are administrators from many other disciplines that hold positions as administrators in human service organizations. Different fields of service seem to attract administrators from different disciplines. It is impossible to cover all of the different disciplines and their codes of ethics, but the following study of ethical codes has implications for human services administration regardless of the area of practice.

In examining adoption services, Babb (1998) "identified the professions most often involved in adoption practice, such as social work, law, medicine, nursing, and mental health, including psychology, counseling, and marriage and family therapy" (p. 124). The codes of ethics of these groups have major implications in the provision of services and in protecting the rights of clients. In reviewing the codes of these professional groups and surveying 75 organizations, Babb found that shared standards for ethical practices could be identified and categorized. Shared standards were found in areas of the professional's role in society, client–employee relations, nondiscrimination, diligence and due care, communication, objectivity/independence, fees, what constitutes the best interest of the child, contract relationships, and some aspects of confidentiality. The overlapping principles in professional groups are significant and, in many ways, very reassuring. There is a great deal of commonality when evaluating ethical practice as it relates to providing human services.

Watson and Cobb (2012), building on the work of Babb (1998), examined the codes of ethics for each of these groups in more detail. For social workers, the basic ethical standards are prescribed by the National Association of Social Workers (2008). Social work's ethical principles are based on social work's core values of service, social justice, importance of human relationships, integrity, competence, and the dignity and worth of the human beings. Similarly, the guiding principles for psychologists include beneficence and nonmaleficence, fidelity and responsibility, integrity, justice, and respect for people's rights and dignity (American Psychological Association, 2010). A fundamental principle that underlies all nursing practice is respect for the inherent worth and dignity of patients and the human rights of every individual. Furthermore, nurses take into account the needs and values of all persons in all professional relationships (American Nurses Association, 2011). The American Counseling Association's (2005) code of ethics asserts that responsible professional counselors should advocate for clients' access to services at the individual, group, institutional, and societal levels. They also should examine potential barriers and obstacles to clients' growth and development. Marriage and family therapists' code of ethics calls for respect for the rights of clients to make decisions and understand the consequences of these decisions. These decisions include cohabitation, marriage, divorce, separation, reconciliation, custody, and visitation (American Association for Marriage and Family Therapy, 2001). Regardless of the affiliation of the major professions involved in the administration of human services, adequate guidance exists for ethical practice.

ASPIRATIONAL ETHICS

Whereas professional codes of ethics have detailed the basic standards of behavior, some codes express aspirational goals for higher levels of ethical standards. For example, the social work code describes professional behavior as behavior to which all professionals should aspire.

Corey, Corey, and Callanan (2003) suggested that all professional groups should look beyond their codes of ethics and endorse the larger issue of aspirational ethics that describe the highest level of ethical functioning and do more than just meet the letter of the ethics code. Candilis and Martinez (2006) affirmed aspirational ideals as "a higher standard for professionals than any minimalist legal requirements. Aspirational ethics are concerned with what the profession ought to be" (p. 244). They conceptualize the professional duty as providing a "structurally stabilizing, morally protective presence" (p. 244). Many ethicists point to Aristotle's emphasis on the "ultimate good" as a principle to which professionals should aspire (Souryal, 1992).

Reamer (2000, p. 76) presents Solomon's (1992) assertion that administrative actions should be based on six core values from Aristotle's writings.

1. Community: "We are, first of all, members of organized groups, with shared histories and established practices governing everything from eating and working to worshiping." (Solomon, 1992, p. 146)

2. Excellence: "It is a word of great significance and indicates a sense of mission to a commitment beyond profit potential and the bottom line. It is a word that suggests 'doing well' but also 'doing good.'" (Solomon, 1992, p 153)

3. Membership: "The idea that an employee or executive develops his or her personal identity largely through the organizations in which he or she spends most of their adult waking life." (Solomon, 1992, p. 161)

4. Integrity: "Integrity is essentially *moral courage*, the will and willingness to do what one knows one ought to do." (Solomon, 1992, p. 168)

5. Judgment: "Aristotle thought that it was 'good judgment' or *phronesis* that was of the greatest importance in ethics." (Solomon, 1992, p. 174)

6. Holism: "The ultimate aim of the Aristotelian approach to business is to cultivate whole human beings, not jungle fighters, efficiency automatons, or 'good soldiers' . . . But one of the problems of traditional business thinking is our tendency to isolate our business or professional roles for the rest of our lives." (Solomon, 1992, p. 180)

According to Solomon (1992), these six values "form an integrative structure in which the individual, the corporation, and the community, self-interest and the public good, the personal and the professional business and virtues all work together instead of against one another" (p. 145).

A MODEL OF ETHICAL DECISION MAKING

There is no one model to guide administrators in making ethical decisions. From the material presented above, you can see that there are many different views to determine what is "ethical." Cottone and Clause (2000) conducted a comprehensive review of the literature on ethical decision-making models from the counseling literature. They found the literature rich with decision-making models, but few that had been assessed empirically. There was a great deal of consistency across the models. Using several of the models presented, and borrowing heavily from the model presented by Forester-Miller and Davis (1996), we present the following model as a starting place for you as you develop your own model of ethical decision making.

1. Identify the problem. What are the facts as opposed to the assumptions, suspicions, or rumors? Is it a legal problem? Do you need to seek legal advice or involve law enforcement?

2. Apply the code of ethics of your professional association. Be clear about your professional obligations and that you are upholding the principles of your organization. Be sure you truly understand your code of ethics. Seek consultation from your professional organization if you need help in interpreting your specific code of ethics.

3. What is the nature of the ethical dilemma? Is it in fact a dilemma, or is it so clear-cut that there are not competing values? Remember that an ethical dilemma "is that situation in which an action is required that reflects only one of two values or principles that are in opposition to one another" (Beckerman, 1997, p. 6). If there is not an ethical decision, you can move forward and make the decision that the situation demands.

4. Generate several scenarios of potential decisions. What are all the different decisions that you might make? Consult with a colleague if you can do so without violating confidentiality of the people involved.

5. Consider the potential consequences of all the options and determine a course of action. What will the impact of your decision be on the individuals involved, on the people you serve, on the organization, and on the community? What will the impact be on you and your career? Would you be willing to make the obvious ethical decision (or refuse to make an obviously unethical decision) if it meant you would lose your job? Hopefully so.

6. Choose the course of action and evaluate it. Stadler (1986) proposes several questions to evaluate the chosen course of action. Is it just? Does it meet the standard of your own sense of fairness? Would you expect to be treated the same way in the same situation? How would your action look if reported on the six o'clock news or on the front page of the newspaper? Finally, would you recommend the same action to a colleague dealing with the same situation?

7. Implement the action. Many times, implementing the action is difficult. In most cases, the stakes are high whether the involved parties be clients, staff, volunteers, or board members. After some time has passed, it is good practice to go back and review the situation to see if there are things you would do differently in the future.

SUMMARY

Human service administrators often are required to make decisions that involve two values or principles that are in opposition to one another. Such situations constitute ethical dilemmas. In this chapter, we have reviewed classic as well as more recent theories of ethics. We have also reviewed a model of decision making for you to use as you face ethical dilemmas in your administrative practice. Having a good understanding of the theories of ethics and an example of a decision-making process will help you as you face these difficult decisions. You should also be aware of the cultural and diversity issues as they relate to ethical decision making. As in all cases, you must be careful not to impose your own cultural or religious beliefs on others, but to be mindful and respectful of cultural differences that come into play in many ethical dilemmas.

REFERENCES

American Association for Marriage and Family Therapy. (2001). Retrieved December 2011 from http://www.aamft.org/imis15/content/legal_ethics/code_of_ethics.aspx

American Counseling Association. (2005). Retrieved December 2011 from http://www.counseling.org/ethics/feedback/ACA2005Code.pdf

American Nurses Association. (2011). Retrieved December 2011 from http://nursingworld.org/MainMenuCategories/EthicsStandards/CodeofEthicsforNurses

American Psychological Association. (2010). *Ethical principles of psychologists and code of conduct including 2010 amendments*. Retrieved December 2011, from http://www.apa.org/ethics/code/index.aspx

American Society for Public Administrators. (2013). Retrieved February 2013 from http://www.aspanet.org/public/ASPA/Resources/Code_of_Ethics/ASPA/Resources/Code%20of%20Ethics1.aspx?hkey=acd40318-a945-4ffc-ba7b-18e037b1a858

Babb, A. (1998). Ethics in contemporary American adoption practice. In V. Groza & K. F. Rosenberg (Eds.), *Clinical and practice issues in adoption: Bridging the gap between adoptees placed as infants and as older children* (pp. 105–155). Westport, CT: Bergin & Garvey.

Beckerman, N. (1997). Advanced medical technology: The ethical implications for social work practice with the dying. *Practice, 3*, 5–18.

Candilis, P. J., & Martinez, R. (2006). The higher standards of aspirational ethics. *Journal of the American Academy of Psychiatry and the Law Online, 34*(2), 242–244.

Chandler, R. C. (2001). Deontological dimensions of administrative ethics revisited. In T. Cooper (Ed.), *Handbook of administrative ethics* (pp. 179–193). New York: Marcel Dekker.

Corey, G., Corey, M. S., & Callanan, P. (2003). *Issues and ethics in the helping professions* (6th ed.). Pacific Grove, CA: Brooks/Cole.

Cottone, R. R., & Clause, R. E. (2000). Ethical decision-making models: A review of the literature. *Journal of Counseling & Development, 78*, 275–283.

Denhardt, K. G. (1991). Unearthing the moral foundations of public administration: Honor, benevolence, and justice. In J. S. Bowman (Ed.), *Ethical frontiers in public management* (pp. 91–113). San Francisco: Jossey-Bass.

Forester-Miller, H., & Davis, T. (1996). A practitioner's guide to ethical decision making. *American Counseling Association*. Retrieved February 2013 from http://www.counseling.org/resurces/pracguide.htm

Fox, C. J. (1994). The use of philosophy in administrative ethics. In T. Cooper (Ed.), *Handbook of administrative ethics* (pp. 105–130). New York: Marcel Dekker.

Gorovitz, S. (Ed.). (1971). *Mill: Utilitarianism*. Indianapolis, IN: Bobbs-Merrill.

Grobman, G. M. (2011). *An introduction to the nonprofit sector: A practical approach for the 21st century* (3rd ed.). Harrisburg, PA: White Hat Communications.

MBA Oath. (2013) Retrieved February 2013 from http://mbaoath.org/mba-oath-legacy-version

National Association of Social Workers. (2008). *Code of ethics*. Retrieved February 2013 from http://www.socialworkers.org/pubs/code/code.asp

Plant, J. (1994). Codes of ethics. In T. Cooper (Ed.), *Handbook of administrative ethics* (pp. 221–242). New York: Marcel Dekker.

Reamer, F. G. (2000). Administrative ethics. In R. Patti (Ed.), *The handbook of social welfare management* (pp. 69–86). Thousand Oaks, CA: Sage.

Solomon, R. C. (1992). *Ethics and excellence: Cooperation and integrity in business*. New York: Oxford University Press.

Souryal, S. S. (1992). *Ethics in criminal justice: In search of the truth*. Cincinnati, OH: Anderson.

Stadler, H. A. (1986). Making hard choices: Clarifying controversial ethical issues. *Counseling & Human Development, 19*, 1–10.

Watson, L., & Cobb, N. (2012). Ethical issues in the use of putative father registries in infant adoption: Implications for administrators and practitioners. *Adoption Quarterly, 15*(3), 206–219.

Aspirational ideals—a higher standard for professionals than any minimalist legal requirements.

Benevolence—disposition to do good and to promote the welfare of others, implying not only actions that promote good and the welfare of others, but also motivation to pursue those ends.

Codes of ethics—a systematic effort to define acceptable conduct (Plant, 1994).

Deontological theories—these claim that certain actions or behaviors are inherently right or wrong, and that actions are good or evil. These theories are based on the idea that there are higher-order principles. From a religious standpoint, this approach is based on the belief that God has determined what is right and what is wrong.

Ethical dilemma—"that situation in which an action is required that reflects only one of two values or principles that are in opposition to one another" (Beckerman, 1997, p. 6).

Honor—defined as adherence to the highest standards of responsibility, integrity, and principle, and denotes a quality of character in which the individual exhibits a high sense of duty, pursuing good deeds as ends in themselves, not because of any benefit or recognition that might be accrued because of the deeds.

Justice—fairness and regard for the rights of others. The rights of others include, most fundamentally, respect for the dignity and worth of each individual. Justice further involves a commitment to developing and preserving rights for individuals that will ensure that their dignity and worth will not be violated by others in society.

Teleological theories—based on the assumption that individuals faced with an ethical dilemma should measure the moral rightness of their actions based on the moral goodness of the consequences. In other words, one should act in a manner that produces the most favorable outcome.

Utilitarianism—a subset of the teleological theories. This approach holds that the proper sets of actions are those that promote the greatest good for the greatest number in society (Solomon, 1992).

Utilitarianism (act)—the rightness of an action is determined by the goodness of its consequences in that individual case (Grobman, 2011).

Utilitarianism (rule)—this requires one to anticipate the long-term consequences and act accordingly in all similar situations (Grobman, 2011).

Below, you will find three situations that demand your attention as a human services administrator. Sit with three or four of your classmates and discuss one of the following scenarios. Your instructor will assign you one or more of the scenarios to discuss. Select a spokesperson from your group, and report your findings to the class. Use the "Model of Ethical Decision Making" to frame your answer.

A. Service Delivery

   You are sitting in your office when the director of family services comes into your office. She has received a request from a couple who had previously adopted a child from your agency. The request is that the agency assist them in their process to adopt an embryo. The couple has found an agency on the Internet that places embryos for adoption. The couple asking your agency for help has learned that the agency they found on the Internet stores embryos produced through fertility treatment because they believe it is morally wrong to destroy the embryos. The couple is requesting that your agency provide the home study for the adoption of the embryo and provide ongoing supervision once the baby is born. Your agency does home studies and provides ongoing supervision but has no experience with embryo adoption. Your agency is religiously affiliated and is pro-life. However, some of the staff members are opposed to providing the service because they believe that fertility treatments are morally wrong.

Can your agency help?

B. Agency Functioning

You are sitting in your office when the phone rings. It is Mr. Warbucks, who is the community relations director of the Acme Tobacco Company, the largest tobacco company in America. They have selected your agency to receive a $100,000 check to remodel the agency's youth services complex. You have recently had the board of directors approve a policy that all facilities in the agency will be smoke free. Some of the employees are very angry that they must leave the property to smoke, and a few have resigned. Since the smoke-free policy has been adopted, you find that fewer of the clients are smoking. Mr. Warbucks would like to come to the next board meeting with his camera crew to present the check. The board will need to agree to have the film footage used in national advertising for the Acme Tobacco Company.

The agency is experiencing financial difficulties, and the youth services complex is badly in need of repair. Do you accept the donation and have your agency featured in the advertising campaign?

C. Relationships

You are sitting in your office when two clerks from the business office come in and tell you that the director of finance is stealing money from the petty cash drawer. You consider the director a dear friend and would trust him with your personal money. You do not believe that this could be true, but, to be on the safe side, you call the independent auditor to come and check the allegation. After the auditor completes his work, he asks to meet with you and the director. As the auditor begins to discuss several questionable transactions, the director asked to speak to you alone. The director tells you that it is true that he has been taking money from petty cash. He had used the money to buy tires and make repairs on his personal automobile. On one occasion, he had given some of the money, about $200, to the two employees who are making the allegations. The director states that he did this because they had worked so hard and were underpaid for what they do. The total amount taken was $1,200, which he said he would pay back immediately. The employee has been with the organization for 18 years. What will you do with the three employees involved?

ASSIGNMENTS

1. Examine the code of ethics for your discipline and compare and contrast it to two of the other codes mentioned in this chapter. Discuss the similarities and the differences in the codes of ethics between the disciplines.

2. Describe an ethical dilemma from either your own experience or a current event. In dealing with the ethical dilemma, would you use a deontological approach or a teleological approach? Why did you choose this approach? What actions would you take

based on the approach you find to be the most appropriate? Use the steps in the "Model of Ethical Decision Making" presented in this chapter to describe how you would deal with the ethical dilemma.

3. Conduct a telephone or a face-to-face interview with a human service administrator. Ask her if she can share an ethical dilemma that she has faced in her administrative practice. Describe the process used to arrive at her decision.

Administrative and Organizational Theories

3

How can theory be helpful and meaningful to an administrator? Why should you care about theory? For theory to be of practical use to you, it must have three critical elements: the capacity to describe, to explain, and to predict (Frederickson & Smith, 2003). Theory attempts to describe a phenomenon in abstract terms rather than attempting to describe a specific situation, setting, or case. The description cannot be highly specific without losing the ability to describe a general phenomenon. To build on a general description, a strong theory will also attempt to explain. The explanatory elements of a theory will explain "why" something happened or is happening. The most important part of a theory is its ability to predict. No theory could be expected to explain every situation, but it should have the ability to describe a range of outcomes that can be expected when applying the theory to real-life situations.

This chapter will give you an overview of some of the most important theories that shape administrative practice. You will then have the opportunity to apply each of the theories to a real-world situation.

Few administrators can describe which theories they use in their work and in their decision-making processes, but all administrators, over time, will develop their own theory of administration and will use different theories of organization and administration depending on their particular values, beliefs, and administrative styles. Therefore, to shape and inform your administrative practice, it is important for you to have a working knowledge of the major theories of administration. At the end of this section, you will be asked to imagine that you have been appointed as the administrator of an organization and to list three of the most important things you would do in your first 100 days based on each theoretical perspective presented in this chapter.

There are many approaches to the study of organization and administrative theory. Some typologies place the different theories on a chronological time line, while others divide the literature into different approaches or "schools." The history of organization and administration theory cannot be easily divided into clearly delineated periods, and therefore, each period must be viewed from the perspective of chronology, subject orientation, and issue orientation, since each period of theory development has built on the work of earlier theorists. Some theorists appeared to be far ahead of their times and gave glimpses of work that was to be further developed many years in the future. There are limits to any classification system, but we will approach the history of organization and administration theory in the following categories: Rational Approach Theories, Human Relations Perspectives, Contingency Theory, Political Economy Perspective, Population Ecology, Institutional Perspective, Organizational Culture and Sense Making, Postmodernism, and Critical Theory (Hasenfeld, 2000).

This chapter provides only a brief overview of several theories of organization and administration. Each of the sections below is a "thumbnail sketch" of the theory presented. There are numerous books written on each of these approaches, and the references at the end of this chapter will guide you to some of these books. This list is by no means complete, but hopefully, it will give you a sense of the use of theory in administrative practice and will lead you to a further in-depth study of the theories that will shape your practice.

RATIONAL APPROACH THEORIES

Rational Approach Theories have their roots in the classical theory of the late 1800s and early 1900s and are, therefore, strongly influenced by the European values of the time. Max Weber identified the elements of bureaucracy as the ideal method of organization (Gerth & Wright, 1946). This highly structured, chain-of-command approach was the model for this period. During this period of time, management viewed workers as intellectually and socially subordinate, and, for the most part, management was indifferent to the human needs of the work force. Workers needed to be controlled.

In this view, organizations existed to accomplish production and to achieve economic goals. As the scientific approach of this time gained acceptance, it was thought that there was one best way to organize work for maximum production and that people and organizations act in accordance with rational economic principles. Workers were viewed not as individuals, but as interchangeable parts. From this perspective, the organization was seen as a machine with interacting, interdependent parts, and workers were seen as incidental "cogs" in the machinery. This orientation was referred to as *mechanistic* by later theorists. Frederick Taylor's (1911) *Principles of Scientific Management* and Henry Fayol's (1916) "Administration industrielle et générale" (published in 1949 as *General and Industrial Management*) were major works of this period. Taylor designed a mechanical way to do a job and concentrated on the mechanics of what was performed rather than who was performing the work. Fayol's approach was to look at methods to promote effectiveness and efficiency. He also put forth the proposition that a university education had implications for one's ability as a manager and, from this position, developed career-development schemes.

Paper on the Science of Administration, edited by Luther Gulick and L. Urwick (1937), brought together in one volume articles of the leading theorists of the time. Many of the concepts from that work still have great influence on management practices today. For example, the work of V. A. Graicunas on "span of control" studied the number of subordinates that a supervisor should supervise. This work still has influence in the design of organizations today. It was also in this publication that Gulick introduced POSDCORB, or the seven major functions of executive management: planning, organizing, staffing, directing, coordinating, reporting, and budgeting.

While other approaches began to appear earlier, it was not until the mid-1940s that Herbert A. Simon wrote "The Proverbs of Administration" (1946), which questioned the relevance on "principles" of administration and challenged the approach. He proposed that the idea of principles was a myth, and that for every principle, there was a contradictory principle. Simon's work was the beginning of a challenge to the Rational Approach Theories and led to the development of other approaches.

HUMAN RELATIONS PERSPECTIVES

In keeping with the classical approach, the management of Western Electric Company contracted with a group of Harvard professors to perform a study to improve effectiveness and efficiency. These studies, known as the Hawthorn Studies (Greenwood, 1994), observed production rates while controlling variables such as lighting, work group membership, and physical position. The researchers were surprised to find that there were many variables other than physical space and lighting that impacted productivity. While it seems obvious to us today, they discovered that interpersonal relationships, supervisory relationships, and informal groups within the organization all had influences on production. These studies led to new thinking about work environments, worker motivation, supervision, and influences on productivity. This was a major event in the development of the social/psychological approaches, even though the studies were completed in 1932, and the social/psychological approaches were still several years in the future.

In this view, management began to view worker relationships as important factors in the work environment, and the power of both formal and informal groups was recognized. Dynamics of group conformity and group loyalty became the new topic of investigation and theory development. Some began to question the bureaucratic structures of the workplace and to view the Industrial Revolution as removing the meaning from work. Human Relations Theory held that workers were more responsible to social pressure of peer groups than to the demands, or even incentives, of management.

In "Toward a Psychology of Being," Abraham Maslow (1943) described his hierarchy of needs: physical security, self-esteem, and self-actualization. Figure 3.1 identifies these needs as physiological, safety, belonging–love, self-esteem, and self-actualization. This period brought about a major shift in the view of workers. Management began to view workers as capable of growth, needing choice to grow and as adaptive. Managers also began to recognize that motivation was important and that the sources of motivation would change over time.

In *The Human Side of Enterprise*, Douglas McGregor (1957) proposed a framework to examine administrative styles that he called *Theory X* and *Theory Y*. The traditional approach to management he labeled as Theory X management. He proposed a Theory Y as an alternative approach in which the task of management was to arrange organizational conditions and methods of operation so that people could achieve their own goals by directing their own efforts toward organizational objectives.

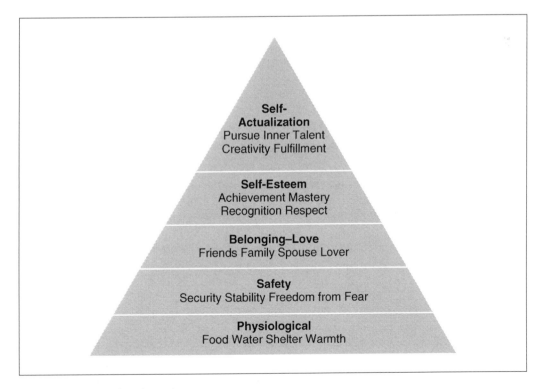

Figure 3.1 Hierarchy of Needs

CONTINGENCY THEORY

What is the best structure for a human services organization? Some of the work in the Human Relations models, such as Theory X and Theory Y, would lead us to the conclusion that an organization with little structure and maximum flexibility would lead to the highest levels of efficiency and effectiveness. Contingency Theory challenges this notion.

Contingency Theory moves toward an open systems perspective as opposed to the closed system view of the Rational Approach. In this theory, the structure of an organization is variable and contingent on the characteristics of the organization's environment, including environmental heterogeneity and stability, technological certainty, organizational size, and power (Mintzberg, 1979). In this theory, the task of the administrator is to create the right "fit" between the contingency and the internal structure of the organization as a strategy to promote effectiveness and efficiency.

A study by Burns and Stalker (1994) examined over 20 firms in the United Kingdom. The purpose of this study was to see what types of management methods and procedures produced the highest level of productivity. They found that the determining factor is the nature of each organization's demands from the environment and the types of tasks and functions necessary to meet those demands. From this work, they developed a new typology of organizations they called mechanistic organizations and organic organizations (Kettner, 2002).

Mechanistic organizations were defined as organizations that were fixed and somewhat rigid, with predictable tasks and relatively stable environments. *Organic organizations* were defined as being less structured. The supervisors in these organizations functioned more as consultants rather than as supervisors. In the organic organization, workers are given expected outcomes to achieve rather than specific tasks. The authors say that these organizations function best in an unstable environment in which inputs are unpredictable and the organization is expected to respond to changing environmental conditions.

What are the implications for the human services administrator? Because we are in the human services field, the tendency may be to lean more toward an unstructured and informal organizational structure that appears more equalitarian and participatory, but Contingency Theory says this is not always the best arrangement. The administrator taking the Contingency Theory approach will look at the inputs to the organization and the expected outcomes, and develop structures to maximize positive outcomes. The administrator will seek to achieve the best fit for the organization.

POLITICAL ECONOMY PERSPECTIVE

Political Economy Perspective states that for organizations to survive and to produce services, they must secure legitimacy and power, as well as production or economic resources. From this perspective, *political economy* refers to a system of distribution not only of resources but also of status, prestige, power, legitimacy, and related social amenities. The Political Economy Perspective views the organization as a collectivity that has multiple and complex goals, paramount among them being survival and adaptation to the environment (Hasenfeld, 2000). The capacity of the organization to survive and to provide services depends on its ability to mobilize power, legitimacy, and economic resources—for instance, money, personnel, and clients (Wamsley & Zald, 1976).

Most organizations are dependent on resources that are controlled by others in the external environment. In this approach, the greater the organization's dependence on these resources, the stronger the influence of external interest groups on processes within the organization (Schmid, 2000).

The human services administrator must manage his environment at least as well as he manages the organization to ensure an adequate resources supply. In this respect, managing the environment may be even more important than managing the organization itself (Aldrich & Pfeffer, 1976). Pfeffer (1992) notes that changes in the external and internal political economies will result in changes within the organization. Internal power relations shape internal structure and resource allocation.

POPULATION ECOLOGY

Population Ecology views the organization within the context of the community of organizations and services. In this view, dynamics of the founding and survival of organizations—that is, the founding and failure of organizations—are explained by population dynamics and density dependence. Population dynamics is seen as a factor in stimulating the founding of new organizations. For example, if there is an identified community need and there is the perception that there are resources to meet this need, then chances are that groups will work to develop a new organization or service to meet this need. Conversely, as new organizations or services are founded, then there is a perception of competition, and therefore, new foundings are discouraged. The concept of density dependence means that an increase in the density of organizations or services signals legitimacy of the services being provided and that resources are available for such services. In this view, the administrator must employ macro strategies to position the organization within the larger community of organizations and services and recognize that environmental forces set limits on the success of administrative practice (Hasenfeld, 2000).

INSTITUTIONAL PERSPECTIVE

In the Institutional Perspective, survival depends on the degree that structure reflects and reinforces the institutional rules shared by the community of organizations.

The more the organization adheres to rules, the greater its legitimacy and chances of survival. The administrator using this approach will focus on the critical relations between the organization and cultural institutions, and the values and norms these institutions are expected to promote (Scott, 1995). In this theory, the more closely the organization mirrors the values of the community, the more likely there will be financial and political support for the organization.

ORGANIZATIONAL CULTURE AND SENSE MAKING

The organizational culture enables members of the organization to make sense of their work and construct common understanding of their internal and external environments. Sense making is the process that ties together the beliefs and actions of the organization and the individuals in the organization. This approach recognizes that powerful sub-cultures exist in organizations and have a powerful socializing function. When new employees enter the organization, they must be socialized into the culture or, in the alternative, leave the organization. Services will be organized to accommodate the culture, and therefore, productivity is strongly influenced by culture. An important task of administrators is to influence the culture through the messages they give and their behavior (Weick, 1995).

POSTMODERNISM

For many administrators, postmodernism is very difficult to understand, yet alone explain. The term *postmodern*, put simply, implies a reaction against the modern condition. There is, however, a deeper meaning that attempts to move to a higher level of social thought. The common denominator to the many meanings of postmodernism is the idea that individuals and societies today have lost the capacity to represent the "real" (Denhardt, 2004). One of the tools of postmodernism is "deconstruction," or the process of finding historical and cultural flaws that mold our thinking and our institutions.

Postmodernists argue against the concepts of rationality or "scientific" knowledge. In this approach, it is the culture that defines and objectifies the values, norms, and knowledge of those in power. Since the culture is defined by those in power, the culture perpetuates the patterns of dominance that exist in the society. Postmodernists examine how things come into being and become self-ratifying. The administrator taking a postmodern approach will attempt to uncover practices that maintain and reinforce patterns of domination over staff and clients, while excluding alternative perspectives. The major limitation of the postmodern approach is that it does not provide a model for administration.

CRITICAL THEORY

Critical Theory is similar to postmodernism in that it views organizations as repressive systems. All Critical Theory is historical in the sense that it tries to analyze the long-term development of oppressive arrangements in society (Turner, 1986). The foundation of Critical Theory is Marxist theory, which says that the very structure of organizations, including hierarchical structures and division of labor, is designed to disenfranchise workers.

According to Marxist theory, human services organizations play a special role in a capitalist economy. In this view, the organization serves as a buffer between the capitalist and the working classes. "The benefits and services they provide are designed to maintain a compliant and complacent working class while defining and isolating as deviant those who might challenge the capitalist system" (Hasenfeld, 2000, p. 105). While this is not a popular notion with human services administrators, it does force an administrator to, at least, examine this proposition. Administrators strive to be agents of positive change, not agents of oppression. While administrators are engaged in "hands-on" service provision, critical theorists are focused on the purpose of their research—to achieve social change. Administrators committed to social change as well as service provision will draw on the lessons of the critical theorists.

SUMMARY

All administrators have a theory of administration. Some are well aware of their theory, and some have no awareness. This chapter has given an overview of some of the major theoretical approaches that shape administrative practice in human services. Administrators will use different theoretical approaches depending on the circumstances in which they find themselves. Sometimes they will act as rationalist, political economist, or critical theorist. Gaining more knowledge about theories of administration and organizations will assist you as an administrator to develop a solid theoretical base for your practice.

REFERENCES

Aldrich, H. E., & Pfeffer, J. (1976). Environments of organizations. *Annual Review of Sociology, 11,* 79–105.

Burns, T., & Stalker, G. (1994). *The management of innovation* (Rev. ed.). New York: Oxford University Press.

Denhardt, R. B. (2004). *Theories of public organization.* Belmont, CA: Thomson Wadsworth.

Fayol, H. (1949). *General and industrial management.* London: Sir Isaac Pitman.

Frederickson, H. G., & Smith, K. B. (2003). *The public administration theory primer.* Boulder, CO: Westview Press.

Gerth, H. H., & Wright, M. C. (Eds.). (1946). *From Max Weber: Essays in sociology.* Oxford: Oxford University Press.

Greenwood, R. G. (1994). Preface: Remembering the Hawthorne experiments. *International Journal of Public Administration, 17*(2), xvii–xxi.

Gulick, L., & Urwick, L. (Eds.). (1937). *Paper on the science of administration.* New York: Institute of Public Administration.

Hasenfeld, Y. (2000). Social welfare administration and organizational theory. In R. J. Patti (Ed), *The handbook of social welfare management* (pp. 89–112). Thousand Oaks, CA: Sage.

Kettner, P. M. (2002). *Achieving excellence in the management of human service organizations.* Boston: Allyn and Bacon.

Lewis, J. A., Lewis, M. D., Packard, T. R., & Souflee, F. (2001). *Management of human service programs* (3rd ed.). Belmont, CA: Brooks/Cole.

Lewis, J. A., Packard, T. R., & Lewis, M. D. (2011). *Management of human service programs* (5th ed.). Belmont, CA: Brooks/Cole.

Maslow, A. (1943). A theory of human motivation. *Psychological Review, 50,* 370–396.

McGregor, D. (1957). *The human side of enterprise.* New York: McGraw-Hill.

Mintzberg, H. (1979). *The structuring of organizations.* Englewood Cliffs, NJ: Prentice Hall.

Pfeffer, J. (1992). *Managing with power: Politics and influence in organizations.* Boston: Harvard Business School Press.

Schmid, H. (2000). Agency–environment relations: Understanding task environments. In R. J. Patti (Ed.), *The handbook of social welfare management* (pp. 133–154). Thousand Oaks, CA: Sage.

Scott, W. R. (1995). *Institutions and organizations.* Thousand Oaks, CA: Sage.

Simon, H. A. (1946). The proverbs of administration. *Public Administration Review, 6*(1), 53–67.

Taylor, F. W. (1911). *Principles of scientific management.* New York: Harper & Row.

Turner, J. H. (1986). *The Structure of sociological theory.* Chicago: Dorsey Press.

Wamsley, G. L., & Zald, M. N. (1976). *The institutional ecology of human service organizations.* Bloomington: Indiana University Press.

Weick, K. E. (1995). *Sensemaking in organizations.* Thousand Oaks, CA: Sage.

HELPFUL TERMS

Contingency Theory—Contingency Theory moves toward an open systems perspective as opposed to the closed system view of the rational approach. In this theory, the structure of an organization is variable and contingent on the characteristics of the organization's environment, including environmental heterogeneity and stability, technological certainty, organizational size, and power (Mintzberg 1979).

Critical Theory—similar to postmodernism in that it views organizations as repressive systems. All critical theory is historical in the sense that it tries to analyze the long-term development of oppressive arrangements in society (Turner, 1986).

Human Relations Perspectives—an approach based on the Hawthorne experiments that illuminated the importance of the human element in organizational life. Dimensions of worker motivation beyond economic incentives and fear were introduced as valid areas of study (Lewis, Lewis et al. 2001).

Institutional Perspective—Survival depends on the degree that structure reflects and reinforces the institutional rules shared by the community of organizations. The more the organization adheres to rules, the greater legitimacy and chances of survival.

Organizational Culture and Sense Making—The organizational culture enables members of the organization to make sense of their work and construct common understanding of their internal and external environment. Sense making is the process that ties together the beliefs and actions of the organization and the individuals in the organization.

Political Economy Perspective—for organizations to survive and to produce services, they must secure legitimacy and power, as well as production or economic resources. The Political

Economy Perspective views the organization as a collectivity that has multiple and complex goals—paramount among them, survival and adaptation to the environment (Hasenfeld, 2000).

Population Ecology—Population Ecology views the organization within the context of the community of organizations and services. In this view, the dynamics of founding and survival of organizations—that is, the founding and failure of organizations—are explained by population dynamics and density dependence. Population dynamics is seen as a factor in stimulating the founding of new organizations.

Postmodernism—The term *postmodern*, put simply, implies a reaction against the modern condition. There is, however, a deeper meaning that attempts to move to a higher level of social thought. The common denominator to the many meanings of postmodernism is the idea that individuals and societies today have lost the capacity to represent the "real" (Denhardt, 2004).

Rational Approach Theories—classical theories of organization from the 19th century. Max Weber's ideal bureaucracy, Frederick Taylor's scientific management, and Henri Fayol's management principles are still influential today (Lewis, Packard, & Lewis, 2011).

EXERCISES

1. In-Basket Exercise

Directions

Work with a group of three or four of your classmates and consider the following memo from the supervisor of Refugee Services to you, the administrator of the organization. Develop a memo in response to this memo. Use Institutional Theory to frame your response memo and then read your response to the class.

Memo

Date: February 13, 20XX

To: Administrator

From: Refugee Services Supervisor

Subject: Television Spots for Refugee Services

Our new public service spots began running on all the local TV stations this week. As you know, the spots are intended to find employers willing to hire our newly arrived refugees. I think the spots are very well done. They open with a shot of the Statue of Liberty with the voiceover saying, "Give us your tired, your poor and your huddled masses longing to breathe free." We have received a few calls from potential employers (two or three calls), but my phone has been ringing off the hook with "hate" calls. The most common complaint is the perception that we are taking away jobs from Americans and giving them to these foreigners. As you know, our program is not very popular in this community. I'm proposing that we pull the spots from the air as soon as possible. Your thoughts?

2. In-Basket Exercise

Directions

Work with a group of three or four of your classmates and consider the following memo from the Parenting Service coordinator to you, the administrator of the organization.

Develop a memo in response to this memo. Use Population Ecology Theory to frame your response memo and then read your response to the class.

Memo

Date: June 29, 20XX

To: Administrator

From: Parenting Service Coordinator

Subject: Request for Letter of Support

I have recently learned that there is a move under way in the community to develop a new parenting services agency. In fact, I received a call today asking if our agency will provide a letter of support that they can use as part of their grant proposal to the local community foundation. I am worried that this will be in direct competition with our service and that they will compete for funds from our funding sources and donors. There is always a need for additional services, but I think we would be in the better position to provide more services rather than have this group start a new agency. They are asking for a letter of support by the end of this week. What shall I do?

3. Exercise

Congratulations! You have been appointed as executive director of Acme Social Services Agency. The agency has 50 employees and a budget of $3.2 million. The agency provides a variety of services, including emergency assistance, refugee resettlement, residential youth services, and counseling services. The agency is facing a $50,000 deficit by year end if things do not change. Some of the staff are very unhappy that the former executive director was forced to resign after 20 years with the agency.

Based on each theoretical perspective, what are the three most important things you will want to do in your first 100 days in office? Why are these three tasks the most important?

Rational Approach Theories

1.

2.

3.

Human Relations Perspectives

1.

2.

3.

Contingency Theory

1.

2.

3.

Political Economy Perspective

1.

2.

3.

Population Ecology

1.

2.

3.

Institutional Perspective

1.

2.

3.

Organizational Culture and Sense Making

1.

2.

3.

Postmodernism

1.

2.

3.

Critical Theory

1.

2.

3.

ASSIGNMENTS

1. Write a brief statement called "My Theory of Administration." Which of the theories presented in this chapter fit with your beliefs and approaches to administration?

2. Write a five-to-seven-page paper on the work of Max Weber and how you see the influence of his work on the administration of human service organizations today.

3. Pick one area of human services such as domestic violence programs, hospice, youth services, or any other service area and, using the concepts of Population Ecology Theory, explain the founding of organizations providing this service.

Part II

Leadership and Communications

Leadership

4

Being a leader in a nonprofit organization is challenging. You must acquire a host of skills and use them well to be successful. There are few "right" answers, and conditions change constantly, bringing new opportunities and issues each day (Hopkins & Hyde, 2002). Part of the genius of successful nonprofit leaders lays in knowing which skills are called for in which situations. Rewards most often come from doing your best to fulfill your organization's mission, not from the pay and benefits, which are often considerably less than comparable work in the for-profit world. This chapter provides guidance for nonprofit leaders to be more successful in their jobs by discussing what leadership is, what it is used for in a nonprofit setting, what skills nonprofit leaders should possess, and other topics.

WHAT IS LEADERSHIP?

The term *leadership* is bandied about so frequently that it is easy to think that strong agreement exists in what it means. Shelves at libraries are filled with books on the subject, some written by business leaders, some by officers in the military, and others by elected officials. Leadership is usually seen as a generic skill—that is, leadership is leadership, whether in the commercial sector, military, or government arenas. Most of this material is not academically rigorous—in fact, it is little more than entertaining storytelling, with a few kernels of wisdom amidst the large amount of chaff that readers have to sift through. Still, leadership is important, and learning more about it is good for organizations and society. Poertner (2006) shows that client outcomes vary in connection with the leadership ability of agency managers. Warren Bennis (2009), a respected business leadership guru, indicates that leaders shape the effectiveness of organizations, provide inspiration and restore hope, and are able to recognize problems, yet rise above the current context of society (and their organizations) to see a better tomorrow.

A classic definition of leadership was given by renowned organizational theorist Richard Cyert (1990): "Leadership is the ability to get participants in an organization to focus their attention on the problems that the leader considers significant" (p. 29). In a similar vein, Shenkman (2007) argues, "The leader's real work is to create followers" (p. 13).

In nonprofits, however, the aim of leadership is not merely to create followers, but rather to create followers to accomplish something useful, such as quality services for clients. The centrality of values in the nonprofit sector is widely recognized and supported (Rothschild & Milofsky, 2006). Thus, being a leader in the nonprofit sector requires a personal commitment to the core values inherent in the nonprofit sector and the particular nonprofit organization in which you work.

Leadership in a nonprofit often requires working closely with staff members, funders, and other stakeholders. A successful executive values their input for the additional insights they have and the opportunities they offer to come to better decisions. In addition, people who are involved in workplace discussions are more likely to go along with the final decision, even if it wasn't their preferred option. While made in a different context, President Dwight D. Eisenhower's observation is apt: "Leadership is the art of getting someone else to do something you want done because he wants to do it" (quoted in Hughes, Ginnet, & Curphy, 2006, p. 405). Leadership in nonprofits is not about commanding but rather influencing others.

ARE THERE DIFFERENCES BETWEEN LEADERS, ADMINISTRATORS, AND MANAGERS?

In this book, we do not make clear distinctions between the terms *leaders*, *administrators*, and *managers*, although there are differences in meanings described in the literature. Foremost among the differences discussed is the sense that leaders chart the overall direction of organizations, administrators lay out the plans for moving forward, and managers get the front-line workers to implement the plans. Naturally, there is less difference in practice as a person who is a manager at one level may be seen as a leader at a different level. We believe that the roles are interdependent and often interchangeable, depending on the exact situation. We also believe that putting too much emphasis on "leadership" compared to "administration" or "management" discourages people from taking on appropriate activities that may be outside of their job description.

WHAT ARE NONPROFIT LEADERSHIP SKILLS TO BE USED FOR?

A question that is often overlooked in thinking about leadership in nonprofit organizations is exactly what leaders should be trying to accomplish. While this may seem to be an easy question to answer, and hardly worth considering, the issues are not as simple as they may first appear.

The common-sense view of nonprofit organizations is that they can best be understood as single goal-maximizing organizations. In the case of human service organizations, their goal would be to eliminate the problems of their clients. For sports nonprofits, the goal would be to maximize the number of youth playing the sport. For arts organizations, the goal might be to expose as many people as possible to theater/opera/music productions or the visual arts. A major problem with this approach is that organizations, as organizations, cannot have goals—only people can have goals (Mohr, 1982). Treating the organization as a person in this way leads to a failure to understand the nuances of what a leader must do to get individuals to align their goals with the organization's mission. Other problems with this organizational goal perspective are that goals often are not very specific, and that unofficial or unstated goals are often as important to the nonprofit's staff as are the professed goals of the organization (Herman & Renz, 1997). For example, an agency leader may try to achieve certain outcomes in an organization, not for the good of the agency, but because it will put him in a good position to get a better job in another organization.

A second theoretical approach to understanding what skills a nonprofit leader is using is the system resources approach, which posits that the key metric for understanding organizational success is the level of resources extracted from the environment to support the organization. In other words, the larger the budget (or the larger the percentage increase in the budget), the more successful the organization (and thus its leader) is said to be (Herman & Renz, 2004). This approach to what nonprofit leaders are trying to achieve would have to be an implicit, rather than an explicit, goal of the leader. Other things, such as the articulated mission, or achieving client outcomes, are what provide a nonprofit with its legitimacy and, thus, its ability to obtain resources from the environment. Donors or other stakeholders would not look kindly on a nonprofit leader espousing the goal of accumulating lots of cash reserves, and funding would probably decrease if this were the leader's announced goal.

A third view of what leaders in the nonprofit sector are working for, the multiple constituency view, says that the different stakeholders of a nonprofit (leader, staff, clients/patrons, funders, general public, and so on) may all have different ideas about what the organization is established for and how it should act. Because each group is important in the nonprofit's work, each of these stakeholders' views about what the organization is for is correct, even if the views are contradictory to another stakeholder's view (Herman & Renz, 2004). The task for the organization's leader is to balance the demands on the agency to accomplish these different goals.

Funders may value organizational effectiveness in solving client problems, clients may want to know that their assigned staff member cares about them as individuals, staff members may want a secure job, and the general public may want to have the agency be free from scandal. The nonprofit leader is thus required to pay attention to different stakeholders sequentially, attending first to one aspect of the organization, then another. This requires a tremendous repertoire of skills and a highly developed dose of political savvy. It also requires understanding theories about leadership.

LEADERSHIP THEORIES

Perhaps the oldest theory of leadership, sometimes known as the *great man* or *trait theory*, is that there are "born leaders" who have the traits that are needed to be effective (Carlyle, 1841). Some of the traits associated with successful leaders are drive, leadership motivation, honesty, integrity, self-confidence, cognitive ability, and knowledge (Kirkpatrick & Locke, 1991), although many additional traits could be added to the list. If you believe in this theory of leadership, and you wanted to develop leaders, you would first identify the traits of leadership you desire, screen the population for people who have these traits, and then provide training and opportunities for these traits to be used. This theory has practically no research support, but does make for powerful storytelling.

Leadership research gives us many more options for understanding the role of leaders and how they can be developed. Lewin, Lippitt, and White (1939/1970) proposed three styles of leadership: authoritarian, democratic, and laissez-faire. (Some authors refer to these styles of leadership as *directive*, *participative*, and *delegative*.) Authoritarian leaders tell others what to do without consulting with them much. Democratic leaders solicit others' opinions and seek to influence their ideas so that a general consensus emerges. Laissez-faire leaders do not put much effort into being leaders and allow others to do as they wish. The subjects in Lewin et al.'s studies generally preferred the democratic leaders, followed by laissez-faire leaders, with lowest levels of approval given to authoritarian leaders.

Despite the popularity of the democratic (or participative) style of leadership, later research indicates that each style of leadership can be effective, given the right circumstances. For example, when time is limited and the leader has all the facts needed to make a decision, the authoritarian approach can (and perhaps should) be used. In other circumstances, such as when staff members have some or all of the information needed to reach a decision, and the leader does not have all the information necessary, a democratic leadership style brings about better results.

The key realization from this research is that there is not just one correct model of leadership; rather, the leadership style must match the situation. This basic idea, as described in Chapter 3, is known as Contingency Theory, of which several different versions have emerged. Perhaps the most influential was developed by Fielder (1967).

Fielder (1967) argued that leadership could be understood as behavior to accomplish tasks. Two approaches (which exist on a continuum) for how to get tasks taken care of exist. On the one hand, a leader can get tasks accomplished by developing positive relationships with people so they will work because they like or trust the leader. This style is called *relationship oriented*. The other end of the spectrum involves focusing on getting things done rather than worrying about relationships. This style is called *task focused*. Neither of these styles works all the time. Fielder's critical insight was to try to determine when an effective leader uses one style and when the other.

According to Fielder (1967), when relations are good between leader and followers, the task is well structured, and the leader has high position power, then task orientation is effective. When the opposite is true (that is, relations are not very good, the task is poorly structured, and the leader does not have very high power from her position), task orientation can also be effective. For situations that are intermediate in relationship, structure, or position power, then relationship-oriented leadership is more effective. A recent restatement of contingency leadership declares that the best outcomes occur when the fit between leader and circumstances is "aligned" (Dym & Hutson, 2005).

Two additional recent leadership approaches include transformational leadership (Burns, 1978) and servant leadership (Greenleaf, 1991). Transformational leadership offers followers a chance to accomplish great things by making large changes in their organization and themselves. Transformational leaders create a vision, sell that vision to followers, and then move forward to enacting the vision, along with their followers, always leading the charge. Transformational leaders are usually charismatic, inspirational, intellectually stimulating, and people oriented, providing individualized attention to others. Servant leadership is described by Greenleaf (1991) as a feeling and a choice that the leader makes to lead, but to lead in a way that is in service to others. The goal for the servant-leader is to serve first and to acquire power or influence later, but only to continue to serve others better.

People employing different theories and styles use different sets of skills. An authoritarian leader requires far fewer "people skills" than does a leader following a servant-leader model. Leaders who want to be successful over the long term must be flexible in how they approach their job based on the needs of the organization. As Rothschild and Milofsky (2006) remind us, the needs of the organization (which can vary according to where it is in its life cycle, the state of its distinctive technologies, and what the demands of its external constituencies are) determine how the leader must act to be effective, and the personal desires of the leader are secondary. For example, a person not normally seen as charismatic may need to use such abilities to develop a following for a large-scale and difficult project. At other times, a visionary leader may need to focus on detailed "running of the ship" to achieve the vision that has come together. (Of course, another option for when a leader's skills do not match the organization's situation is to find a different leader.)

PUTTING TOGETHER THE PIECES: UNDERSTANDING NONPROFIT LEADERSHIP

Contingency theory argues that different leadership styles are more or less effective depending on the situation facing an organization. Schmid (2006) has assembled an excellent empirically based approach to linking organizational situation to leadership duties required.

According to Schmid (2006), leaders can locate themselves and their organization's needs on a two-axis plane (see Figure 4.1). One axis is labeled people-oriented vs. task-oriented, while the other axis is labeled internal orientation vs. external orientation. This creates four quadrants that we will examine, each in turn.

Quadrant I represents "task-oriented with an internal focus." The leader with such an approach will be focused on achieving organizational goals using standard work processes.

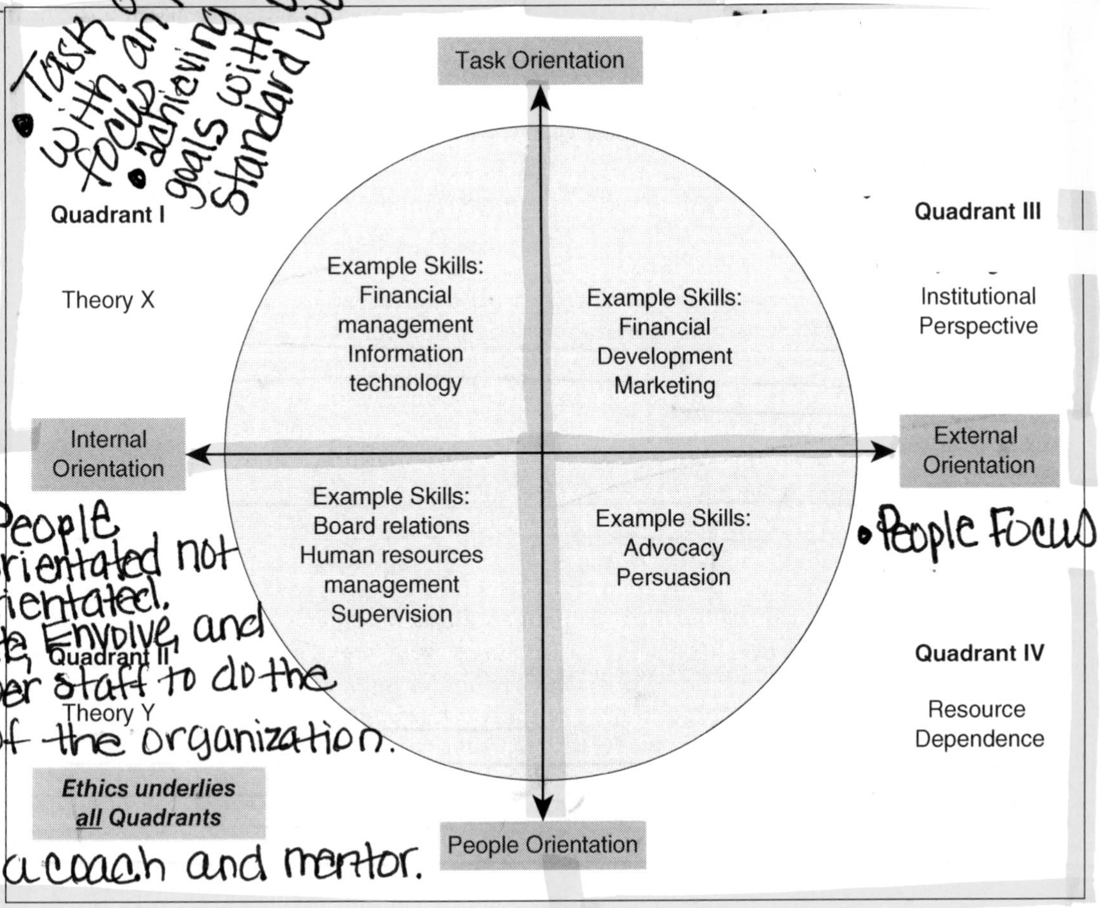

Handwritten annotations (top):
- Directive and Authorative
- Task oriented with an internal focus on achieving organizational goals with using standard work procedures
- Authoritarian leadership style.

Figure 4.1 content:

Task Orientation

Quadrant I

Theory X

Example Skills:
Financial management
Information technology

Example Skills:
Financial Development
Marketing

Quadrant III

Institutional Perspective

Internal Orientation ← → External Orientation

Example Skills:
Board relations
Human resources management
Supervision

Example Skills:
Advocacy
Persuasion

Quadrant II

Theory Y

Ethics underlies all Quadrants

Quadrant IV

Resource Dependence

People Orientation

Figure 4.1 A 4-Quadrant View of Leadership, Needed Skills, and Linked Theory

Handwritten annotations (left/right margins):
- People orientated not task orientated. motivate, Envolve, and Empower staff to do the work of the organization.
- acts a coach and mentor.
- People Focus
- Authurative Leadership Style
- Putting Together the pieces: understanding nonprofit Leadership!

Centralization will be used most often, with few opportunities for others to be involved in the decision-making process. The leader will keep subordinates on a short leash, with strict attention to meeting organizational goals and objectives. The leader will demand that staff members strictly follow organizational rules and processes. This type of leader is likely to use Theory X (McGregor, 1957), which was discussed in Chapter 3.

While this type of leader does not sound very much in tune with nonprofit values of democracy and openness, Schmid (2006) argues that such a set of behaviors in a leader has its place. Residential boarding institutions, for example, require strict following of rules to protect residents' rights, maintain legitimacy, and assure an adequate flow of resources into the organization. Reports of abuses by staff of dependent clients (such as in prisons, state schools, or nursing homes) are far too common and reflect a breakdown in the control of the organization, leading to lawsuits, governmental inquiries, and possible elimination of the organization.

Quadrant II also has an internal orientation, but the leader in this case is people oriented, not task oriented. Leadership behaviors in this quadrant are designed to motivate, involve, and empower staff to do the work of the organization. The leader acts as coach and mentor, seeking to develop staff members to achieve more and to be committed to improving themselves as they accomplish the goals of the organization. This type of leader seems closely aligned with the Human Relations model of leadership, or Theory Y (McGregor, 1957), both discussed in the previous chapter.

Schmid (2006) argues that the most appropriate time for Quadrant II leadership is during the early years of a nonprofit organization's existence. This is when rules are not yet written, patterns are not yet fully established, and the founders of the organization have the most direct influence on the organization and its members/clients/staff. An internal focus for leadership is necessary to stabilize the organization and to create routine job processes and procedures that can lead to routines being established at the organization.

● Quadrant III sets aside the internal focus of Quadrants I and II to look outside of the organization, while remaining task oriented as in Quadrant I. Quadrant III can be seen as the leader "conquering" the world outside of the organization—the push is to acquire legitimacy and resources from external sources so as to institutionalize the nonprofit. Leaders in this situation tend to be very directive and authoritative, and rely on their formal authority much more than their ability to influence indirectly or through the use of inducements. Because the task of organizational institutionalization is seen as so important, staff members and volunteers are frequently narrowly seen as resources to be used to achieve the goal, rather than as important actors in the process. This is squarely in line with the Institutional Perspective (Scott, 1995) mentioned in Chapter 3.

● Quadrant IV represents the convergence of an external orientation with a people focus. Leaders in this area of the model seek to control the future of their organization by reducing its dependence on others for resources even while making other organizations more dependent on them. Considerable attention is paid to developing staff members to improve their ability to handle the external environment's constraints. Because the leader is using so much time and energy to build coalitions and alliances outside of the organization, lower-level staff members must be trained to handle as many issues themselves as possible. Resource dependency theory (Pfeffer & Salancik, 1978) fits well in this quadrant.

It is important to remember that none of the quadrants is "better" than another. But working in each quadrant presents a different set of challenges and requires a different set of skills to be successful. None of the sets of skills described is inferior to another. Just as a carpenter uses many different tools, depending on the job to be done, nonprofit managers must have a basic set of skills at their disposal to be able to employ the ones that fit the situation best.

WHAT ARE THE BASIC SKILLS OF NONPROFIT LEADERSHIP?

Nonprofit organizations come in a variety of sizes, fields, and purposes. Obviously, some are small local organizations, aiming to affect one neighborhood or community by providing services to a marginalized group. Contrast this with international organizations whose purpose is worldwide in scope, such as trying to reverse the process of global climate change. While the exact skills of being a leader may be somewhat different in different types of nonprofits, the literature has some clear guidelines regarding what skills are necessary. Chief among these are being able to work with a board of directors (Herman & Heimovics, 2005). This topic is so important for nonprofit administrators that it has an entire chapter devoted to it (Chapter 10).

Besides being adept with board relations, Herman and Heimovics (2005) make additional suggestions for successful leadership at the executive director level in the nonprofit world:

- Spend time on external relations.
- Develop an informal information network, particularly regarding future events.
- Know your agenda.
- Improvise and accept multiple, partial solutions.
- Use a political framework to understand issues.

In summary, Herman and Heimovics (2005) declare that "board-centered, external and political skills are what distinguish particularly effective nonprofit chief executives" (p. 169). However, lest one believes that nonprofits should operate under a "great leader" model, where all the responsibility for success or failure rests on the shoulders of one person, Grant and Crutchfield (2008) describe the importance of leadership being shared. These authors studied 12 nonprofit organizations extensively for a number of years, developing lessons about what made these organizations so high-impact. One of the most important of these lessons is "leaders of these organizations are able to *share power and inspire others to lead. Leadership doesn't stop at the top;* rather, it extends throughout the organization and a larger network or movement" (p. 46). The analogy used by Grant and Crutchfield is important: They describe the nonprofit director not as the person on top of the hierarchy, but rather the person at the hub of many people, all working to accomplish the mission of the organization.

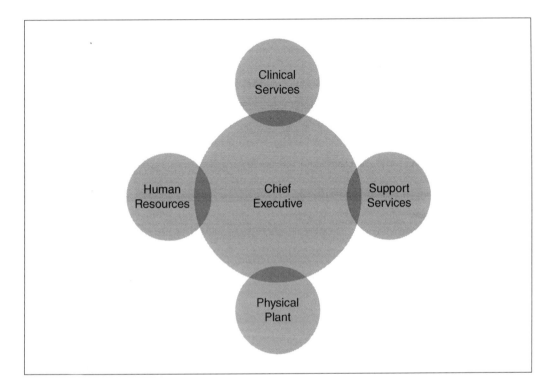

Figure 4.2 The Nonprofit Leader as Hub

STUDIES OF WHICH SKILLS NONPROFIT MANAGERS SHOULD HAVE

The mid-1990s saw considerable research to answer basic questions in the field of nonprofit administration. Hoefer (1993, with a follow-up article in 2003) addresses the question of what should be taught to prepare students to be effective nonprofit leaders. His results show that 37 skills, attitudes, and knowledge areas found in the literature could be rated individually in terms of importance. They could also be condensed into four categories (people skills, attitudes and experiences, substantive knowledge, and management skills) to determine what human services administrators should know how to do. Hoefer (2003) develops three primary conclusions based on the ratings of the skills:

- "Strong agreement exists regarding which skills are most important at the three different levels of administration across disciplines and types of administrators." (p. 41)
- The desired knowledge, skill sets, and attitudes of human service administrators do not change very much as they move from lower levels of administration to higher levels. But it is important to become more accomplished in each of the areas as one reaches a higher level of administration.

- "For all respondents, at all levels, 'people skills' are the most important, and 'management' skills are the least important." (p. 38)

Another conceptualization of what social work managers should know was developed by the National Network for Social Work Managers (NNSWM, 2004) and discussed in Wimpfheimer (2004). Developed through a lengthy process of consultations with practitioners and academics, 14 competency areas are considered vital for social work managers. To receive the "Certified Social Work Manager" credential from the NNSWM, applicants must demonstrate their abilities in these areas. The standards of the NNSWM are not minimum standards but are the competencies that are for experienced and academically trained managers. These standards have solid face validity given the process used to develop and refine the list.

LEADERSHIP SKILLS AT DIFFERENT LEVELS OF AN ORGANIZATION

Most people do not move directly from graduating from college or graduate school to becoming the executive director of a nonprofit organization. They move up the ranks, just as in the corporate and government worlds. Still, leadership skills are necessary at all levels of nonprofits. Thus, it is vital to remember that your leadership skills should be improved throughout your career at whatever organization you are currently working in and throughout your life.

FUTURE DIRECTIONS

Leadership is a fascinating topic for those in the nonprofit field. Given the difficult-to-define nature of nonprofits, and the multiplicity of theories about how to be a good leader, continued research is imperative. Besides better defining which skills might be most important in what type of situations, other areas for research are needed. One of the important topics is assessment of the way students and current leaders can learn new skills and improve current basic levels of leadership skills. One area of needed research is perhaps the most difficult of all: How does improved leadership link to improved outcomes for clients, students, or the public at large? Because nonprofits are legally chartered to enhance the public good, we must always keep sight of the connection between what leaders do and how the public benefits from those actions.

SUMMARY

In the end, we must echo Tschirhart's (1996) words as she ends her book on leadership in nonprofit arts organizations: "There are no simple formulas to adopt" (p. 84). Despite this warning, we have identified what leadership is and what it can be used for, and described a four-quadrant system (and associated leadership theories) to show how different skills can be categorized and used in nonprofit leadership. We have also identified basic leadership skills that are needed across the spectrum of nonprofit organizations (particularly human service agencies) and the situations in which they are most useful. With this as a guide, organization leaders may find it easier to have a positive impact, despite daunting challenges in their everyday work.

REFERENCES

Bennis, W. (2009). *On becoming a leader* (4th ed.). New York: Basic Books.
Burns, J. (1978). *Leadership*. New York: Harper & Row.

Carlyle, T. (1841). *On heroes, hero-worship and the heroic history.* Boston: Houghton Mifflin.

Cyert, R. (1990). Defining leadership and explicating the process. *Nonprofit Management and Leadership, 1*(1), 29–38.

Dym, B., & Hutson, H. (2005). *Leadership in nonprofit organizations: Lessons from the Third Sector.* Thousand Oaks, CA: Sage.

Fielder, F. (1967). *A theory of leadership effectiveness.* New York: McGraw-Hill.

Grant, H., & Crutchfield, L. (2008). The hub of leadership: Lessons from the social sector. *Leader to Leader, 2008*(48), 45–52.

Greenleaf, R. (1991). *The servant as leader* (Rev. ed.). Indianapolis, IN: Robert K. Greenleaf Center.

Herman, R., & Heimovics, R. (2005). Executive leadership. In R. Herman (Ed.), *The Jossey-Bass handbook of nonprofit leadership and management* (2nd ed., pp. 153–170). San Francisco: Jossey-Bass.

Herman, R., & Renz, D. (1997). Multiple constituencies and the social construction of nonprofit organization effectiveness. *Nonprofit and Voluntary Sector Quarterly, 26*(2), 185–206.

Herman, R., & Renz, D. (2004). Doing things right: Effectiveness in local nonprofit organizations: A panel study. *Public Administration Review, 64*(6), 694–704.

Hoefer, R. (1993). A matter of degree: Job skills for human service administration. *Administration in Social Work, 17*(3), 1–20.

Hoefer, R. (2003). Administrative skills and degrees: The "best place" debate rages on. *Administration in Social Work, 27*(1), 25–46.

Hopkins, K., & Hyde, C. (2002). The human service managerial dilemma: New expectations, chronic challenges and old solutions. *Administration in Social Work, 26*(3), 1–15.

Hughes, R., Ginnet R., & Curphy G. (2006), *Leadership: Enhancing the lessons of experience.* New York: McGraw-Hill.

Kirkpatrick, S., & Locke, E. (1991). Leadership: Do traits matter? *Academy of Management Education, 5*(2), 48–60.

Lewin, K., Lippitt, R., & White, R. (1970). Patterns of aggressive behavior in experimentally created social climates. In P. Harriman (Ed.), *Twentieth century psychology* (pp. 200–230). Manchester, NH: Ayer Publishing. (Original work published 1939)

McGregor, D. (1957). *The human side of enterprise.* New York: McGraw Hill.

Mohr, L. (1982). *Explaining organizational behavior.* San Francisco: Jossey-Bass.

National Network for Social Work Managers (NNSWM). (2004). *Leadership and management practice standards.* Retrieved on October 8, 2007, from http://www.socialworkmanager.org/Standards.htm

Pfeffer, J., & Salancik, G. (1978). *The external control of organizations: A resource dependence perspective.* New York: Harper and Row.

Poertner, J. (2006). Social administration and outcomes for consumers: What do we know? *Administration in Social Work, 30*(2), 11–24.

Rothschild, J., & Milofsky, C. (2006). The centrality of values, passions and ethics in the nonprofit sector. *Nonprofit Management and Leadership, 17*(2), 137–143.

Schmid, H. (2006). Leadership styles and leadership changes in human and community service organizations. *Nonprofit Management and Leadership, 17*(2), 179–194.

Scott, W. (1995). *Institutions and organizations.* Thousand Oaks, CA: Sage.

Shenkman, M. (2007, March–April). Defining your leader brand. *Nonprofit World,* 13–14.

Tschirhart, M. (1996). *Artful leadership: Managing stakeholder problems in nonprofit arts organizations.* Bloomington: Indiana University Press.

Wimpfheimer, S. (2004). Leadership and management competencies defined by practicing social work managers: An overview of standards developed by the National Network for Social Work Managers. *Administration in Social Work, 28*(1), 45–56.

HELPFUL TERMS

Authoritative leadership style—a leadership style marked by telling people what to do without providing many opportunities for feedback and suggestions by those being affected.

Contingency leadership theory—a theory regarding leadership that says that the effectiveness or appropriateness of a leader's behaviors is determined to some degree by the leader's environment.

Democratic leadership style—a style of leadership where the leader seeks out others' opinions and attempts to influence others so that a general consensus around a decision emerges.

Directive leadership style—see "authoritative leadership style."

"Great man" leadership theory—a theory regarding leadership that posits that "leaders are born, not made." In other words, people have the innate ability to be a "great leader" or not.

Laissez-faire leadership style—a style of leadership where the leader puts little effort into being the leader or affecting decisions, allowing others to do as they wish.

Multiple constituency theory—a theory of leadership that indicates that leaders must attend to the needs and desires of a number of stakeholders (constituencies) rather than having only one constituency to satisfy.

Organizational effectiveness—a concept that is usually linked to the ability of an organization to accomplish its stated goals. Sometimes the concept is operationalized differently, however, such as "an effective organization is one that has survived" or "an effective organization is one that is growing."

Participative leadership style—see "democratic leadership style."

Servant leadership style—an approach to leadership where the leader chooses to lead in a way that is in service to others. The goal for the servant leader is to serve first and to acquire power or influence later, but only to continue to serve others better.

Single goal-maximizing organization theory—the idea that an organization can be thought of as a unitary entity pursuing one goal to the utmost. Other theories dispute this.

Stakeholder—any individual or outside organization with a vested interest in what occurs within an organization. Typical stakeholders in a nonprofit include service recipients, funders, employees, board members, and the public at large.

System resources theory—a theory of organizations that indicates that the key measure of organizational success is the amount of resources extracted from the environment, with a larger budget indicating a more successful organization.

Trait leadership theory—a theory of leadership characterized by lists of individual traits that are said to be associated with being a good leader.

Transformational leadership style—a style of leadership where the leader creates a vision, sells that vision to followers, and then moves forward to enact the vision with the followers.

EXERCISES

1. In-Basket Exercise

Directions

Read the following memo from a consultant you have hired to help you get your bearings straight in your new position as CEO of Bound for Success, Inc. (BfS), a youth-serving agency specializing in assisting teen foster children successfully transition to independent adulthood by the time they are 22 years of age. As you will read, your agency faces many challenges, and it is up to you to provide guidance to the consultant so he can provide information on possible paths for agency sustainability. You will, of course, need to work closely with the board of directors of BfS, but you would like to have some concrete ideas to start the conversation with them.

Your assignment is to write a memo to your consultant that indicates your top three priorities (in rank order) and the specific actions you believe should be taken to implement these priorities. Provide clear rationales for your decisions so that the consultant can be most helpful to you in his next report. As you write your memo to the consultant, be clear in your mind which stakeholder group(s) you have in mind as your primary reference point. Are you looking more to satisfy the board of directors of BfS, donors and other funders (current and potential), clients, staff members, or some combination of these? You will find that knowing who you are trying to satisfy most will have a large impact on the clarity of your thinking.

Memo

Date:	September 21, 20XX
To:	Rebecca Mayes, CEO, Bound for Success, Inc.
From:	Jim Kreslin, Consultant
Subject:	Strategic Planning Ideas

As requested, I have completed a preliminary analysis of BfS's current situation. Before moving forward, I need direction from you regarding your priorities and the options you feel are most in line with your desired strategy.

The external environment has several important trends impacting BfS. The first is the anticipated decrease in opportunities for federal and state grants. As you know, government sources of funding are becoming fewer and fewer as elected officials promise to reduce taxes, "get back to basics," and let private donors and foundations take more of the funding role for social services. At the same time, many foundations are still unable to provide as much funding as they have in the past due to difficult times in the stock market, where much of their assets are invested. Private donors are also barely keeping their levels of funding even as the economic situation is unsettled for so many. Even BfS's own board's giving has dwindled.

To address these factors, BfS could choose from among the following options:

- Increase its spending on marketing to the general public so that our name recognition and good work is more widely known
- Hire an external grantwriter (at a significant fee) to supplement current fundraising efforts
- Improve and expand current communication channels with important stakeholders and potential donors (we have not used social media outlets such as Facebook and Twitter to any extent, and our web page has not been updated for six months)
- Join coalitions of human service agencies to advocate for more funding for human services in general and agencies serving our client population in particular
- Engage the BfS board more actively to donate at previous or even expanded levels
- Recruit more donors by training board members to fundraise amongst their peers more effectively

At the same time that BfS must understand and deal with these external issues, a number of other issues are important within the organization. As you are aware, no raises have been given to staff for the past three years. Not only has this impacted morale among the agency's workers, but it is also leading to higher levels of staff turnover and increased costs in recruiting new staff members. The high quality applicants we would like to hire are not attracted by our starting salaries, yet the persons willing to work for what we currently offer do not have the skills we need. If we were somehow able to increase our starting salaries for the type of employee we have had, their salaries would be higher than those of loyal workers who have been on the job many years. I am afraid this would lead to a loss of our more senior workers. Another aspect of the job that is important is that proper building maintenance has been deferred for several years. The building's age shows, and both residents and staff see this general deterioration as a negative.

Additionally, it has been at least six years since BfS took a serious look at its programming. A great deal of research has been conducted in this time, and our programs are no longer using the evidence-based information that made them so attractive to funders only a few years ago. The programs we use are not necessarily culturally relevant to the many youth of color we serve, and funding for training to improve staff members' ability to be culturally competent has not kept up with the needs we face, particularly with the high turnover noted earlier.

We should be implementing what are seen to be the most effective services available at the current time, but we have no one assigned the task to stay abreast of the research literature on this topic. Regaining the reputation for being at the forefront of effective service delivery is an important task.

Some steps that BfS could take to handle these (mainly internal) issues include the following:

- Work with a salary and benefits consultant to come into line with local averages for employee compensation
- Hire a researcher from Southeastern University's School of Social Work (or other university) to determine what are currently the most effective, evidence-based services for our clients
- Revamp our service delivery system to be more efficient and to require fewer front-line employees. Savings from having fewer staff could be used to fill a rainy day fund or increase salaries for current and future employees
- Restructure our entire agency to reduce the need for (relatively) expensive administrative positions such as separate directors of "Clinical Services" and "External Relations and Development"
- Engage trainers to assist staff with issues of cultural and racial diversity

Also at your request, I interviewed representatives of some of the important stakeholder groups at BfS. Board members are most concerned with financial stability and organizational sustainability. Staff members would like to see a stronger focus on pay and working conditions, and on being able to assist clients more effectively. Current donors express no negative feelings, but many of them have been surprised at a lack of outreach to them, whether to communicate future plans or even to give thanks for past contributions. Current clients are so focused on their problems that they have few opinions regarding the direction of the agency, as long as their existing needs are met.

I would appreciate it if you would provide guidance as to which issues are your most important priorities and which options I should explore further to address those priorities. If you would also explain the reasons for your decisions, that will greatly benefit me as I work to provide you and the board with a viable plan for agency sustainability.

2. Follow the Leader

Purpose: to experience the difficulty of directing other people to perform specific tasks.

One aspect of leadership is being able to communicate clearly and directly. This exercise shows how challenging a task this can be!

Preparation: You will need an open area (as in the middle of a room) to conduct this exercise. Have participants get in pairs standing together to one side of the open area. One person from each pair should be blindfolded or must promise to keep his or her eyes closed during the exercise. The other person is the "leader." On the floor in the open area, scatter a number of sheets of paper.

Task: The leader in each pair must direct the follower to walk across the open space without the follower touching any of the scattered sheets of paper. The follower must not be able to see the paper. The leader may not use any guidance techniques except for telling the follower what to do. No touching or guiding with props is allowed. Of course, the leader may not touch the sheets of paper either!

Variations:

A. The task can be made more or less challenging depending on the number of sheets of paper used. Having to navigate a few sheets of paper can be thought of as the "front-line supervisor level," a moderate number can be the "department or program leader level," while a large number would be the "CEO level" of leadership. This exercise works best if both members of the pair take turns being leader and follower, and if everyone experiences at least two levels of leadership to show how the process gets more complicated with increasing responsibility.
B. The leader may be allowed to be beside the follower, or may be forced to stay 5–10 feet away from the follower.
C. Add a time dimension by allowing only a certain amount of time for the task to be completed.
D. The leader may become responsible for more than one follower simultaneously. If any of the followers touch the paper on the floor, all are out.
E. Add a competitive element by timing each pair. The pair that completes the task most quickly without touching the paper wins a small prize.
F. The leader may choose a leadership or management theory to implement during this process. Thinking about the ways different theories would try to elicit particular follower behaviors can bring home differences in how management and leadership theories are "in real life." The instructor can start with discussing the differences between how an authoritarian leader and a laissez-faire leader would approach leading a follower from one side of the room to the other, and allow students to try out these approaches or use other leadership theories and perspectives in their efforts.

3. Discuss Your Passion for Nonprofit Leadership

Purpose: to facilitate students' thinking about and ability to express why they would like to be a nonprofit leader.

Understanding your own motivation and passion to be a nonprofit leader can be challenging. Discussing such topics in front of a group can be embarrassing. To succeed in a nonprofit leadership position (or to be hired in the first place), it is important to be able to speak fluidly and with ease about these topics. With practice, discussing these topics becomes easier.

Preparation: Students form into pairs. One is the interviewer, and one the interviewee. (Note: A person can practice answering questions on his or her own, if desired or needed.) Develop a set of two or three questions as a class or small group. The following are some suggested questions:

• What makes you excited to be a nonprofit leader?
• What motivates you to work in a nonprofit rather than a for-profit organization?

- If you were interviewing for a leadership position in a nonprofit agency, what would you say makes you a good fit for such a job?
- Fill in the blanks: "My preferred style of leadership is _____ because _____."

Task: The two students in each pair practice asking and answering the chosen questions. When they are comfortable with their ability to answer the questions, have the students do this in front of the class (or have only volunteers do this).

Variations:

A. Have students make videos of themselves answering the questions in class (using their cell phones if available). Have them critique their own performance with their partner. Have students discuss what they would do to improve their performance.

B. Students can be assigned to make a video outside of class of themselves answering the questions. This would then be posted to a class wiki or other area to be viewed by the instructor and/or other students. This variation works well for online courses.

4. Being the "Dancing Guy"

Purpose: One definition of being a leader is having one or more followers. Leadership occurs at all levels of organizations, not just at the top of the organizational chart. Leadership skills need to be developed throughout your career, as many of them are similar in nature no matter where in an organization your current position is. This exercise shows the way leadership can emerge anywhere and at any time.

Preparation: Go to YouTube and search for the term "Leadership Lessons from the Dancing Guy." Select any one of the versions of the video available. (They are all copies of the original one by Derek Sivers at http://youtube/fW8amMCVAJQ.) Cue up the video for your class or group. Announce that you are going to demonstrate that anyone can be a leader.

Task: First, watch the video without sound. Lead a discussion with students about what they saw. Then discuss the sorts of things that they can do in the spirit of being the "dancing guy" at their job or in their volunteer time. Discuss the differences between formal leadership positions and informal leadership. Then show the video again, with sound, to listen to the commentary by Derek Sivers.

Variations:

A. Have students try being "the dancing guy" in some part of their lives (for extra credit), perhaps starting a dancing mob or by engaging in some other non-dangerous behavior, even just looking up at the top of a building. Have them debrief for the class what occurred and how it felt.

B. Have students take the exercise one step further by pre-organizing the "spontaneous" first and second followers to join in. What other ways can they think of to improve their perceived leadership abilities by using theory and knowledge in their work?

1. A huge number of sources exist regarding leadership, and more become available constantly. This assignment asks you to "curate" information for yourself and others in your class or group. Be willing to post the results of these assignments to a class or group wiki or other method of dissemination.

    A. Find two to three books on leadership or by leaders you'd be willing to read. What makes them attractive to you? What can they tell you about how to be a better leader?

    B. Find four to five videos on leadership in nonprofits, searching in YouTube, Vimeo, or other free sources. Write a synopsis of what each video is about. Rate each video from 1 (not good at all) to 5 (excellent source of information) and explain your rating.

    C. Search for a nonprofit leadership training or seminar you could attend, live or virtually. Try to find participant reviews of it. Describe the training and reviews for others in your class or group.

2. Think about leaders you are aware of, whether you have known them or only read or seen information about them. These people may be as varied as a Scout leader, an historical leader such as Jane Addams or Abraham Lincoln, an instructor or teacher, or a boss in one of your jobs. Make a list of the qualities that you see that are good leadership traits, skills, or behaviors. Have at least 15 different entries. Look over this list and group the individual items into a smaller number of overarching behaviors or skills. Label these groups. Write or find a definition that matches your idea of what YOU mean by that term. Be prepared to discuss your list and definitions in class or other group setting.

3. Select a person who is in a leadership position in the nonprofit world. (This position may be paid or volunteer.) Arrange to interview him or her. Find out about that person's journey to the current leadership position. What led to starting in this position? What training does your interviewee have (formal or informal)? Does this person follow any "theories" of leadership, such as being directive, participative, or delegative? Did the person you talked with have a mentor? (Note: This assignment works best if several or all students or group members ask similar questions so that, after sharing what was discussed in the interview, generalizations can be made about the processes of becoming a leader in the nonprofit world.)

Personal Communication

5

According to research, oral and written communication skills are among the most important skills for nonprofit leaders to have (Hoefer, 2003). This chapter provides information about understanding what you want to communicate and communicate well, primarily in one-on-one and collegial situations. Communication is such a vital skill for nonprofit leaders that we also have Chapter 13, "Persuasion," and Chapter 14, "Advocacy," which also deal with communication. Those chapters are geared toward communication with the purpose of moving others to agree with you and to take certain actions. The skills in this chapter are important for being able to be persuasive as well, so these interpersonal skills really form the foundation for communication of all types.

Before moving forward, it is important to remember that the techniques of "communication" are rarely important for their own sake. Communication, at its core, is sending and receiving messages—messages of praise, correction, affirmation, hope, affection, or belonging, for example. Leaders must know the techniques of effective communication to make connections with others within and outside their organization, and to provide a means of accomplishing organizational goals through the work of those others. The most well-written and delivered speech, for example, even if it is a wonderful application of "communication theory," will fall flat if personal connection is not made.

In this chapter, we have three underlying topics. First, we examine the need for managers to use active listening techniques; second, we examine management of emotions; finally, we look at storytelling as a method of making your message resonate. All of these techniques, when used to communicate with others, are important in developing your leadership capacity.

ACTIVE LISTENING

Arguably the most important skill for effective personal communication (as a manager or otherwise) is to be able to use active listening. Based on the work of Carl Rogers, this process is seen as part of a manager's job, but the listener must have true empathy for and trust in the speaker's ability to self-direct, or else it is impossible to truly listen actively. Rogers and Farson (1987) indicate that active listening is "the art of listening for meaning" (p. 1) and that this requires careful listening, but even this alone is not sufficient.

Active listening, according to Rogers and Farson (1987), brings about better self-understanding for the speaker who becomes "more emotionally mature, more open to their experiences, less defensive, more democratic and less authoritarian" (p. 1). The listener also benefits by obtaining more information from the speaker, developing deep positive relationships, and constructively improving attitudes.

To achieve these results, the active listener must use the following techniques.

- **Listen for meaning, not just content.** Messages and conversations have content, but content can be surrounded by additional contextual information. For example, a colleague could tell you, "I just completed the quarterly report for the new project we're starting," and you would be likely to give a positive response. Suppose that colleague told you instead, "I finally got done with the quarterly report for the director's pet project—now I can do some real work!" You would probably understand that a significantly different set of meanings was intended by your colleague. Even if you gave the same content response, such as "Congratulations!" it might be construed differently in the two situations by your colleague. In the first situation, you might find the meaning given to your word as a straightforward and supportive acknowledgement. In the second situation, however, your coworker might assume you are being ironic, which could still be seen as supportive, but might be interpreted as disrespectful by the director if you were overheard.

- **Respond to feelings.** For active listening to take place, you must let the speaker know that you have comprehended both the content of the statement and the feelings that emerge with the content. In the same example, you could be a better listener if you replied, in the first instance, "Congratulations! That must feel good to have that finished!" and, in the second, "You sound like you're not too happy with having to do that job. It must be a relief to move on to something else." Neither of these responses takes much longer to say, but both indicate that you are trying to understand how your coworker feels about what has just been said.

- **Note nonverbal cues.** Communication happens through many channels, including voice tone, speed of talking, volume level, vocal hesitations, facial expressions, hand gestures, and other body language. To completely understand someone else's meaning, you must decode what all these nonverbal signals mean.

While the benefits of active listening are many, there are at least three reasons why people do not listen actively. Multitasking is a common behavior where we try to do something else while the speaker is talking. This frequently results in miscommunication because important nonverbal and emotional cues are not noticed. It is best to lay aside other things and focus on the speaker when you wish to listen carefully. Some people are unable to actively listen to a speaker because they are formulating their own responses to the previous statement the speaker said. They may even be lining up the reasons why the speaker is wrong instead of following along with what is being said. Remember that you are not engaging in a debate, but rather attempting to understand the other person's viewpoint.

Another barrier to active listening that frequently occurs at work is that the person speaking is of lower status than the listener. While we would all like to believe this is not true about ourselves, the facts are otherwise. Our supervisors and leaders usually receive our attention because what they say can affect our job situation positively or negatively. It is more difficult to listen attentively to someone who reports to you, particularly when you have a lot of other work to complete. It can be even worse if the person speaking is in a different department or is unknown to you. Unfortunately, we may respond to communications from clients with a lack of attention as well. Despite our best intentions, we may also harbor biases and prejudices about certain populations that get in the way of listening to them. The best way to guard against these tendencies is to stay aware of our own biases and to feel deeply that each person has inherent worth, just as Carl Rogers taught.

Becoming skilled in active listening techniques will not solve every problem you encounter as a manager. You will still need to work with employees who are not performing well. Some employees may expect you to understand them using ESP, so they don't need to explain to you what they are thinking. This is a challenge. Over time, however, using active listening will make your job easier because you will at least understand what your coworkers want to tell you. This will go a long way to making every day smoother because your colleagues will learn to trust that you will listen to them before you make decisions that affect them. Your colleagues will have seen you seeking to understand their views first before you take action. Even if they don't agree with your final decision, they will be more likely to follow your lead because their ideas have been heard.

MANAGING YOUR EMOTIONAL SELF

Related to the need to be a skilled active listener, and thus to understand what other people want to communicate, is the need to manage your own emotional self. While the idea of emotional intelligence is currently heatedly debated on both conceptual (Eysenck, 2000; Locke, 2005) and methodological (Brody, 2004) grounds, managers need to understand their own emotions (as they occur) and be able to handle them appropriately. Managers and leaders are frequently put into positions where conflict is either raging or bubbling under the surface. Frequently, tough decisions must be made. The outcomes of these decisions can have severely negative repercussions for some people—staff members might be laid off or fired, client services reduced, or programs eliminated entirely.

Even if you have used active listening to its fullest, sometimes people are going to be very distraught and angry. They may yell at you, threaten you, or start other unpleasant or even dangerous situations. It is at times such as this that your ability to notice how you are feeling (angry, frightened, irritated, afraid, withdrawn, and so on) is vital. Strong emotions can result in an "emotional hijacking" (Goleman, 2006) where your feelings literally avoid the rational parts of your brain and affect your "primitive brain" directly. Such a hijacking can cause you to invoke the "flight or fight" response, which motivates you to run away or to lash out. Hormones and adrenaline are immediately released by your body, which then stimulate action without thought. While this type of reaction is important if one is about to be attacked by a predator, it has less use in a nonprofit office. Being unable to take control back after an emotional hijacking can be quite damaging to your career and have negative effects for your organization.

In this type of situation, being able to note and classify your emotional state allows you to re-route your hijacked brain so that your thoughts go through the rational parts of the cortex, and allows you to regain the ability to think logically about how to respond to the perceived danger you face. It may be that you are not threatened nearly as much as you first thought. Taking the time to calm down enough to think again will usually save considerable amounts of time later on as you will not need to retrace your steps or attempt to undo hasty actions.

Once the emotions are noted, they have less power to control you. You can also take four additional steps when confronted with an emotionally difficult situation at work. First, take control of yourself. If you are not under control, you won't be able to assist others. One way to manage yourself is to breathe deeply and slowly, forcing oxygen into your system (which is good for thinking) and preventing you from rashly taking action. In situations like this, it is better to take slow steps, even taking a step back mentally, than to jump ahead quickly without thinking things through. Second, you can also take a few moments to think about how you would like the situation to end and the steps you can take to achieve that preferred end. Third, by engaging your active listening skills, you can determine what your colleague wants from the situation. This act will take time and also help pacify the other person to some extent. Finally, you can try to interject some humor into the situation. This must be genuine humor, and preferably self-deprecating, rather than a sarcastic or snide sort of joking about the other person. While not always an easy thing to do, finding a way to comment on something funny about yourself or the situation relieves tension and allows for a peaceful resolution. Many times, a mild disagreement can escalate into something much worse, a situation that causes lasting damage to relationships and job performance. These few simple acts on your part can keep communication open.

As a leader, you will at times need to manage your team and their feelings in group (rather than one-on-one) situations. You must be clear about your own feelings, as noted earlier, and you can use similar techniques to bring about good results in meetings. One of the more important elements of communicating during group sessions is to be clear about what others in the group are thinking and feeling. Often, when there is conflict within a group, or as options are being discussed, frustrations arise if participants do not feel they are being heard. You need to ask for clarification and use your active listening skills in these situations. You should also ask questions and be willing to challenge ideas that are put forth so that pros and cons can be brought out ahead of any decisions. In addition, it is wise to have the group discuss issues such as what are "best case" solutions, and what alternative solutions are acceptable. By separating out these two levels of results, solutions meeting different needs or views can often be found. By modeling what you expect from others, you will help create a higher functioning group. In the end, your final decision probably will not make everyone happy. Still, if the process is open and people have a chance for meaningful participation, you can usually retain good working relationships.

A final way to keep emotional hijacking from occurring is to take the surprise element out of the situation. It may not be that your fight-or-flight response is related to the actual topic (as conflictual as it might be) but rather that your emotions are aroused because of the suddenness or unexpectedness of the issue arising at that moment. It is often appropriate to take a step back and request a short break or to schedule a separate meeting time for topics with high emotional loads. You will have time to consider what you want to accomplish with the discussion, as will everyone else involved. By lowering the stress levels for yourself and others, better decisions will be made.

If you have introduced the concept of emotional hijacking to your coworkers and explained how our emotions can bypass our logical thinking processes, leading to unnecessary escalation of responses to issues, everyone on the team can be on guard to keep the whole group or a member of the group from succumbing to this common problem. It can even turn into a group practice that a certain phrase can be used to signal to people that they may need to check and monitor their emotional situation. When used in this way, the power of the group is enhanced and individuals within it can be nudged by colleagues to become more self-aware and productive.

STORYTELLING

Humans have used stories and storytelling since we developed the ability to communicate. It continues to be a primary means for helping people listen and remember important messages (Heath & Heath, 2007). Listening to carefully crafted stories has been shown to create changes in the listener's brain chemistry, increasing both cortisol (which focuses attention) and oxytocin (which improves the ability to empathize and create feelings of care) (Zak, 2011).

Excellent stories have advantages for communicating ideas because they have a clear narrative and so are easy to follow, they are concrete, they are credible, they contain a surprising element, and they pack an emotional jolt. Even mediocre stories that have just some of these elements help people retain key, simple points that help them act in desired ways (Heath & Heath, 2007). Stories are seen to be more captivating, conversational, outwardly focused on the audience, entertaining, compelling, textured, and real than typical organizational communications (Hoffman, 2011).

Different types of stories exist for different purposes. Simmons (2007) describes many types of stories that are useful to achieve different types of goals. We look at four here. The first, "Who I am," is useful when you want to get across your values and the kind of leader or person you are. You open yourself up a bit to allow those around you to see who you are. This type of story is important in job interviews, for example, when interviewers might ask you to describe a time when you overcame an obstacle, or approached a new situation. Political candidates have a well-rehearsed story of "Who I am" so they can connect with the electorate, particularly as they start wooing new sets of voters.

A second type of story is called the "Why I am here" story, and can be related to the first type. When you are a leader, people working with and for you want to know not only who you are, but also why you are in your current position. You've chosen to be a part of an organization, in fact, to be a leader within it. People rightly want to have insight into what you want to accomplish.

Teaching stories are the third type Simmons (2007) discusses. For millennia, the parables of Jesus, such as the Good Samaritan, or the parables of Aesop, with the story of the Boy Who Cried Wolf, have become shorthand ways of communicating the right way or the wrong way to live. If you can encapsulate "best practices" for your organization in a teaching story, you can be sure that the message will get through.

The fourth type of story communicates a vision. Martin Luther King Jr.'s "I Have a Dream" speech is such a story, but so is John Kennedy's speech about sending a man to the moon and returning him safely. When you and your organization can develop a story of where you want to go, such inspiration will help you keep going through even massive difficulties. In Chapter 6, you will read about the value of an organizational vision. Remember that your vision is only a set of words unless you can get people to act to achieve it. A vision story provides just the means to make the vision "sticky"—easily remembered and thus capable of being worked toward (Heath & Heath, 2007).

When you have an important message to deliver to your coworkers, a story might be the best way to begin. When using storytelling in this way, you need to prepare—few of us are able to speak extemporaneously in an effective way (although we can get better with practice). Good stories, even very short ones, often have the following features in common:

1. A protagonist in a situation

2. A challenge (internal and/or external)

3. A resolution to the challenge

4. Moral or application

The first three features together are called the *dramatic arc*. Longer stories have more challenges that need to be dealt with, and have smaller resolutions and setbacks along the way, leading eventually to the ultimate showdown and climax to the story. In the end, something has changed, whether it is the situation, the protagonist, or both. When stated plainly, this becomes the moral of the story. Sometimes it is left up to the listeners to determine the moral for themselves, especially if the story is left unfinished as part of a current situation or as a way of stimulating engagement in the decision-making process.

Naturally, you will need to speak and write in other ways as well, for example, when communicating a set of facts or options that are being considered. Even here, however, you can incorporate a look at challenges, emotions, and successes in narrative forms that will hold your audience's attention and stick in their heads. Once you begin communicating with stories, you will find that people remember what you have to say and you have more of an impact (Simmons, 2007).

One of the beneficial aspects of storytelling is that you are forced to determine what point you wish to make before you can effectively communicate it. We have all been in conversations with people who want to tell a story that is lacking a dramatic arc, rambles endlessly, and has no point. As you begin to use stories in your work life, remember to describe a person or situation, the challenges to be faced, the difficulties in overcoming obstacles, and the benefits that ensue when the deeds are successfully accomplished.

SUMMARY

This chapter has described three areas of interpersonal communication skills that leaders need to master. The first, active listening, allows you to learn what others think and make good use of their knowledge because you are listening for meaning. You will be able to make better decisions with a broader set of facts and emotional understanding by listening actively. Becoming skilled in emotional management and emotional intelligence was the second topic. Learning to take charge of your emotions in the service of your work and organization represents an important aspect of leadership. If you are not in charge of yourself, you are really not in charge of much at all. Finally, we presented information about storytelling, and the benefits it can bring to your ability to communicate about yourself, the organization's view of best practices, and the future you are working towards.

REFERENCES

Brody, N. (2004). What cognitive intelligence is and what emotional intelligence is not. *Psychological Inquiry, 15*, 234–238.

Eysenck, H. (2000). *Intelligence: A new look.* Piscataway, NJ: Transaction Publishers.

Goleman, D. (2006). *Emotional intelligence* (10th anniversary ed.). New York: Random House.

Heath, C., & Heath, D. (2007). *Made to stick: Why some ideas survive and some die.* New York: Random House.

Hoefer, R. (2003). Administrative skills and degrees: The "best place" debate rages on. *Administration in Social Work, 27*(1), 25–46.

Hoffman, L. (2011). Storytelling vs. corporate speak [Web log post]. Retrieved from http://www .ishmaelscorner.com/2011/09/22/infographic-storytelling-vs-corporate-speak

Locke, E. (2005). Why emotional intelligence is an invalid concept. *Journal of Organizational Behavior, 26*(4), 425–431. doi:10.1002/job.318.

Rogers, C., & Farson, R. (1987). Active listening. In R. Newman, M. Danzinger, & M. Cohen (Eds.), *Communicating in business today.* Lexington, MA: D.C. Heath & Company. Retrieved from http:// www.go-get.org/pdf/Rogers_Farson.pdf

Simmons, A. (2007). *Whoever tells the best story wins: How to use your own stories to communicate with power and impact.* New York: American Management Association.

Zak, P. (2011). Trust, morality—and oxytocin [Video file]. Retrieved from http://www.youtube.com/ watch?v=rFAdlU2ETjU

HELPFUL TERMS

Active listening—a type of listening that seeks to understand the meaning behind words rather than just the words themselves.

Emotional hijacking—a situation where your feelings are strong enough to overcome your rational thought process.

Emotional intelligence—the concept that there exists a set of skills that allow people to understand their own and others' emotions, help them regulate their emotions, and help them plan and achieve goals in their life.

Teaching story—a type of story that has an explicit moral or lesson that will help listeners behave in the desired manner after hearing it.

Unconditional positive regard—a term associated with the work of psychologist Carl Rogers, meaning acceptance of a person as a person, even when you may not agree with his or her behavior. It is a way for the manager to point out and seek to correct employee mistakes or errors without the employee feeling less worthy as a person.

Vision story—a type of story that communicates the preferred future that you or your organization is working to achieve.

Why I am here story—a type of story that communicates your reason for being in the position you are in and what you hope to accomplish.

Who I am story—a type of story that communicates who the storyteller is by revealing personal values, beliefs, and history. It is very useful in allowing others to become comfortable with you as a person because they feel they know you and can perhaps more easily trust you.

1. In-Basket Exercise

Directions

For this exercise, pretend you are Becky Jones, Communications Director for your organization. Your boss, the CEO of the entire agency, needs your help. Using the ideas presented in this chapter, craft a 3 minute presentation with PowerPoint slides (or other visual aids) or a speech (without visual aids) that will give the CEO something "compelling, entertaining, and (hopefully) lucrative" as he requests.

Memo

Date: September 1, 20XX

To: Becky Jones, Communications Director

From: Shawn O'Malley, CEO, Youth Services of Eastern Oklahoma

Subject: Message for End of Year Fundraising Kickoff

In two weeks, I will provide the closing talk to the End of Year Fundraising Kickoff Dinner with some of our best donors. Usually, I list off the goals and objectives we set at the start of the year and how we've done in accomplishing them so far. In the past few years, I have found that we are not getting the financial benefits from these events that are expected by members of the board and what our agency needs. I've looked in the mirror and found what I think is the reason for this lack of success. Frankly, I have given boring speeches, but I don't know how to make them better.

This year, I am asking for your help to take the usual list of goals, objectives, and results and turn it into a compelling, entertaining, and (hopefully) lucrative communication with our best donors. Here are the facts—I would like to hear back from you with your draft by next week.

I know people like to hear how their money is spent, so I have gotten this information for you. So far this year, we have served 147 youth (85 boys and 62 girls). We have served over 132,000 meals, washed sheets nearly 7,000 times, administered 219 prescriptions, and bought 46 pairs of glasses, 93 dresses, 151 pairs of pants, 289 shirts/tops, 308 pairs of shoes, and many dozens of socks and pieces of underclothing. Our cleaning supplies budget is $12,000. Office supply purchases have topped $14,000, due mainly to the need to upgrade the computers we have in the residences and offices. Luckily, we were able to get a good price on those from the local Best Buy store. Grounds-keeping with all this snow we had last winter has run over budget, and stands at $7,450. Utilities are also high this year, costing about $21,000 so far. We are hoping for a mild winter this year.

The economy of the state has been poor this year, with the economic downturn lingering in its effects. Unemployment is at 12%, job losses are in the thousands in our area, and natural disasters are sucking potential donors dry. Our foundation supporters have reduced funding by 15% over the past three years, and government reimbursements are running six months behind. Our total income for the year is down 4%, after previous dips of 1% and 6%.

We anticipate that we will exhaust our cash reserves within six months and be forced to do something drastic to continue serving the same number of clients. We are not likely to be forced to close our doors next year, but the future after that is rather grim.

Typical client 1: Sally, a 12-year-old girl who has been abused for a period of 10–12 months by a family member. Parents have relinquished rights. Adoption for this type of client is rare. She is under our care and protection for perhaps the next six years.

Typical client 2: Nicodemus, a 16-year-old boy who is looking at the end of his time with us in less than two years. He came to our facility after being orphaned a year ago and attempting to live on the streets. He wants to be independent but doesn't have strong social or living skills.

Here is our mission, for your easy reference: "We protect children and youth from abuse and neglect by providing a safe, caring residential alternative when needed."

As the largest provider of services to youth in the eastern Oklahoma area, we strive to ensure that no child is left in an unsafe situation for more than 24 hours. We do this through three emergency shelters, one residential facility, and 43 staff members. We also provide parent-training programs to prevent problems before they begin. We don't turn children away, calling on an extensive network of emergency foster care parents when other resources are full or otherwise unavailable to meet the needs of impacted children.

See what you can do with this information, will you?

2. How Was Your Day?

Sitting with a partner, tell the story of what you did this morning to get to school or work on time. Don't make anything up, just stick to the facts. Complete this task in two minutes or less. This is the sort of typical "how was your day?" approach to conversation and communication. Listen to your partner's story. Now, take a 10-minute break and revise your story, keeping in mind the following prompt: What obstacles did you face to get to or school or work (internal or external)? How did you address each issue? Were you successful or not? What lessons can you draw from this experience? Retell the story of your morning.

3. Emotional Self-Management

Think of a situation at work or school where you were quite irritated or angry and you let it show. Discuss with a colleague or two what happened and what you did. If you were to find yourself in a similar situation, how could you apply some of the tools for emotional self-management? Do you think they would be effective in this situation?

4. Active Listening

Active listening is very helpful in many workplace situations. Working with the same person you talked with in Exercise 3, pretend that you are that person's instructor or supervisor who witnessed the situation. Role-play how you would work with your colleague to resolve the situation.

ASSIGNMENTS

1. The concept and measurement of Emotional Intelligence (EI) is controversial. Some authors say that it doesn't really exist as an "intelligence." Write a four- to five-page paper discussing the main arguments about the validity of EI as a concept. Which side of the argument do you believe is correct? What are the implications of your position as a nonprofit manager?

2. The idea of active listening is derived from the work of psychologist Carl Rogers. Unconditional positive regard is another concept he developed and embraced. Write a short paper (four to five pages) of the pros and cons of Rogers' work as it applies to being a manager or leader in a nonprofit organization. Which techniques, if any, would you like to incorporate into your management and leadership style?

3. Storytelling is an art and a profession. There are storytelling events and workshops across the country. If possible, attend one to gain a deeper understanding of this ancient craft. If you cannot attend one live, locate a book or other training aid about storytelling. Write a review of what you saw, heard, or read, and how you can apply the principles to your own life, particularly your life as a nonprofit leader and manager.

Part III

Leadership Skills

Agency Planning

6

Human service administrators must provide leadership in developing tools that keep the organization moving in the right direction. From time to time, we need to ask our key stakeholders, "What direction do we want to take?" Many times, this question comes during the process of strategic planning. While there are variations in the approach to strategic planning, the basic steps are, typically, as follows:

STEPS IN THE STRATEGIC PLANNING PROCESS

1. Determination of nonprofit values, vision, and mission
2. Setting goals and objectives to accomplish the mission
3. Conducting a SWOT Analysis or other analytical assessment
4. Developing strategies to meet goals and objectives
5. Evaluating performance in meeting goals
6. Learning from evaluation and making necessary corrections

Source: Adapted from Vaughan and Arsneault (2013).

Strategic planning allows an organization to evaluate the vision, mission, and all that the organization does to accomplish its goals and objectives. Without a clear and up-to-date vision and mission for the organization, there is the danger that there will be a great deal of activity but very little accomplished. If we don't a have good idea about our ultimate destination, it doesn't make a lot of difference what direction we take to get there. Alice learned this lesson from the wise cat in *Alice's Adventures in Wonderland*.

"Would you tell me, please, which way I ought to go from here?"

"That depends a good deal on where you want to get to," said the Cat.

"I don't much care where—," said Alice.

(Continued)

(Continued)

"Then it doesn't matter which way you go," said the Cat.

"—so long as I get SOMEWHERE," Alice added as an explanation.

"Oh, you're sure to do that," said the Cat, "if you only walk long enough."

(Carroll, 1898)

As a human services administrator, you don't want to get "somewhere"—you want to get to a clearly defined future state. Planning (many times within the context of strategic planning) involves formulating a course of action that will move the organization from its present state to some desirable future state. Such planning is important in the agency being able to get things done because it allows the board, administration, and staff to have an "end-in-mind" perspective that helps to orchestrate the day-to-day decisions that are made throughout the agency to minimize the possibility of activity without purpose. Such planning involves creating and articulating a vision of a desirable and attainable future state, having a clear and concise mission, and articulating the guiding values of the organization. Once these are developed in the form of a vision statement, mission statement, and a statement of guiding principles, the organization can move on to identifying appropriate goals, objectives, and activities to accomplish these goals.

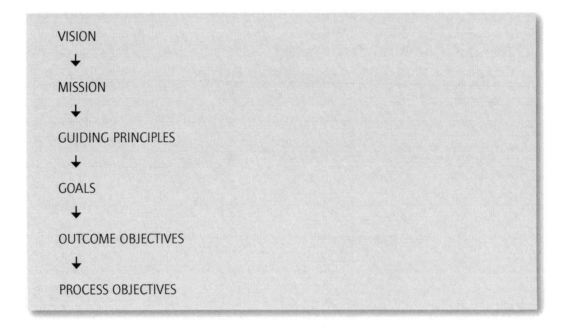

VISION

↓

MISSION

↓

GUIDING PRINCIPLES

↓

GOALS

↓

OUTCOME OBJECTIVES

↓

PROCESS OBJECTIVES

GOVERNING IDEAS

Peter Senge (1990) presents the concept of "governing ideas" in an organization in his work *The Fifth Discipline*. He states that the mission should answer the question "Why do we exist?" and the core values should answer "How do we want to act?" He presents vision as the way to describe the ideal future for the organization and as the foundation of the planning process that includes strategic planning, setting goals and objectives, and designing programs (cited in Lewis, Packard, & Lewis, 2011). Let us more closely examine the concepts of vision, mission, and values and their associated documents: the vision statement, the mission statement, and the values statement.

VISION STATEMENT

Helen Keller, probably the most recognized blind person who has ever lived, once said, "What would be worse than being born blind? To have sight without vision." With guidance from Helen Keller and Alice's Cheshire Cat, we must conclude that having a clear mission is an important thing!

Developing a vision statement is a powerful way to frame the agency's mission, goals and objectives, and activities; provide a powerful image of the future for the organization; and provide the foundation for planning activities (Lewis, Packard, & Lewis, 2011). A key component of developing a vision statement is that it is developed from throughout the organization. It is not something that you can write in isolation sitting in your office. The vision statement is really the "shared vision" of the organization. The vision is what you and your stakeholders believe or dream that your organization can be in the future. It answers the question, "What do we want the organization to be?" What would the organization look like in the next 10 to 15 years if there were no resource constraints? What would you want your organization to mean in the lives of your clients? An organization is more likely to succeed when as many stakeholders as possible share the same vision of the future. The process of developing a vision statement to describe that shared vision can be an important event in the life of the organization (Worth, 2009). The purpose of a vision statement is to give the organization a vision of the future. The real value in developing a vision statement is to engage the board, staff, and other stakeholders in the process to develop a shared vision of their future. Those participating in the process should not be constrained in their creativity by thinking about the resources available at the present time. The assumption needs to be made that the agency will have all it needs in money, staff, and other resources to reach the agreed-on vision (Austin & Solomon, 2009). The following are examples of vision statements from some leading human services organizations.

> ## EXAMPLES OF VISION STATEMENTS
>
> **Boy Scouts of America:** To prepare every eligible youth in America to become a responsible, participating citizen and leader who is guided by the Scout Oath and Law.
>
> **Goodwill:** Every person has the opportunity to achieve his/her fullest potential and participate in and contribute to all aspects of life.
>
> **Amnesty International:** Amnesty International's vision is of a world in which every person enjoys all of the human rights enshrined in the Universal Declaration of Human Rights and other international human rights instruments. (Top Nonprofits, n.d.)

MISSION STATEMENT

Simply put, the mission statement explains why your organization exists. Drucker (1992) has stated that one of the most common mistakes in developing a mission statement is to make it into a "kind of hero sandwich of good intentions" (p. 5). He cautions that the statement needs to be simple and clear. A mission statement according to Smith, Bucklin & Associates, Inc. (2000) is "[a] succinct statement that sets forth the organization's purpose and philosophy. Although brief, the mission statement will specify the fundamental reasons for the organization's existence;

establish the scope of the organization; and identify the organization's unique characteristics" (p. 13). A good mission statement should be inspiring but, at the same time, be concise and easily understood and remembered (Brody, 2005). It is sometimes said that the mission statement should be short enough to fit on the back of a business card. It is the mission statement that gives the organization a sense of direction.

The ongoing and constant question should be, "Does this fit within our mission?" This question often arises in organizations when new funding opportunities arise. The alternative to evaluating funding opportunities in light of the agency mission is to be involved in "chasing dollars." Just because funding is available or a new service opportunity emerges does not mean that it is right for the agency. All such opportunities need to be evaluated within the context of the mission of the organization. The mission statement gives direction and continuity (Kettner, Moroney, & Martin, 2008).

A key component of the mission statement is that it focuses on the future state of the clients if the agency is successful in addressing their problems or meeting their needs (Kettner et al., 2008). For anyone reading the mission statement, it should be clear to them as to why the organization exists and what difference it will make to the clients they serve. Take a look at the following examples of mission statements. Do they meet the requirements of a good mission statement?

EXAMPLES OF MISSION STATEMENTS

American Red Cross: Prevents and alleviates human suffering in the face of emergencies by mobilizing the power of volunteers and the generosity of donors.

Wounded Warrior Project: To honor and empower wounded warriors.

March of Dimes: We help moms have full-term pregnancies and research the problems that threaten the health of babies.

Make-A-Wish: We grant the wishes of children with life-threatening medical conditions to enrich the human experience with hope, strength and joy. (Top Nonprofits, n.d.)

It is important to know that it is the board of trustees (or, in the case of public agencies, the legislative body) that determines the mission of the organization. The development of the mission statement is and should be a collaborative effort between the human services administrator, the board, and the staff. However, the reality is that the mission statement is a policy statement and, therefore, is within the responsibility of the board. Mission statements are not static documents; they can and do change over time, but those changes must be made in a systematic and thoughtful way as part of a planning process. The board should constantly ask, "Is this within the mission of our agency?" If the answer is "No," then the activity should not be undertaken or the mission should be modified. Likewise, the board must always ask, "Is our mission still relevant?" If the original purpose of the organization is no longer relevant, the board must decide whether the agency has a reason to exist.

A CASE STUDY IN CHANGING MISSIONS

The Methodist Mission Home in San Antonio, Texas, was established in 1895. For most of its history, the agency served as an unwed mothers' home. It had started out in a small house and by the mid-1960s was serving over 300 young women each year with residential services. In 1968, the agency moved from the small facility to a beautiful new 30-acre campus with six buildings. However, by the time the new facility opened, there were only six women in residence. Many things had changed: birth control, abortion, single parenthood, and changing societal views. The need for which the facility was built was no longer valid. After a long period of planning, the board made the decision to continue the original mission of serving unwed mothers (but on a smaller scale) and to expand their mission to serve deaf adults in need of independent living and job skills training. The agency continues to serve both populations today and has expanded to serve other people with disabilities.

GUIDING PRINCIPLES

A statement of principles describes the values that will guide the organization. These are the things that will not be compromised and are often based on deeply held convictions and traditions. Many times, agencies will find themselves caught between the policies, needs, and desires of funders or their contract agencies and their own agency principles. Human services administrators need to be clear in knowing the guiding principles of their organization and carrying out their responsibilities to uphold them. For that reason, it is very important to be sure that your personal values are in sync with the agency where you work. Can you support the principles of the organization even if they are not exactly the same values that you hold? If you are working for an organization that is religiously affiliated and you are not a member of that religious group, can you support and uphold the guiding principles of the organization? These are important questions to ask yourself when considering where you want to work.

In addition to the guiding principles of an organization, we each have professional values and ethics that come into consideration. As a human services administrator, you will work with professionals from many different disciplines that come with different codes of ethics and work from different guiding principles.

EXAMPLE OF GUIDING PRINCIPLES (VALUES)

We understand that a child's needs are best met in a family environment. We believe that all families have strengths and that focusing on these strengths can create new possibilities for change. We strive to partner with families and support their efforts to provide environments for children to thrive. We work to secure a family setting when one is unavailable to children. (ACH Child and Family Services, 2013)

GOALS AND OBJECTIVES

Goals describe future outcomes or states of being and, typically, are not measurable or achievable. Instead, goal statements are focused on outcomes and are ambitious and idealistic. The goals must support the vision and mission statements and be consistent with the guiding principles of the organization. The goal statements are the overarching framework for the outcome and process objectives that flow from them. Goals are intended to address the problems and needs of the agency's target population and to articulate an ideal outcome (Coley & Sheinberg, 2008). Goals are the linkage between identified needs and the actions taken by the organization to address those needs. If the goals are well formulated and flow from the governing ideas, then the specific objectives will flow naturally from the goals.

Objectives are the related results that are expected as the organization works toward its stated goals. In essence, objectives are the steps that will be taken to reach the stated goal (Coley & Scheinberg, 2008). It is common to have three or four (or more) objectives related to each program goal.

Unlike the lofty and, sometimes, unattainable goal statements, objectives should be clear, specific, and concrete. A useful acronym to remember when developing objectives is SMART. Objectives need to be *specific* (S), *measurable* (M), *achievable* (A), *realistic* (R), and *timely* (T).

SMART OBJECTIVES

Specific—clear and concrete

Measurable—how many, how much

Achievable—can be achieved with appropriate program activity and resources

Realistic—high enough that there is a possibility that the objective can be reached, but not so low that achieving the stated objective would be meaningless.

Timely—time limited, within what timeframe will the objective be achieved? (Lewis et al., 2011)

Generally, there are two subcategories of objectives: process objectives and outcome objective. *Process objectives* have to do with the things you will need to do to reach your program goals. Process objectives quantify the usage of the services and identify how much service will be provided. Process objectives are designed to determine whether the program is doing what it says it will do. They describe the services that are to be provided and in what quantities in what time frames. For example, the process objective might be to deliver 250 counseling hours to 75 clients within a six-month period of time. *Outcome objectives* answers the "so what?" question. If you deliver the 250 counseling hours to 75 clients, the question you want to answer is, "So what?" What difference did it make in the lives of the people served? How are they different? The outcome objectives become the basis of the outcome evaluation for your program. Outcome objectives indicate what will be different after the service is delivered. These may be stated as improved behavior, increased skills, changed attitudes, increased knowledge, or improved conditions. The well-developed outcome objective will follow the SMART formula and include the target group, number of program recipients, the expected results, and the geographic location (Coley & Scheinberg, 2008). The following are examples of goals and related process and outcome objectives.

EXAMPLE OF A GOAL AND ASSOCIATED PROCESS AND OUTCOME OBJECTIVES

GOAL

Runaway and homeless youth will be safe in transitioning to stable living conditions.

PROCESS OBJECTIVES

To provide 75 hours of street-based counseling services to 150 runaway and homeless youth by December 31, 20XX.

To provide home-based services for 50 families of runaway and homeless youth by December 31, 20XX

> To provide 25 drug abuse education and prevention training sessions to 100 runaway and homeless youth by September 1, 20XX
>
> OUTCOME OBJECTIVES
>
> One hundred runway and homeless youth will be reunited with their parents or be living in other stable living environments with adult supervision by December 31, 20XX.
>
> Forty youth participating in in-home family services will have no further incidents of separation from their families within one year after receiving services.
>
> One hundred runway and homeless youth will increase their knowledge by 65% about the danger of drug abuse by December 31, 20XX.

SWOT ANALYSIS

In the beginning of this chapter, we outlined the steps of the strategic planning process. Step 3 is to conduct a SWOT Analysis (examining the organization's Strengths, Weaknesses, Opportunities, and Threats) or other assessment tool. Typically, the SWOT Analysis will be conducted in a group setting. For example, a board retreat could be devoted to a strategic planning process including a SWOT Analysis. The executive team or the entire staff can be valuable in the SWOT process. After listing the many strengths of the organization, it is then time to turn to the weaknesses. While this can be a painful process, it is critical to take a hard and realistic look at the organization. Weaknesses could be such things as the lack of visibility of the organization in the community or inadequate fundraising plans. After examining the internal strengths and weaknesses, it is then time to examine the environment in which the organization exists to identify opportunities and threats. Is there a new identified need in the community that we can address? In the "strengths" section, do we have resources to bring to bear on this identified need? Are new funding opportunities on the horizon? Are there opportunities for mergers or collaborations with other organizations? After reviewing the opportunities, it is important to look at threats in the environment. Are there political trends that are a threat to the organization? Is the agency vulnerable to economic downturns? Are there issues with any of the major funding sources?

The purpose of the SWOT analysis it to assess how internal strengths and weaknesses are related to external opportunities and threats (Bryson, 1995; Lewis, Lewis, Packard & Souflee, 2001). The planning process is undertaken to maximize the strengths and opportunities and to realistically address the weaknesses and threats.

Internal	
Strengths	Weaknesses

(Continued)

(Continued)

External	
Opportunities	Threats

SWOT Analysis Summary

Source: "SWOT Analysis" (2009).

SUMMARY

Agency planning is a critical skill for you as a human services administrator. Without careful planning, the organization can be like a vessel adrift at sea without a clear destination. Your job is to provide leadership to the board and staff in assuring that the organization is moving forward in a direction to best serve the clients of the organization.

REFERENCES

ACH Child and Family Services. (2013). Retrieved from http://www.achservices.org

Austin, M. J., & Solomon, J. R. (2009). Managing the planning process. In R. Patti (Ed.), *The handbook of social welfare management* (pp. 321–338). Thousand Oaks, CA: Sage.

Brody, R., (2005). *Effectively managing human services organizations* (3rd ed.). Thousand Oaks, CA: Sage.

Bryson, J. (1995). *Strategic planning for public and nonprofit organizations* (Rev. ed.). San Francisco: Jossey-Bass.

Carroll, L. (1898). *Alice's adventures in wonderland.* London: Macmillan.

Coley, S. M., & Scheinberg, C. A. (2008). *Proposal writing: Effective grantsmanship* (3rd ed.). Thousand Oaks, CA: Sage.

Drucker, P. F. (1992). *Managing the non-profit organization: Principles and practices.* New York: HarperCollins.

Kettner, P. M., Moroney, R. M., & Martin, L. L. (2008). *Designing and managing programs: An effectiveness-based approach.* Thousand Oaks, CA: Sage.

Lewis, J. A., Lewis, M. D., Packard, T. R., & Souflee, F. (2001). *Management of human service programs* (3rd ed.). Belmont, CA: Brooks/Cole.

Lewis, J. A., Packard, T. R., & Lewis, M. D. (2011). *Management of human service programs* (5th ed.). Belmont, CA: Brooks/Cole.

Senge, P. M. (1990). *The fifth discipline: The art and practice of the learning organization.* New York: Doubleday/Currency.

Smith, Bucklin & Associates, Inc. (2000). *The complete guide to nonprofit management* (2nd ed.). New York: Wiley.

SWOT Analysis. (2009). Retrieved from http://www.whatmakesagoodleader.com/swot_analysis_template.html#SimpleSWOTAnalysisTemplate

Top Nonprofits. (n.d.). Retrieved from http://topnonprofits.com/examples/vision-statements

Vaughan, S. K., & Arsneault, M. (2013). *Managing nonprofit organizations in a policy world.* Thousand Oaks, CA: CQ Press.

Worth, M. J. (2009). *Nonprofit management.* Thousand Oaks, CA: Sage.

HELPFUL TERMS

Goals—descriptions of future outcomes or states of being that typically are not measurable or achievable. Instead, goal statements are focused on outcomes and are ambitious and idealistic.

Governing ideas—Peter Senge (1990) presents the concept of "governing ideas" in his work *The Fifth Discipline.* He defines the governing ideas as the vision statement, the mission statement, and the statement of guiding principles.

Guiding principles—a statement of principles that describes the values that will guide the organization—the things that will not be compromised based on deeply held convictions and traditions.

Mission statement—according to Smith and Bucklin (2000), "[a] succinct statement that sets forth the organization's purpose and philosophy."

Objectives—the results that are expected as the organization works toward its stated goals. Objectives are the steps that will be taken to reach the stated goals.

Outcome objectives—answers the question "so what?" What difference did it make in the lives of the people served? Outcome objectives are stated as improved behavior, increased skills, changed attitudes, increased knowledge, or improved conditions.

Process objectives—quantify the usage of the services and identify how much service will be provided. Process objectives are designed to determine whether the program is doing what it says it will do. It describes the services that are to be provided and in what quantities in what time frames.

SMART—a useful acronym to remember when developing objectives. Objectives need to be *specific* (S), *measurable* (M), *achievable* (A), *realistic* (R), and *timely* (T).

SWOT Analysis—a process for examining the organizations Strengths, Weaknesses, Opportunities and Threats usually in the context of a strategic planning process.

Vision statement—a governing statement that answers the question, "What do we want the organization to be?"

EXERCISES

1. SWOT Analysis

Work with a group of three or four students in your class to develop a SWOT Analysis of this class. What are the strengths and weaknesses internally, and what are the opportunities and threats in the external environment? Use the SWOT template and report your findings to the class.

2. In-Basket Exercise

Directions

Read the following memo from your board chair. Work with a group of three or four of your classmates and frame a response memo based on this chapter. Read your memo to the class.

Memo

Date:	August 4, 20XX
To:	Administrator
From:	Board Chair
Subject:	Our Mission Statement

As we are preparing for our strategic planning retreat, I have been thinking that the two of us need to be on the same page about our mission statement. I know that we have not revised the mission statement in several years, but I think it does a pretty good job of saying what we do. The statement, "To help people realize their full potential" seems to capture what we do in helping people with multiple disabilities to live and work independently. I'm advocating that we keep the same mission statement as we move forward to develop new goals and objectives. Please share your thoughts with me.

3. Guiding Principles

If you were starting a new agency, what values would guide you in your administration of the agency? Write a guiding principles statement for your new agency, and read your statement to the class.

ASSIGNMENTS

1. Examine the websites of three human service organizations in your community. Analyze the mission statements of the three organizations by comparing and contrasting them. What are the strengths and weaknesses of each? What recommendations would you make for improving each of the mission statements?

2. Make an appointment to interview a human services administrator and interview him or her about a recent strategic planning process. Write a five-page paper that describes the process. Pay special attention to the role of the administrator in the planning process.

3. Find an agency that has changed its mission statement in the past five years. Compare the old and the new statements. How are they different? How are they similar? Write a three-page paper that describes the reasons behind the change in the mission statement and the human service administrator's thoughts on the change.

Logic Models and Program Evaluation

7

INTRODUCTION

Nonprofit administrators both develop and evaluate programs. A logic model is useful for both, even though development happens before the program begins and evaluation happens after it has been in operation. A good evaluation, however, is planned at the same time that the program is designed so that necessary data is collected along the way, rather than annually or after the program finishes. This chapter first describes the process of logic modeling using an example of the logic model. Then, it discusses how to use the logic model to plan an evaluation.

LOGIC MODELS

The idea of logic models as an adjunct to program evaluation extends at least as far back as 2000 when the Kellogg Foundation published a guide to developing logic models for program design and evaluation. According to Frechtling (2007), a logic model is "a tool that describes the *theory of change* underlying an intervention, product or policy" (p. 1). While one can find many variations on how a logic model should be constructed, it is a versatile tool that is used to design programs, assist in their implementation, and guide their evaluation. This chapter describes one basic approach to logic modeling for program evaluation and links the planning and evaluation aspects of human service administration.

You should understand that not all programs have been designed with the aid of a logic model, although that is becoming less common every year. Federal grants, for example, often require applicants to submit a logic model, and their use throughout the human services sector is growing through academic education and in-service training. If there is no logic model for a program you are working with, it is possible to create one *after* a program has been implemented. You can thus bring the power of the tool to bear when changing a program or creating an evaluation plan.

Logic model terminology uses system theory terminology. Because logic models are said to describe the program's "theory of change," it is possible to believe that this refers to something such as social learning theory, cognitive-behavioral theory, or any one of a number of psychological or sociological theories. In general, though, logic models have a much less grand view of theory. We begin with the assumption that any human services program is created to solve a problem. The problem should be clearly stated in a way that does not predetermine how the problem will be solved. The utility of a logic model is in showing how the resources used (inputs) are changed into a program (activities) with closely linked products (outputs) that then lead to changes in clients in the short, medium, and long terms. The net effect of these client changes is that the original problem is solved or at least made better for the clients in the program. An example of a logic model is shown as Figure 7.1.

The problem being addressed by the example program is, "School-aged youth have anger management problems leading to verbal and physical fights at school and home." This problem statement is specific about who has a problem (school-aged youth), what the problem is (anger management problems leading to verbal and physical fights), and where it is a problem (school and home). It also does not prejudge what the solution is, allowing for many possible programs to address the problem. An example problem statement that is not as good because it states the problem in a way that allows only one solution is, "There is a lack of anger management classes in schools for school-aged youth."

Another way to make the problem statement good is to phrase the statement in such a way that almost anyone can agree that it is actually a problem. The example problem statement might make this point more clearly by saying, "There are too many verbal and physical fights at school and home among school-aged youth." Phrased this way, there would be little doubt that this is a problem, even though the statement is not specific about the number of such fights or the cause of the fights. If the program personnel want to focus on anger management problems, this way of stating the problem might lead to a host of other issues being addressed instead that might be leading to fights—such as overcrowding in the halls, gang membership, conflict over curfews at home, or anything else that might conceivably cause youth to fight at school or home. Be prepared to revisit your first effort at the problem statement and seek input from interested stakeholders to be sure that you are tackling what is really considered the reason for the program. The problem statement is vital to the rest of the logic model and evaluation so take the time to make several drafts to get full agreement.

After the problem statement, the logic model has six columns. Arrows connect what is written in one column to something else in the next column to the right or even within the same column. These arrows are the "logic" of the program. If the column to the left is achieved, then we believe that the element at the end of the arrow will be achieved. Each arrow can be considered to show a hypothesis that the two elements are linked. (The example presented here is intentionally not "perfect" so that you can see some of the nuances and challenges of using this tool.)

The first column is labeled "Inputs." In this column, you write the major resources that will be needed or used in the program. Generically, these tend to be funds, staff, and space, but can include other elements such as type of funds, educational level of the staff, and location of the space (on a bus line, for example), if they apply to your program. The resource of "staff," for example, might mean MSW-level licensed counselors. In the end, if only staff members with bachelor degrees in psychology are hired, this would indicate that the "staff" input was inadequate.

The second column is "Activities." In this area, you write what the staff members of the program will be doing—what behaviors you would see them engage in if you sat and watched them. Here, as elsewhere in the logic model, there are decisions about the level of detail to include. It would be too detailed, for example, to have the following bullet points for the case management activity:

- Answer phone calls about clients
- Make phone calls about clients
- Learn about other agencies' services
- Write out referral forms for clients to other agencies

This is what you would see, literally, but the phrase "case management" is probably enough. Somewhere in program documents, there should be a more detailed description of the duties of a case manager so that this level of detail is not necessary on the logic model, which is, after all, a graphical depiction of the program's theory of change, not a daily to-do list.

Problem: School-aged youth have anger management problems leading to verbal and physical fights at school and home.

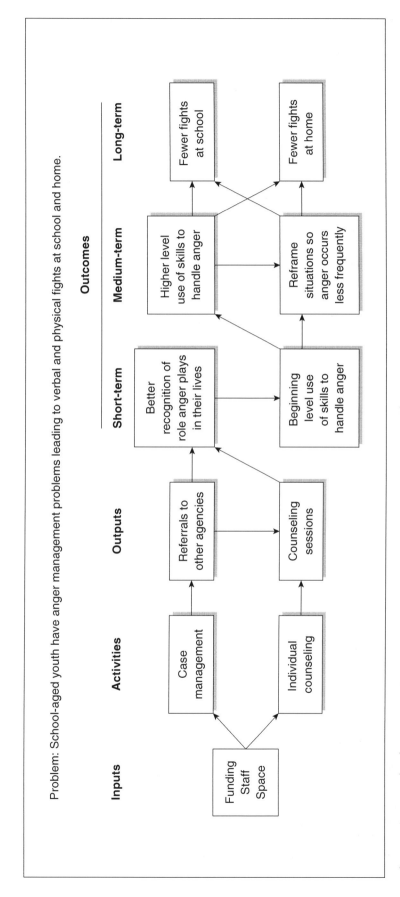

Figure 7.1 Example of a Logic Model

The other danger is being too general. In this case, a phrase such as "provide social work services" wouldn't be enough to help the viewer know what the employee is doing as there are so many activities involved in social work services. Getting the correct level of specificity is important in helping develop your evaluation plan here and throughout the logic model.

As you can see from the arrows leading from the inputs to the activities, the program theory indicates that, given the proper funds, staff, and space, the activities of case management and individual counseling will occur. This may or may not happen, however, which is why a process evaluation is needed and will be discussed later in this chapter.

The third column lists "Outputs." An output is a measurable result of an activity. In this example, the activity of "case management" results in client youth being referred to other agencies for services. The output of the activity "individual counseling" is counseling sessions. It is important to note that outputs are not changes in clients—outputs are the results of agency activities that may or may not then result in changes to clients. The connection between agency activity and outputs is perhaps the most difficult part of putting together a logic model because many people mistakenly assume that if a service is given and documented, then client changes are automatic. This is simply not true.

The next three columns are collectively known as "Outcomes." An outcome is a change in the client and should be written in a way that is a change in knowledge, attitude, belief, status, or behavior. Outcomes are why programs are developed and run—to change clients' lives. Outcomes can be developed at any level of intervention—individual, couple or family, group, organization, or community of any size. This example uses a program designed to make a change at an individual youth level, but could also have changes at the school or district level if desired.

Outcomes are usually written to show a time dimension with short-, medium-, and long-term outcomes. The long-term outcome is the opposite of the problem stated at the top of the logic model and thus ties the entire intervention back to its purpose—to solve a particular problem. The division of outcomes into three distinct time periods is obviously a helpful fiction, not a tight description of reality. Still, some outcomes are expected to come sooner than others. These short-term outcomes are usually considered the direct result of outputs being developed. On the example logic model, the arrows indicate that referrals and individual counseling are both supposed to result in client youth better recognizing the role that anger plays in their life. After that is achieved, the program theory hypothesizes that clients will use skills at a beginning level to handle their anger. This is a case where one short-term outcome (change in self-knowledge) leads the way for a change in behavior (using skills).

OUTCOMES AND GOALS AND OBJECTIVES: WHAT'S THE DIFFERENCE?

Logic models use the term *outcome*, but many people use the terms *goals and objectives* to talk about what a program is trying to achieve. In the previous chapter, you were told that an outcome objective answers the question, "What difference did it make in the lives of the people served?" In this chapter, you are told that an outcome is a "change in the client." What's the difference?

In reality, there is not much difference. Goals and objectives are one way of talking about the purpose of a program. This terminology is older than the logic model terminology and more widespread. But it can be confusing, too, because an objective at one level of an organization may be considered a goal at another level or at a different time.

Outcomes are easier to fit into the logic model approach to showing program theory by relating to resources, activities, and outputs. Systems theory terminology is more widespread than before and avoids some of the conceptual pitfalls of goals and objectives thinking.

We present both sets of terms so that you can be comfortable in all settings. But you should realize that both approaches are ultimately talking about the same thing: the ability of an organization to make people's lives better.

The element "beginning level use of skills to handle anger" has two arrows leading to medium-term outcomes. The first arrow leads to "higher level use of skills to handle anger." In this theory of change, at this point, there is still anger, but the youth recognize what is occurring and take measures to handle it in a skillful way that does not lead to negative consequences. The second arrow from "beginning level use of skills to handle anger" indicates that the program designers believe that the skills youth learn will assist them to reframe situations they are in so that they feel angry less frequently. This is a separate behavior than applying skills to handle anger, so it receives its own arrow and box.

The final column represents the long-term outcomes. Often, there is only one element shown in this column, one indicating the opposite of the problem. In this logic model, since the problem is seen to occur both at school and at home, each is looked at separately. A youth may reduce fights at home but not at school, or vice versa, so it is important to leave open the possibility of only partial success.

This example logic model shows a relatively simple program theory, with two separate tracks for intervention but with overlapping outcomes expected from the two intervention methods. It indicates how one element can lead to more than one "next step" and how different elements can lead to the same outcome. Finally, while it is not necessarily obvious just yet, this example shows some weak points in the program's logic that will emerge when we use it as a guide to evaluating the program.

PROGRAM EVALUATION

As you can see from this discussion, we have used a logic model to represent what we believe will happen when the proper inputs are applied to the correct client population. In the end, if all goes well, clients will no longer have the problem the program addresses, or at least the degree or extent of the problem will be less.

Evaluation is a way to determine the worth or value of a program (Rossi, Lipsey, & Freeman, 2003). There are two primary types of evaluation: process and outcome. The first, *process evaluation*, examines the way a program runs. In essence, a process evaluation examines the first three columns of a logic model to determine whether required inputs were available, the extent to which activities were conducted, and the degree of output accomplishment. Another aspect of a process evaluation, called *fidelity assessment*, examines whether the program being evaluated was conducted in accord with the way the program was *supposed* to be conducted. If all components of a program are completed, fidelity is said to be high. Particularly with evidence-based and manualized programs, if changes are made to the program model during implementation, the program's effectiveness is likely to be diminished.

The value of the logic model for evaluation is that most of the conceptual information needed to design the evaluation of a program is in the logic model. The required inputs are listed, and the evaluator can check to determine which resources actually came into the program. Activities are similarly delineated, and an evaluator can usually find a way to count the number of activities that the program completed. Similarly, the logic model describes what outputs are expected, and the evaluator merely has to determine how to count the number of completed outputs that result from the program activities.

Looking at the example logic model shows us that we want to have in our evaluation plan at least one way to measure whether funding, staff, and space (the inputs) are adequate; how much case management occurred and individual counseling was conducted (the activities); and the extent to which referrals were made (and followed up on) and the number of individual counseling sessions that happened (the outputs). This information should be in program documents to compare what was planned for with what was actually provided. Having a logic model from the beginning allows the evaluator to ensure that proper data are being collected from the program's start, rather than scrambling later to answer some of these basic questions.

As noted earlier, this is not a perfect logic model. The question in the process evaluation at this stage might be to determine how to actually measure "case management." The output is supposed to be "referrals to other agencies," but there is much else that could be considered beneficial from a case management approach. This element may need careful delineation and discussion with stakeholders to ascertain exactly what is important about case management that should be measured.

The second primary type of evaluation examines program outcomes. Called an *outcome evaluation*, it focuses on the right half of the logic model, where the designated short-, medium-, and long-term outcomes are listed. The evaluator chooses which outcomes to assess from among the various outcomes in the logic model. Decisions need to be made about how to measure the outcomes, but the logic model provides a quick list of what to measure. In the example logic model, the short-term outcome "better recognition of the role anger plays in their lives" must be measured and could be accomplished using a set of questions asked at intake into the program and after some time has passed after receiving services. One standardized anger management instrument is called the "Anger Management Scale" (Stith & Hamby, 2002). A standardized instrument, if it is appropriate for the clients and program, is a good choice because you can find norms, or expected responses, to the items on the instrument. It is helpful to you, as the evaluator, to know what "average" responses are so you can compare your clients' responses to the norms. Sometimes, however, it can be difficult to find a standardized instrument that is fully appropriate and relevant to your program.

Another way of measuring is to use an instrument you make up yourself. This has the advantage of simplicity and of being directly connected to your evaluation. In this case, for example, you could approach this outcome in at least two ways. First, you could request a statement from the case worker or counselor indicating that the client has "recognized the role that anger plays" in his or her life, without going into any detail. A second approach would be to have the client write a statement about the role anger plays in his or her life. Neither of these measurements will have a lot of practical utility. Going through the logic model in this way actually shows that this link in program logic is difficult to measure and may not be totally necessary.

WHAT IS AN UNANTICIPATED OUTCOME?

Outcome evaluations also sometimes include a search for unanticipated outcomes. An unanticipated outcome is a change in clients or the environment that occurs because of the program, intervention, or policy, but that was not thought would result and so is not included in the logic model.

While it may seem startling to have an example in a text that shows a less-than-perfect approach, it is included here to show that using a logic model is very useful in showing weak spots in the program logic. This link to "better recognition" is not a fatal problem, and may indeed be an important cognitive change for the client. The issue for evaluation is how to measure it, and whether it really needs to be measured at all.

Of more importance is the next link, which leads to "learn skills to handle anger." The evaluation must ensure that clients understand skills to help them handle anger and so document these skills. It is not enough to indicate that skills were taught, as in a group or individual session. Teaching a class is an activity and so would be documented in the process evaluation portion of the overall evaluation, but being in a class does not guarantee a change in the client. In this evaluation, we would like to have a measure of skill that can show improvement in the ability to perform the anger management skill. This attribute of the measure is important because we expect the clients to get better in their use over time and include more skillful use of the techniques as a medium-term outcome in the logic model.

The other medium-term outcome expected is that clients will be able to reframe situations so that they actually get angry less frequently. The program logic shows this outcome occurring as a result of both beginning and higher level use of skills. Because this element is broken out from the use of skills to "handle anger," it will need a separate measure. As an evaluator, you can hope that an established, normed instrument is available, or that this is a skill that is measured by a separate item on a longer scale. If not, you will need to find a way to pull this information from staff members' reports or client self-assessments.

The final links in the logic model connect the medium-term outcomes to the long-term outcomes of fewer fights at school and fewer fights at home. Because youth having too many fights was identified as the problem this program is addressing, we want to know to what degree fights decreased. The measure here could be client self-reports, school records, or reports from people living in the home.

Implicit in the discussion of the use of this logic model for evaluation purposes is that measurements at the end will be compared to an earlier measure of the same outcome. This is called a *single group pretest-posttest evaluation* (or research) design. It is not considered a strong design due to the ability of other forces (threats to internal validity) to affect the results. The design could be stronger if a comparison group of similar youth (perhaps at a different school) were chosen and tracked with the same measures. The design could be *much* stronger if youth at the same school were randomly assigned to either a group that received the program or a different group that did not receive the program. It is beyond the scope of this book to cover in detail all the intricacies of measurement and evaluation design, but we hope this brief overview whets your appetite to learning more.

Measurement of outcomes, while alluded to earlier, is an important part of any evaluation effort. If measures are not appropriate or have low validity and reliability, the value of the evaluation will be seriously compromised. It is suggested that anyone designing an evaluation look at a book on research methods such as Rubin and Babbie (2012), and also have access to books about measures, such as Fischer and Corcoran (2007). (The cost of a new book on research methods may be pretty high, but used editions contain much the same information and can be found for much lower prices.)

SUMMARY

Using an example, this chapter has covered the components of a logic model and how to develop one. It also demonstrates how to use a logic model to design an evaluation plan, including how it raises issues of comprehending program logic, measurement, and evaluation design.

REFERENCES

Fischer, J., & Corcoran, K. (2007). *Measures for clinical practice and research: A sourcebook* (4th ed.). New York: Oxford University Press.

Frechtling, J. (2007). *Logic modeling methods in program evaluation.* San Francisco: Jossey-Bass.

Preskill, H., & Russ-Eft, D. (2004). *Building evaluation capacity.* Thousand Oaks, CA: Sage.

Rossi, P., Lipsey, M., & Freeman, H. (2003). *Evaluation: A systematic approach* (7th ed.). Thousand Oaks, CA: Sage.

Rubin, A., & Babbie, E. (2012). *Essential research methods for social work* (3rd ed.) Brooks-Cole.

Stith, S., & Hamby, S. (2002). The anger management scale: Development and preliminary psychometric properties. *Violence and Victims, 17*(4), 383–402.

HELPFUL TERMS

Activities—elements of a logic model that describe what is done in the program, intervention, or policy with the inputs allocated.

Fidelity evaluation or **fidelity assessment**—a type of process evaluation specifically designed to determine the fidelity with which a program, intervention, or policy was implemented. In other words, a fidelity evaluation (or fidelity assessment) determines the degree to which the program was conducted in the way it was supposed to be conducted.

Goals—descriptions of future outcomes or states of being that typically are not measurable or achievable. Instead, goal statements are focused on outcomes and are ambitious and idealistic (see Chapter 6).

Inputs—elements of a logic model that describe the resources that will be used to address the problem described in the problem statement. Inputs typically include funding, staff, and space.

Logic model—"[a] tool that describes the *theory of change* underlying an intervention, product or policy" (Frechtling, 2007, p. 1). Using systems theory concepts, relationships between resources, activities, and desired outcomes are displayed.

Measurement—the act of operationalizing concepts (such as a particular change in clients) and assigning a score or value to the level of that concept.

Objectives—the results that are expected as the organization works toward its stated goals. Objectives are the steps that will be taken to reach the stated goals (see Chapter 6).

Outcome evaluation—a type of evaluation where the focus is answering questions about the achievement of the program's stated desired outcomes. Sometimes, efforts are included to measure "unanticipated outcomes," that is, effects of the program that were not included in the logic model.

Outcomes—elements in logic models that describe changes in recipients' knowledge, attitudes, beliefs, status, or behavior. These are often divided into short-, medium-, and long-term outcomes to show that some outcomes come before others.

Outputs—elements of a logic model describing the measurable results of program, intervention, or policy activities.

Problem statement—an element of a logic model that describes the problem that the program, intervention, or policy is trying to improve.

Process evaluation—a type or part of a larger evaluation that examines the way a program, intervention, or policy is run or is implemented.

Program evaluation—using a set of research-based methods to determine the worth or value of a program.

1. In-Basket Exercise

Directions

For this exercise, you are Roberta McIntosh, a social work intern who has received a memo from Jonas Sigurdson, a grant writer. He requests for you to develop a logic model, using the information from the chapter and in the memo.

Memo

Date: October 30, 20XX

To: Roberta McIntosh; Social Work Intern

From: Jonas Sigurdson, Grantwriter

Subject: Logic Model Needed

As you know, we are working away on a grant application for a program. The funder wants to see a logic model as part of the application. Since I know you have studied how to do a logic model in your classes, and I am a bit unsure what is required, I would like you to read over the draft program description and develop a logic model by Thursday. Be sure to include all the required elements of a logic model, and use only outcomes that we can measure without too much trouble. I should warn you that this is a fairly complicated program, so developing a logic model will likely take you a pretty good chunk of time and several drafts before you get one that really captures what we're trying to do.

Serve More Project Program Description

The Serve More Project of Urban AIDS Services, Inc. (UAS), the largest nonprofit provider of HIV/AIDS case management services in the Northwestern U.S., is designed to reduce the incidence of HIV infection and increase the engagement of at-risk King County, Washington Blacks and Latinos, including subpopulations of women and children, returning prisoners, injection drug users, and men having sex with men (MSM) who are not injection drug users in preventive, substance abuse treatment, and medical services.

The Serve More Project expands and enhances UAS' Integrated HIV/AIDS-Substance Abuse Treatment (IHASAT) program, funded by the Substance Abuse and Mental Health Services Administration (SAMHSA), with special focus on the burgeoning Hispanic population. UAS' robust HIV/AIDS services are linked with dual disorders treatment providers.

Serve More's **objectives** are to (1) apply evidence-based practices; (2) enhance cultural competency of services; (3) create new bilingual outreach and case management positions located strategically in collaborating agencies; (4) create a bilingual community resource specialist position; (5) create a community action council to plan collaborative response to the focus population needs; (6) improve services to returning prisoners; (7) increase outreach to women and engagement services; and (8) increase and enhance collaborative partnerships.

Serve More's **project goals** include both *process* and *client* outcomes. **Process** goals are to (1) expand outreach efforts, with emphasis on Latinos, Blacks and women, to reach an additional 3,060 (1,440 to 5,000) of the focus populations each grant year; (2) increase the number of individuals receiving HIV testing by UAS' staff by 220 annually (280–500); (3) provide case management to at least 160 project clients annually; (4) provide substance abuse treatment to at least 60 project clients annually; (5) track for evaluation follow up 75 individuals each year of the grant period, focusing on Latinos and Latinas; (6) refer 100% of outreach contacts requesting substance abuse and/or mental health treatment; (7) link 95% of all positive HIV case findings who receive their test results to HIV care and services; (8) achieve at least 50% medical adherence; and (9) achieve 80% substance abuse treatment adherence.

Project **client outcomes** are to **increase** the percentage of clients who (1) do not use alcohol or illegal drugs; (2) are currently employed or attending school; (3) have a permanent place to live in the community; (4) experience no alcohol or illegal drug-related health, behavioral or social consequences; or (5) have no involvement with the criminal justice system; and to **decrease** the percentage of clients who (6) inject illegal drugs; (7) engage in unprotected sexual contact; or engage in unprotected sexual contact with (8) a person high on drugs; (9) an injected drug user; or (10) a person who is HIV+ or has AIDS.

Target Population and Geographic Area Served—The focus populations to be served by the Serve More Project are Hispanics/Latinos and Blacks/American Americans. Subpopulations include (1) men who inject drugs, including non-Intravenous Drug Using (IDU) men who have sex with men (MSM); (2) women, including women and children; and (3) the recently incarcerated. The geographic area for the project is King County, Washington.

2. The Chocolate Chip Cookie Evaluation Exercise [This idea is adapted from Preskill and Russ-Eft (2004). It is one of my students' favorite exercises, and they now use it with their students.]

Have participants get into small groups of no more than four people. This works well in work settings as well as in classes. The task of each group is to develop an evaluation system to determine the "ideal" chocolate chip cookie. The only caveat is that all members of the group must agree to the process developed. Each group should develop a set of criteria that individual members will be able to use to rate how closely any individual chocolate chip cookie nears "perfection." This means the criteria must be understood similarly by all, with an agreed-on benchmark. For example, one student group I gave this exercise to indicated that "shape" was an important attribute of the perfect cookie. I challenged them on this because the group did not indicate what shape was preferred, and I correctly pointed out that all cookies have a shape. After all group members have agreed to a set of criteria, the leader gives each group a cookie from several different varieties of store-bought or home-made cookies. Group members must then individually go through all of the criteria for each cookie and, based on the criteria chosen, choose the "best" cookie from amongst those they were given.

Often, groups come up with very different criteria and individuals, using the same criteria, rate the same cookie very differently. This variation in criteria and ratings provides a very good basis for understanding the underlying principles of criterion-based evaluation and measurement issues.

3. Design Your Own Logic Model

It can be a very helpful exercise in understanding how to construct a logic model to use a program or intervention with which you are very familiar. With one or two other people who share your knowledge, develop a logic model (if you are a student, you might choose your educational program; if you are employed, use the program you are employed by). Be sure to construct a problem statement—what problem is being addressed? (Knowing the purpose is sometimes a difficult question to answer, but it is essential.) When you are done, show your work to another group or talk about it in class. What were the easier parts of the process, and which were the more challenging?

4. Using a Logic Model to Plan an Evaluation

Using the logic model that you just created in Exercise 3, discuss how you would ideally evaluate this intervention. What are the most important process and client outcomes to measure? What measures will you use? Who will collect the information? How will it be analyzed to determine whether the recipients of the intervention changed? Which were the easier parts of the process, and which were the more challenging parts?

ASSIGNMENTS

1. Do an online search for "logic model" (you'll find millions of results, including YouTube videos). Find three different sources (not including Wikipedia) describing what a logic model is and how to develop one. Compare and contrast these with the information in this chapter. Make two different logic models of a simple program you're familiar with, following the guidelines from two different sources. Which variations make the most sense to you?

2. Conduct an online search for a program evaluation of a program that you are either familiar with or that you would like to know more about. Write a paper about the evaluation, answering these questions: What is the program being evaluated? What are the results of the evaluation, both process and outcome? How strong do you think the evaluation research design was? What measures were used, and what are their strengths and weaknesses? How much credence do you place in the results? Finally, how does this evaluation affect your willingness to try the program with the clients in your (possibly hypothetical) agency?

3. Find a set of three to four program objectives or outcomes for a program you're familiar with and briefly describe them. Look for standardized instruments to be able to accurately measure these objectives. Describe the source of the instruments and what makes them good measures for the objectives or outcomes you have found. Write up the information as a memo recommending these instruments to the lead researcher of the program evaluation team.

Budgeting and Finance

8

INTRODUCTION

Most human service administrators start their careers as direct service providers and come to human services with a desire to make a difference in people's lives through service, advocacy, and policy reform. Very few start with the goal of becoming financial managers and, therefore, have little formal education or training in financial management. However, new human services administrators learn very quickly, and sometimes painfully, that financial management is a major part of their job.

Human service administrators do not have to give up their natural inclination toward client services to adopt a financial management perspective. Financial management is a skill critical to assure quality services for clients and is as important as policy analysis, social planning, casework, and program evaluation (Martin, 2001). Human services administrators do not need to be accountants, but they must be able to prepare a budget and to read and understand financial reports. Budgets and financial reports are important management tools in assuring the financial health of the organization. Financial management is a critical skill needed to provide quality services for the clients of the organization.

This chapter will present the basic accounting terms you will need as a human services administrator and give you the tools you need to read and understand the key elements of a budget and financial statement. You will also learn the basic steps in preparing a budget, including identifying multiple funding sources, projecting income and expenses, and concepts of program accounting. After reading the chapter, you will work with a balance sheet and a financial statement to complete the exercises.

UNDERSTANDING FINANCIAL STATEMENTS

Generally Accepted Accounting Principles (GAAP) are basic sets of rules governing how the financial books and records of an organization are to be maintained, including how revenues, expenditures, and expenses are to be accounted for and how financial statements are to be prepared. The Financial Accounting Standards Board (FASB) establishes the GAAP for nonprofit and for-profit organizations. The FASB rules require all private nonprofit organizations to prepare "general purpose external financial statements" at least once each fiscal year and must be reflective of the overall financial activities in their entirety during that fiscal year (American Institute of Certified Public Accountants, 1998).

The FASB requires four types of financial statements be prepared annually by nonprofit human services organizations. The required reports are (1) a statement of activities, (2) a statement of financial position, (3) a statement of cash flows, and (4) a statement of functional expenses by functional and natural classifications. In most cases, these reports are prepared by an independent auditor, hired by the organization to examine the financial records of the organization each year. These reports are based on the monthly statement prepared by the organization throughout the fiscal year.

Statement of activities. In simple terms, the statement of activities is the profit and loss statement for the organization. It is essentially the same report that a business would use to report its profit and losses for the year. The report tells the reader that, for example, there was "excess of revenues over expenses" or a profit, or that the expenses exceeded the revenues, and, therefore, the organization lost money for the fiscal year.

Can a nonprofit organization make a profit? Absolutely, they can and should. There is much confusion about this point. Many believe that a nonprofit human service agency is prohibited from making a profit; to the contrary, it is acceptable and desirable for the organization to bring in more revenue than it spends. The issue is what the organization does with the excess income. The revenues must be used to promote the mission of the organization. For example, the profits cannot be paid to the board members as dividends, but it is perfectly alright to develop a reserve fund, buy equipment, or establish an endowment—anything that furthers the mission of the organization.

To understand the statement of activities, it is necessary to understand several terms used in the report.

Balance sheet (statement of financial position). A balance sheet is a statement of the financial position of an organization that states the assets and liabilities at a particular point in time. The balance sheet illustrates the financial "worth" of the organization. The statement presents the assets and liabilities of the organization. Statements can be prepared as often as the administrator of the board of trustees wants, but must be prepared at least annually on the last day of the fiscal year. The annual audit will include a balance sheet and will, in most cases, compare the current year to the year before to see if there has been a change in the financial position of the organization. The organization's assets, minus its liabilities, give a picture of the organization's net assets or the "net worth" of the organization.

Statement of cash flows. The cash flow statement is used to analyze the cash inflows and outflows (where the money went) during a designated time period. From the monthly statement of activities report, you will find there are certain items that may not affect your statement of activities for some time, such as the following:

- Substantial increase in inventory purchases
- Increase in accounts receivable (money owed to you)
- Purchase of equipment
- Lump sum payment of debt

A cash flow statement will highlight these activities in a way that an income statement will not. Without the cash flow statement, you will have an incomplete picture of your organization. The cash flow statement is used to analyze the cash inflows and outflows (where the money went) during a designated time period. This is especially important for nonprofit agencies where donated funds come at specific times of the year rather than throughout the year (Women's Economic Self-Sufficiency Team–Albuquerque, NM, 2001).

Statement of functional expenses. All voluntary health and welfare organizations must provide a statement of functional expenses. FASB requires that the statement include the organization's total expenses for the fiscal year and that the expenses be separated out by functional categories such as program, management, general, and fundraising, and by natural categories such as salaries, and fringe and other operating expenses. Many times, this report also presents revenue and expenses for each program of the organization.

The independent audit. The independent audit is an important part of the financial management of an organization. As a part of this process, the independent auditor examines the financial records for the fiscal year and makes a report to the board of trustees. If the report does not find any significant problems in the financial reporting of the organization, it is said to be a "clean" audit. Auditors often will make recommendations for changes in the financial procedures of an organization to strengthen the "internal control" processes. These recommendations assure checks and balances in the financial system of the organization. The report is made, not to the administrator, but to the board of trustees. It is the board that has the ultimate responsibility to protect the financial health of the organization.

As mentioned earlier, the financial reports and the independent audit are based on the organization's fiscal year. A *fiscal year* is usually a 12-month period of time for which the financial records of the organization are maintained. The organization can decide on the fiscal year in which it will operate. Some organizations choose to use the calendar from January through December as their fiscal year. Others choose to use the fiscal year of their primary funders. For example, the federal government's fiscal year is October through September. Some states operate on a July to June fiscal year, and others on a September to August fiscal year.

CASH AND ACCRUAL ACCOUNTING

Two major types of accounting are cash accounting and accrual accounting. For our purposes we will be dealing with accrual accounting since this is the method used by most human services organizations and businesses. In cash basis accounting, transactions are recognized (recorded) only when cash is received and only when cash is paid out. This is an acceptable but simplistic method and has serious limitations as a planning tool for human services administrators.

Accrual accounting means that transactions are recognized (recorded) when revenues are earned and when expenses are incurred. Accrual accounting provides a more complete financial picture through the use of accounts receivable and accounts payable. Accrual is the preferred method of accounting.

EXAMPLES OF CASH AND ACCRUAL ACCOUNTING

Think of cash accounting as keeping the money in a shoebox. When the money comes in, you put it in the shoebox, and when you spend money, you take it out of the shoebox. In accrual accounting, you recognize the income when you earn it. So, for example, if you have a contract to provide counseling services you recognize the income in the month you provide the services. For example, during the month of June, you provide 100 yours of counseling services and send a bill to the contract agency. Since you have provided the services, you record the income in June, not in August when the check finally comes. The same is true of expenses. If you receive $1,000 worth of office supplies in June, you recognize the $1,000 expense in June, not when you pay the bill in July.

Financial Statement Examples

The following financial statements are examples of the monthly statements prepared by organizations. These are the basis of the financial reports prepared by the independent auditor. Take a few minutes to examine the following financial statements. Look at the heading of each column and the line items in each statement. Don't be intimidated by the numbers. Just look at each row and number, and think about the purpose of the report and what information the report is giving you.

To understand the report, you will need to know the meaning of several terms used in the reports. Here are a few you will need now. There is a more extensive list of terms at the end of this chapter.

Assets—anything owned by an organization that has economic value. Assets may include cash, bank accounts, accounts receivable (see definition below), equipment, buildings, property, and automobiles.

Liabilities—obligations to pay somebody something. All debts or amounts owed by an organization in the form of accounts payable (see below), loans, mortgages, and long-term debts are liabilities.

Net assets—what is left over when liabilities are subtracted from assets.

Revenues—usually in the form of cash and checks and may come from many sources, such as fees for service, contracts, grants, donations, third-party payments, insurance, managed care firms, or investment income.

Revenue classifications—There are three classifications of revenues to human services.

1. Permanently Restricted Funds—Some funds may be permanently restricted to a specific use. Endowment funds are usually in this category. A donor may give a gift to the organization, but requires that only the earnings from those funds be used by the organization. For example, a donor gives a $100,000 gift to the organization's endowment fund. Let's assume that the interest rates or earnings rate on the $100,000 is 5%. This means that the organization can use $5,000 each year and still have the original $100,000 intact.

2. Temporarily Restricted Funds—These funds are given for a specific project. For example, a donor might give $50,000 to the organization to renovate a building owned by the organization. The donor might choose to give the entire $50,000 at one time and then the organization could pay the contractors for the work as the project progressed. The $50,000 would be temporarily restricted and could be used only to renovate the building.

3. Unrestricted Funds—These are funds on which the donor has placed no restrictions. An example of these funds is operating funds raised in an annual campaign. A donor may respond to a direct mail solicitation by sending a $500 check. Unless the donor specifies that the gift is to be used by a specific program or for a specific purpose, the $500 is unrestricted and can be used by the organization as needed.

Expenses/expenditures—There is a difference in the terms *expenses* and *expenditures*. Expenditures are cash that goes out of the agency. For example, the salaries paid for staff are an expenditure to the organization Expenses are resources consumed by an agency (insurance, computer equipment, etc.). To understand this concept, think about buying a new computer for the organization. You will pay for the computer with cash, but you will use the computer over several years. You have traded one asset (cash) for another asset (the computer). Assume the life of the new computer will be three years. If you paid $3,000 for the computer, you will have an "expense" of $1,000 per year for each of the three years.

While there is a difference in expenditures and expenses, you often hear the terms used interchangeably. The important concept to grasp from this discussion is the concept of "depreciation."

Depreciation—an estimate of the decrease in the value of an asset. Depreciation takes into account the reality that equipment, buildings, automobiles, and so on, become obsolete or simply wear out over time. It is a method to show how much of the value of an asset remains.

Accounts receivable—revenues earned by a human service agency, but not yet received. For example, if services have been provided and a contract has been billed for that service, the amount of the bill is an account receivable. It remains as an account receivable until the cash is received by the organization.

Accounts payable—money owed by the organization to someone else, but not yet paid. For example, if office supplies are received but have not yet been paid for, that amount is an account payable for the organization. Employee vacation time that has accumulated but not been taken is carried on the financial statements as an account payable.

Spend some time looking at the balance sheet. The two columns of numbers are a "snapshot" of the current year's financial picture compared to the prior year. Look at each of the line items in the report. The first section lists all of the assets. The second section lists all of the liabilities and the fund balances (also called the *equity*). The formula for the balance sheet is Assets = Liabilities + Fund Balances.

What assets does this organization have (own) and in what form? What are the liabilities of the agency? How does the financial picture for the current year compare to the last fiscal year?

Now look at the monthly statement of revenue and expenses report. This imaginary organization has two major program components, plus the administrative structure. The first report is the combined report of the two programs and the administration. The columns give information about the current period (last month) and then compare the actual figures to the budgeted amounts. For now, look only at the current period. Which of the income categories exceed the budgeted amount? Which income items are falling short of the budgeted amounts? Now look at the "year to date" columns. Are the same items that were under or over budget for the month also over or under for the year? We will use these financial reports in the exercises at the end of this chapter.

BE PATIENT

You will often hear people say, "I am just not mechanical," meaning that they are not good at making repairs or working on equipment. What they should say is, "I don't have the patience or take the time to see how things work." It is much the same when dealing with financial statements. Saying, "I can't understand financial statements" is really saying, "I don't have the patience or take the time to study financial statements." As you work on the exercises and assignments at the end of this chapter, make a commitment to be patient and invest the time in understanding the financial statements.

ABC NONPROFIT CORPORATION

COMPARATIVE BALANCE SHEET

AUGUST 31, 20XX

	YEAR TO DATE	
ASSETS	ACTUAL	PRIOR YEAR
CURRENT ASSETS		
Cash	507,058	156,314
Accounts receivable	329,561	342,035
Prepaid expenses	51,462	67,015
TOTAL CURRENT ASSETS	888,081	565,364
INVESTMENTS		
Perm endowment assets	1,748,432	1,618,953
Investments	227,657	243,963
TOTAL INVESTMENTS	1,976,089	1,862,916
FIXED ASSETS		
Land & buildings	3,809,845	3,708,297
Equipment, vehicles, furniture	796,436	846,205
Less: accumulated depreciation	(1,966,301)	(1,822,562)
TOTAL FIXED ASSETS	2,639,980	2,731,940
TOTAL ASSETS	5,504,150	5,160,220
LIABILITIES AND FUND BALANCES		
CURRENT LIABILITIES		
Accounts payable	55,801	55,293
Accrued expenses & payroll	110,773	106,471
Notes payable	1,095,531	
Interagency transfers	70,000	821,540
Designated funds	117,412	74,517
TOTAL CURRENT LIABILITIES	1,449,517	1,057,821
FUND BALANCES		
Unrestricted	2,242,049	2,723,851
Retained earnings—current year	57	(317,345)
Temporarily restricted	73,293	81,659
Permanently restricted endow.	1,739,234	1,614,234
TOTAL FUND BALANCES	4,054,633	4,102,399
TOTAL LIABILITIES AND FUND BALANCES	5,504,150	5,160,220

UNAUDITED FINANCIAL STATEMENTS FOR INTERNAL USE ONLY

ABC NONPROFIT CORPORATION

MONTHLY STATEMENT OF REVENUE AND EXPENSES—ALL DEPARTMENTS COMBINED

FOR THE EIGHT PERIODS ENDING AUGUST 31, 20XX

	PERIOD TO DATE		YEAR TO DATE	
	ACTUAL	CURR BUDGET	ACTUAL	CURR BUDGET
INCOME				
Fees for services—Dept. A	98,343	81,000	808,068	648,000
Fees for services—Dept. B	30,965	48,508	422,075	388,067
Church contributions	3,155	6,390	126,958	120,065
Individual contributions	13,501	3,690	124,589	74,936
Foundation/corp./board	7,900	8,333	197,018	216,667
Wills & estates—unrestricted	3,750		48,950	
Grants & contracts	7,452	6,417	58,526	51,333
Rental income	2,935	8,333	71,260	66,667
Investment income	2,816	3,500	31,437	28,000
TOTAL INCOME	170,817	166,171	1,888,881	1,593,735
OPERATING EXPENSES				
Salaries	132,005	118,691	1,021,329	949,526
Benefits	20,366	21,988	167,367	179,908
Advert./promo/printing/postage	7,713	17,657	62,966	90,072
Auto exp	2,158	1,231	16,189	9,853
Computer exp	30		13,435	
Contract services	11,021	5,998	90,941	48,539
Dues/memberships	382	1,156	4,752	10,882
Food	9,499	6,250	99,110	50,550
Insurance	3,937	4,025	31,061	32,199
Interest exp	6,121	7,554	57,491	60,430
Legal & professional	780	871	7,399	8,966
Maintenance & repair	6,125	2,849	35,472	24,400
Office/other supplies	3,991	3,781	37,305	30,958
Recruiting exp		106	12,057	1,496
Rent exp	2,894	1,694	15,154	13,352
Staff development	80	1,133	8,380	10,367
Travel	2,546	7,023	30,641	56,180
Telephone/communications	3,654	5,180	35,588	41,836
Utilities	8,475	9,500	73,525	62,200
Other	322	1,533	46,003	17,716
TOTAL OPERATING EXPENSES	222,099	218,220	1,866,165	1,699,430
NET INCOME (LOSS)	(51,282)	(52,049)	22,716	(105,695)

UNAUDITED FINANCIAL STATEMENTS FOR INTERNAL USE ONLY

ABC NONPROFIT CORPORATION

MONTHLY STATEMENT OF REVENUE AND EXPENSES—ADMINISTRATION

FOR THE EIGHT PERIODS ENDING AUGUST 31, 20XX

	PERIOD TO DATE		YEAR TO DATE	
	ACTUAL	CURR BUDGET	ACTUAL	CURR BUDGET
INCOME				
Fees for services—Dept A				
Fees for services—Dept B				
Church contributions	3,155	6,390	126,958	120,065
Individual contributions	8,186	3,690	118,574	74,936
Foundation/corp./board			173,318	95,000
Wills & estates—unrestricted	3,750		48,951	
Grants & contracts	7,452	6,417	58,526	51,333
Rental income	2,935	8,333	70,960	66,667
Investment income	2,815	3,500	31,336	28,000
TOTAL INCOME	28,293	28,330	628,623	436,001
OPERATING EXPENSES				
Salaries	41,830	49,065	356,901	392,519
Benefits	6,693	9,333	63,306	75,665
Advert./promo/printing/postage	2,480	11,342	19,652	39,690
Auto exp	2,158	1,190	16,189	9,520
Computer exp			12,134	
Contract services	5,103	4,517	44,890	36,133
Dues/memberships	175	346	1,875	3,117
Food	9,451	6,250	98,270	50,000
Insurance	3,137	3,258	24,617	26,067
Interest exp	6,085	7,554	57,137	60,429
Legal & professional	780	700	6,910	7,600
Maintenance & repair	6,125	2,083	34,918	18,267
Office/other supplies	3,786	2,592	31,943	20,733
Recruiting exp		10	11,115	330
Rent exp	1,561	1,089	14,378	8,512
Staff development	80	263	3,767	4,500
Travel	784	2,188	5,386	17,500
Telephone/communications	2,206	2,005	20,958	16,439
Utilities	8,475	9,500	73,526	62,200
Other	(79)	397	30,490	8,523
Allocation of indirect o/h	63,937	(18,214)	(300,173)	(145,709)
TOTAL OPERATING EXPENSES	164,767	95,468	628,189	712,035
NET INCOME (LOSS)	(136,474)	(67,138)	434	(276,034)

UNAUDITED FINANCIAL STATEMENTS FOR INTERNAL USE ONLY

ABC NONPROFIT CORPORATION

MONTHLY STATEMENT OF REVENUE AND EXPENSES—DEPT A

FOR THE EIGHT PERIODS ENDING AUGUST 31, 20XX

	PERIOD TO DATE		YEAR TO DATE	
	ACTUAL	CURR BUDGET	ACTUAL	CURR BUDGET
INCOME				
Fees for services—Dept A	98,343	81,000	808,068	64,8000
Fees for services—Dept B				
Church contributions				
Individual contributions	5,290		5,290	
Foundation/corp./board	7,900	8,333	23,700	121,667
Wills & estates—unrestricted				
Grants & contracts				
Rental income				
Investment income				
TOTAL INCOME	111,533	89,333	837,058	769,667
OPERATING EXPENSES				
Salaries	64,563	42,494	439,360	339,951
Benefits	9,090	8,139	65,176	65,116
Advert./promo/printing/postage	520	1,114	4,203	8,675
Auto exp				
Computer exp	30		1,070	
Contract services	4,065	1,122	39,240	9,539
Dues/memberships	167	120	925	1,645
Food	10		565	350
Insurance	400	384	3,222	3,066
Interest exp	36		354	
Legal & professional		25		200
Maintenance & repair		666	516	5,334
Office/other supplies	66	530	3,728	4,350
Recruiting exp		63	82	500
Rent exp		605	(2,206)	4,840
Staff development		450	3,657	3,250
Travel	409	1,735	7,313	13,880
Telephone/communications	573	1,015	5,156	8,118
Utilities				
Other	103	176	4,039	1,413
Allocation of indirect o/h	51,517	13,733	239,671	109,861
TOTAL OPERATING EXPENSES	131,549	72,371	816,071	580,088
NET INCOME (LOSS)	(20,016)	16,962	20,987	189,579

UNAUDITED FINANCIAL STATEMENTS FOR INTERNAL USE ONLY

ABC NONPROFIT CORPORATION

MONTHLY STATEMENT OF REVENUE AND EXPENSES—DEPT B

FOR THE EIGHT PERIODS ENDING AUGUST 31, 20XX

	PERIOD TO DATE		YEAR TO DATE	
	ACTUAL	CURR BUDGET	ACTUAL	CURR BUDGET
INCOME				
Fees for services—Dept A				
Fees for services—Dept B	30,965	48,508	422,075	388,067
Church contributions				
Individual contributions	25		725	
Foundation/corp./board				
Wills & estates—unrestricted				
Grants & contracts				
Rental income			300	
Investment income			100	
TOTAL INCOME	30,990	48,508	423,200	388,067
OPERATING EXPENSES				
Salaries	25,612	27,132	225,069	217,056
Benefits	4,583	4,516	38,885	39,127
Advert./promo/printing/postage	4,713	5,201	39,111	41,707
Auto exp		41		333
Computer exp			231	
Contract services	1,853	359	6,811	2,867
Dues/memberships	40	690	1,953	6,120
Food	38		275	200
Insurance	400	383	3,222	3,067
Interest exp				
Legal & professional		146	489	1,166
Maintenance & repair		100	38	800
Office/other supplies	139	659	1,634	5,874
Recruiting exp		33	860	666
Rent exp	1,333		2,982	
Staff development		421	957	2,617
Travel	1,353	3,100	17,942	24,800
Telephone/communications	875	2,160	9,473	17,280
Utilities				
Other	298	960	11,474	7,780
Allocation of indirect o/h	12,421	4,481	60,502	35,847
TOTAL OPERATING EXPENSES	53,658	50,382	421,908	407,307
NET INCOME (LOSS)	(22,668)	(1,874)	1,292	(19,240)

UNAUDITED FINANCIAL STATEMENTS FOR INTERNAL USE ONLY

BUDGETING

A *budget* is a plan for anticipating income and expenses to achieve specific objectives within a certain time (Brody, 2005). Some view budgeting as a planning process, while others see budgeting more as a political process. As a planning process, budgeting can be seen as a process to make rational decisions about the allocation of resources. Those who view budgeting more as a political process see competition between different factions for scarce financial resources. In this chapter, we will focus on the mechanics and planning aspects of budgeting, but it is important to always remember that there is a political element to the process.

Budgeting Systems

There are many different types of budget systems, but there are three major types that you will need to understand.

Line-item budget. The line-item budget is the simplest and most common form of budgeting and the form used by most human service organizations. This budget type is concerned with expenditures and revenues related to commodities. The question is, "How much do things cost, and how much of each thing do we need?" This question relates to everything from number of employees to amounts of office supplies. The major purpose of this approach is economy and control of costs. A major purpose of the line item is to identify all sources of anticipated funding and then allocate that funding to the different units of the agency for the next fiscal year.

Performance budget. Performance budgeting is based on the output of each department of the agency. The typical measure is based on a "unit of service." Unit of service can be defined in many ways. Some examples are counseling hours, foster placements, housing units developed, or however the product of the agency is defined. To develop a performance budget, it is necessary to determine the total program costs for a fiscal year and divide the total cost by the units of service to be provided for the fiscal year. If a department's total budget is $1,000,000 and they provide 10,000 counseling hours, the unit cost for this service is $100. Performance budgeting helps evaluate the productivity of an agency. In our example, if the department provided only 2,500 counseling sessions for the year and the budget remained at $1,000,000, then the unit cost would be $400 per counseling hour. As the administrator, this would likely raise concerns for you, which would lead you to reduce expenses or increase productivity. The counseling hour example is a simple and straightforward unit of service. Unfortunately, most units of service are not as easily defined. Even if an agency does not adopt a true performance budget, it is essential that the administrator have a method to monitor the unit costs for each department of the agency.

Program budgeting. A program system budget is built by examining the expenses of each program in the organization, defining the measures of program outcomes, and calculating the cost to the program to achieve the desired outcomes. The program budget computes the total program cost for the fiscal year and divides that cost by the number of outcomes to establish a cost per outcome. Much like performance budgeting, program budgeting is effectiveness budgeting. The primary difference is that performance budgeting is based on *outputs*, whereas program budgeting in based on *outcomes* (Martin, 2001; see also Chapter 7, this volume).

A Comprehensive Budgeting System

Line-item budgeting, program budgeting, and performance budgeting are all important tools for the human services administrator. Each provides important information essential to the management of a human services organization. Each provides data and information from a different perspective. The line-item budget emphasizes financial control, whereas the program budget stresses effectiveness, and the performance budget focuses on productivity. The competent administrator will use elements from all three of the major budgeting systems (Martin, 2001).

THE BUDGETING PROCESS

As stated earlier, budgeting has both a planning and a political component. When we think of the politics of budgeting, we often think of the budget battles in Congress or in the state legislatures, but we should also remember that there is a political component to the decisions made about how much one unit of an organization will get as compared to another unit. The complex interplay between budget planning and budget politics makes it difficult to reduce the budgeting process to a few simple steps, but it is important to have a framework when engaging the process of developing a budget.

In this section, we will concentrate on developing a line item budget since it is the most common budget system in human service organizations and is the base from which you as an administrator can build measures of performance using program and performance budgeting techniques. There are several steps in the budget process. For our purposes, we will use the steps outlined by Ralph Brody in *Effectively Managing Human Service Organizations* (2005)

Step 1: Set Organizational Objectives

The budget is one of the tools to help an organization carry out its mission and achieve its objectives. Building the budget is a process of setting priorities and defining what is important to the organization. The old saying "follow the money" is good advice when developing a budget. To allocate resources of one activity over another is to declare that activity to be a higher priority than another. It is critical to be clear on the mission, goals, and objectives of the organization before engaging in the budget building process.

Step 2: Establish Budget Policies and Procedures

Budget building is a complex task and requires the same level of organization and planning as other major projects. As the administrator, you should develop a budget time line so all the parties involved in the process can coordinate their efforts. You, the program directors, the finance committee, and the board all have a role in the budget process. As the leader of the budget building process, you will assign responsibilities for gathering the needed information. There will be many questions to be answered: What are the staffing needs for the next year? Will the cost of medical insurance be going up? How accurate were our predictions in the last budget year? In which line items did we overspend or underspend? Were our income projections realistic, and what is the outlook for the coming year? Finally, you will need to develop the budget format to be used by each person involved in the process. In most cases, you will provide each person working on the budget with a report that compares the actual income and expenses to date in the current year to the current year's budgets. From this information, program directors are asked to project their needs for the next fiscal year. You may also set guidelines for preparing the budget. For example, you set a guideline that the budget increases may not exceed 3% (or 5% or whatever is appropriate).

Step 3: Set Annual Income and Expense Targets

The arithmetic of developing a budget is very simple: Projected income – projected operation expenses = projected operating surplus or deficit. Remember that it is perfectly acceptable for nonprofit organizations to have a surplus at the end of the year. In most cases, the budget presented to the board is a balanced budget where the projected income and projected expenses are equal, but there are times when an agency may adopt a deficit budget. It is very common for organizations to budget a surplus to build cash reserves for the organization.

The first section of the budget deals with the projected income for the coming fiscal year. Sources of income can include donations, corporate gifts, foundation grants, government contracts or grants, fees for service, and third-party payments. Any money anticipated to come to the agency should be included in the income budget. Remember that the expenses you budget are dependent on meeting the income goals in the budget. You can budget all the expenses you want, but if the income is not available, you will be forced to cut budget expenses to be within the projected income.

The next section of the budget is the expense side, which includes all of the cash operation expenses of the organization. Salaries, fringe benefits, office supplies, rent, utilities, advertising, liability insurance, and any other expenses are to be categorized and included in the expense side of the budget.

Once the administrator has examined the income and expenses to date and made preliminary projections about the following year, the individual departments or units are given the information so they can propose their departmental budget. Your work will be the basis on which they will make their recommendations for their departmental budgets.

Step 4: Each Unit Proposes Their Budget

Each unit head will go through the same process in projecting income and expenses for the department and must justify increases in expenses. If new expenses are proposed, the program director must specify what new income will be generated to support the expenses. When this process is completed, the management team meets to develop the final draft of the budget document.

Step 5: Management Team Proposes Budget to Board

It is the responsibility of the administrator to develop the final budget proposal to the board. While there is a great deal of work from many parts of the organization to develop the budget, it is ultimately the responsibility of the administrator to present a budget to the board. The administrator will also be held accountable for carrying out the budget plan.

In this step, the administrator presents the budget proposal to the finance committee of the board. This is the place for the representatives of the board to take a hard look at the budget proposal. The finance committee should be asking certain questions: Are the income projections realistic? Are the expenses reasonable? Does this budget advance the mission of the organization? Any adjustments required by the finance committee are made, and then the finance committee presents the budget to the full board with a recommendation. Finally, the board adopts the budget for the next fiscal year.

SUMMARY

This chapter examined one of the most challenging tasks for administrators of human service organizations. There are great needs to be addressed by a human services organization, but there are always limited resources. Budgeting and financial management are the tools used to plan and use the resources of the organization in the most effective way. The administrator must manage many tasks at the same time, but financial management must be a priority or the organization will have little chance to live up to the challenges of its mission.

This chapter will surely not make you an accountant, but it will give you the basic tools to learn the art of financial management. As the administrator, you will depend on the expertise of the chief financial officer of the organization who is an important member of the management team. In addition to a strong "in-house" financial person, every organization should have a contract agreement with a certified public accountant (CPA).

REFERENCES

American Institute of Certified Public Accountants. (1998). *AICPA audit and accounting guide: Not-for-profit organizations.* New York: Author.

Brody, R. (2005). *Effectively managing human service organizations.* Thousand Oaks, CA: Sage.

Martin, L. L. (2001). *Financial management for human services administrators.* Needham Heights, MA: Allyn & Bacon.

Women's Economic Self-Sufficiency Team–Albuquerque, NM. (2001, October 10). *Preparing your cash flow statement.* Retrieved June 28, 2005 from http://www.onlinewbc.gov/docs/finance/cashflow.html

HELPFUL TERMS

Accounts—classifications of transactions into one category. Accounts can be for income or expenses, such as fees collected, salaries, or equipment purchased.

Accounts payable—money owed by the organization to someone else, but not yet paid. For example, if office supplies are received but have not yet been paid for, that amount is an account payable for the organization. Employee vacation time that has accumulated but not been taken is carried on the financial statements as an accounts payable.

Accounts receivable—revenues earned, but not yet received. For example, if services have been provided and a contract has been billed for that service, the amount of the bill is an account receivable. It remains as an account receivable until the cash is received by the organization.

Accruals—transactions are recognized (recorded) when revenues are earned and when expenses are incurred. Accrual accounting provides a more complete financial picture through the use of accounts receivable and accounts payable.

Assets—anything owned by an organization that has economic value. Assets may include cash, bank accounts, accounts receivable (see definition above), equipment, buildings, property, and automobiles.

Balance sheets—a snapshot in time of an organization's assets and liabilities, produced monthly, quarterly, or annually. These reports subtract liabilities from assets to show the organization's worth.

Budget—a plan for anticipating income and expenses to achieve specific objectives within a certain time.

Depreciation—an estimate of the decrease in the value of an asset. Depreciation takes into account the reality that equipment, buildings, automobiles, and so on, become obsolete or simply worn out over time. It is a method to show how much of the value of an asset remains.

Financial projections—reports that look and forecast or estimate future income and expenses.

Financial reports/Financial statements—reports on historical financial transactions. Examples include budget reports, activity reports, and balance sheets.

Generally Accepted Accounting Principles (GAAP)—basic sets of rules governing how the financial books and records of an organization are to be maintained, including how revenues, expenditures, and expenses are to be accounted for, and how financial statements are to be prepared.

Liabilities—obligations to pay somebody something. All debts or amounts owing by an organization in the form of accounts payable (see above), loans, mortgages, and long-term debts are liabilities.

Net assets—what is left over when liabilities are subtracted from assets.

Permanently restricted—funds permanently restricted to a specific use. Endowment funds are usually in this category. A donor may give a gift to the organization, but requires that only the earnings from those funds be used by the organization.

Revenues—usually in the form of cash and checks and may come from many sources such as fees for service, contracts, grants, donations, third-party payments, insurance, managed care firms, or investment income.

Temporarily restricted funds—funds given for a specific project.

Unrestricted funds—funds on which the donor has placed no restrictions.

EXERCISES

1. In-Basket Exercise

Read the following memos from your in-basket. For each memo, draft a reply outlining your decision or the action you plan to take.

Memo

Date:	June 25, 20XX
To:	Administrator
From:	Finance Committee Chair
Subject:	Financial Report to the Board of Directors

I will be presenting the financial report to the full board at our next meeting. I have received the financial statements (the monthly statement of activities and the balance sheet), but I need your help in preparing my report. Please prepare a narrative report that explains the financial statements. I need an overall statement about the financial condition of the agency so far this fiscal year and how we are doing compared to last year. Also, please explain any variances in the budget in both income and expenses, and give me your recommendations for any adjustments that will be needed for the remainder of the fiscal year.

Write your answer here: Use the ABC Monthly Statement of Revenue and Expenses—All Departments Combined as the basis for your answer.

Memo

Date: August 31, 20XX

To: Administrator

From: Board Chair

Subject: Budget for Next Fiscal Year

In reviewing the income statements for August, I noticed there are some rather large variances between the budget to date amounts and the actual amounts. I know we will be starting the formal budgeting process next month, but it would be helpful if you could give me some advance information on our financial picture. Please look at the administration statement, the Department A statement, and the Department B statement and project what you think our income and expenses are likely to be next fiscal year. I don't need a lot of detail. Just give me a one-page projected budget for ABC NonProfit Corporation by using the actual income and expenses for the first eight months of this year and projecting next year's 12-month budget.

Write your answer here: Remember the year to date actual and the current budget are only for the first eight months of the year. Your task is to examine the eight months' actual income and actual expenses and project what next year's budget might look like. Use the same line items from the Monthly Statement of Revenue and Expenses—All Departments Combined.

2. Exercise

Working in a small group in class, discuss your personal strengths and weaknesses related to financial management and budgeting. Report to the class how you plan to better prepare yourself for the financial functions you will need to perform as a human services administrator.

ASSIGNMENTS

1. Go online to Guidestar.org and search for a local nonprofit agency. Examine the IRS 990 form and write a two-page summary that describes the financial position of the organization.

2. Prepare a line-item budget for a fictitious agency with a budget of $2 million per year. Assume the $2 million in income comes from the United Way, fees for service, and donations. Develop an income and expense budget that reflects the most common expenses for an organization.

3. Call the finance director of a local organization and ask him or her for a telephone interview concerning the organization's budgeting process. Ask the director to describe his or her role in the process and the role of the administrator and the board of directors. Write a three-page summary explaining what you learn from the interview.

Human Resources

9

Productive employees are truly the heart of any human services organization. One of the major functions of a human services administrator is to recruit, hire, and train productive employees. One of the less pleasant tasks of an administrator is to deal with unproductive employees through processes of discipline and termination. This is a difficult, but necessary, administrative function. Hiring and firing are tools that human services administrators use to either maintain existing norms in the organization or to change them (Wiener, 1988). Agency administrators often say that the most challenging part of their jobs is dealing with employee issues. As an administrator, you will be challenged not to get bogged down in staff issues that will take you away from the mission of your organization.

How do you find the right people for the jobs you have to fill? Remember that every vacancy that occurs is an opportunity for you to assess the vacated position and, if warranted, to restructure or reorganize in some fashion. Staff openings provide opportunities to bring in new perspectives, energy, and diversity to the organization. You may want to look close to home to fill the vacancy. Are there people in the organization who would like to move up or to take on a different challenge in the organization? One of the advantages (and sometimes disadvantages) is that you and the employee know each other. You know their strengths and weaknesses, and they know the reality of working for the organization. If it's a good fit, then this kind of arrangement can strengthen the organization. This chapter will cover the current rules and policies regarding hiring and recruitment, compensation and benefits, training and development, and performance management. Techniques for developing and retaining productive employees will be covered as well as tools for dealing with employee lack of productivity. Making the organization a challenging and positive place to work will be the central theme throughout the chapter.

HIRING AND RECRUITMENT

Human services administrators must have the skills for hiring and recruiting new employees. The ability to identify, recruit, and hire high-performing employees is essential for the long-term success of the human services agency. Your task as a human services administrator is to find the best people you can find to work in your organization. You can only achieve this task by making the organization a challenging and positive place to work. You want potential employees to *want* to work at your organization, and you want to retain the valuable employees you have. What are the elements that make an organization a challenging and positive place to work?

Montana and Charnov (1993) identified 25 factors that motivate employees and then examined a number of studies to determine perceptions about motivation and how these perceptions compared to the 25 factors. From this analysis, they identified the following nine factors as the most important motivating factors:

1. Respect for me as a person

2. Good pay

3. Chance to turn out quality work

4. Chance for promotion

5. Opportunity to do interesting work

6. Feeling my job is important

7. Being told when I do a good job

8. Opportunity for self-development

9. Large amount of freedom on the job

These nine factors represent the *perception* that employees have of what motivates them in their workplace. Psychological climate describes an employee's perception of the psychological impact of the work environment on her/his well-being. When employees in an organization agree in their positive perception of their work environment, their shared perceptions can then be said to form the organization's *climate* (Jones & James, 1979; Glisson, 2000; Glisson & Hemmelgarn 1998). The organizational culture is the shared values, beliefs, and behavioral norms in an organization (Ouchi, 1981). The norms and values of the organization that influence the behavior of service provider employees create a social and psychological context that shapes tone, content, and objectives of the services provided (O'Reilly & Chatman, 1996). The organizational climate has a direct impact on how well the clients of the organization are served.

Are these nine factors important for you as you decide where you want to work? If they are important to you, then it makes sense that these are the same things that will be important to the people you hire and the people you wish to keep working for your organization.

Employment Laws

To be an effective administrator in the area of personnel management, you must have a basic understanding of employment law. Below are several of the major federal laws that govern employment practices and prohibit job discrimination. Review the applicable employment laws at the U.S. Equal Employment Opportunity Commission (EEOC) website at http://www.eeoc.gov/laws/statutes/index.cfm.

Title VII of the Civil Rights Act of 1964 (Title VII)

This law makes it illegal to discriminate against someone on the basis of race, color, religion, national origin, or sex. The law also makes it illegal to retaliate against a person because the person complained about discrimination, filed a charge of discrimination, or participated in an employment discrimination investigation or lawsuit. The law also requires that employers reasonably accommodate applicants' and employees' sincerely held religious practices, unless doing so would impose an undue hardship on the operation of the employer's business.

The Pregnancy Discrimination Act

This law amended Title VII to make it illegal to discriminate against a woman because of pregnancy, childbirth, or a medical condition related to pregnancy or childbirth. The law also makes it illegal to retaliate against a person because the person complained about discrimination, filed a charge of discrimination, or participated in an employment discrimination investigation or lawsuit.

The Equal Pay Act of 1963 (EPA)

This law makes it illegal to pay different wages to men and women if they perform equal work in the same workplace. The law also makes it illegal to retaliate against a person because the person complained about discrimination, filed a charge of discrimination, or participated in an employment discrimination investigation or lawsuit.

The Age Discrimination in Employment Act of 1967 (ADEA)

This law protects people who are 40 or older from discrimination because of age. The law also makes it illegal to retaliate against a person because the person complained about discrimination, filed a charge of discrimination, or participated in an employment discrimination investigation or lawsuit.

Title I of the Americans with Disabilities Act of 1990 (ADA)

This law makes it illegal to discriminate against a qualified person with a disability in the private sector and in state and local governments. The law also makes it illegal to retaliate against a person because the person complained about discrimination, filed a charge of discrimination, or participated in an employment discrimination investigation or lawsuit. The law also requires that employers reasonably accommodate the known physical or mental limitations of an otherwise qualified individual with a disability who is an applicant or employee, unless doing so would impose an undue hardship on the operation of the employer's business.

Sections 102 and 103 of the Civil Rights Act of 1991

Among other things, this law amends Title VII and the ADA to permit jury trials and compensatory and punitive damage awards in intentional discrimination cases.

Sections 501 and 505 of the Rehabilitation Act of 1973

This law makes it illegal to discriminate against a qualified person with a disability in the federal government. The law also makes it illegal to retaliate against a person because the person complained about discrimination, filed a charge of discrimination, or participated in an employment discrimination investigation or lawsuit. The law also requires that employers reasonably accommodate the known physical or mental limitations of an otherwise qualified individual with a disability who is an applicant or employee, unless doing so would impose an undue hardship on the operation of the employer's business.

The EEOC enforces all of these laws and also provides oversight and coordination of all federal equal employment opportunity regulations, practices, and policies. Once you have a basic understanding of the law, you are in a better position to be sure that you do not discriminate in the interview process. Employment laws change over time, and it is not likely that you will become an expert in employment law. However, as a human services administrator, you should be committed to value and promote diversity in the workplace and to strive for social justice in your employment practices. As a human services administrator, you should be committed to the spirit of the nondiscrimination laws and, therefore, committed to fairness and nondiscrimination in the workplace. Sometimes, this is not as easy as it sounds.

A human services administrator was interviewing a candidate for the position of vice president for finance in the human services agency. Since this person would have a great deal of interface with the board of trustees, the administrator asked the board chair to join in an interview of the candidate. The interview was going well until the board chair asked the candidate, "By the way, Mr. X, how old are you?" Mr. X paused for a moment and then said, "Well, I've been around for a while." Not to be deterred, the board chair said, "No, really—how old are you?" More reluctantly, Mr. X said, "I'm 62." Fortunately, Mr. X was a great candidate and was hired for the job. However, if he had not been hired, the board chairman had given Mr. X a great opportunity to file a complaint against the agency based on age discrimination.

In conducting a job interview, you should focus only on what is essential to the job. In the example above, Mr. X's age had nothing to do with the essential job functions of the position. You should think through the way that you will ask questions in an interview. You cannot ask applicants about their child care arrangements or even if they have children. You can, however, legitimately ask if the candidate is available for working nights and weekends if those hours are a requirement of the job. In conducting an interview and in your hiring decisions, you must avoid discrimination based on race, gender, age, place of origin, sexual orientation, and disability.

COMPENSATION AND BENEFITS

Human services administrators are responsible for the management of compensation and benefit plans. Pay and benefits are two critical factors that will determine how employees and potential employees feel about the organization. Administering an effective compensation system and determining the best benefits package for all of the agency employees are vital administrative skills. The perception by employees that there is unfairness in the system has proved to be a powerful disincentive to optimum performance. Montana and Charnov (1993) say perceptions of fairness and equity are affected by two factors: (1) comparison of pay received to such factors as effort, job performance, education, experience, skill, and seniority; and (2) comparison of the perceived equity of pay and rewards received to those received by other people.

Ethical issues can arise at both ends of the salary spectrum (Grobman, 2011). Does the organization pay a living wage to those at the lower end of the salary scale? Is the compensation just? Does the compensation live up to the social justice standards that the organization professes to promote? What about the salaries that will be paid to you and other top administrators? Are the salaries of the top administrators excessive, or are they fair based on the required skills, experience, education, and the size and complexity of the organization? Human services administrators should be well paid, but compensation should not be excessive. Administrators must be mindful of being good stewards of money that comes to the agency whether it comes from tax payers, donors, insurance companies, or clients.

In addition to the base compensation, there are issues and financial considerations related to indirect compensation that employers are required to provide. Indirect compensation includes:

Social Security—Employers are required to cover employees under a comprehensive program of retirement, survivor, disability, and health benefits (OASDHI).

Workers' Compensation Laws—These require that employers finance a variety of benefits such as lost wages, medical benefits, survivor benefits, and rehabilitation services for employees with work-related illness or injuries.

Federal Unemployment Tax—Employers must pay taxes to cover laid-off employees for up to 39 weeks with additional extensions possible.

Family Medical Leave Act of 1993—This requires employers to continue providing health care coverage to employees who are on leave for up to 12 weeks per year for a specified family emergency. (Bernardin, n.d.)

Optional employee benefits are those benefits that many employers choose to offer their employees that are not mandatory. Such benefits include health care insurance, disability insurance, life insurance, retirement plans, flexible compensation, and paid leave (vacation, sick leave, etc.). While these benefits are optional, in reality, most of these are considered the basic benefits expected by potential employees. With the passage of the Affordable Care Act, more employers will be required to provide health care insurance for their employees. For many employers, providing health care will not be an option but, rather, a required part of employment compensation.

TRAINING AND DEVELOPMENT

Training programs that improve employee performance and minimize performance problems can be a valuable asset for an organization. Well-designed and well-presented training can produce tangible results. Providing consistent employee feedback is necessary to meet the goal of continuous quality improvement in the organization. Van Wart (1998) suggests a seven-step organizational needs analysis as a means of determining the greatest need for training and development.

These seven elements are:

1. Ethics assessments or audits to look for gaps between stated values and organizational performance

2. Examining the organization's values, vision, mission, and planning statements to identify possible gaps in the needs

3. Customer and citizen assessments to find emerging needs

4. Employee assessments to reveal employee opinions and values

5. Performance assessments to identify gaps between stated and actual performance

6. Benchmarking to examine best practices (evidence based practices) elsewhere and using them as standards

7. Quality assessment reviews

After conducting the needs analysis using the elements above, the human services administrators and other appropriate top administrators will design the training program for the organization. The complexity and comprehensiveness of the training plan will depend on the size of the budget and the size of the organization. When budgets are tight, training and staff development are often the first place that administrators look to make budget cuts. While this approach is tempting, it can be very damaging to the organization. The following guidelines are presented by the World Health Organization (2005) and outline 10 steps for the development of a training program:

- Define the target population for training.
- List the tasks to be performed by the target population on the job.
- List the skills and knowledge needed to do the tasks.
- Select the skills and knowledge to be taught. (These are the training objectives.)
- Organize the selected skills and knowledge into suitable teaching units (modules) and develop the training design including brief outlines of modules content and planned training methods.
- Draft expanded outlines of modules, including instructional objectives, main body of text, and descriptions of training methods, examples, and exercises.
- Have experts provide realistic examples and information for use in exercises.
- Draft the complete modules, facilitator guidelines, and course director guidelines.
- Field-test the training materials.
- Revise and finalize training material based on the field test.

While training is most often the "in-house" method for improving staff functioning of specific tasks and functions within the organization, professional development is more typically offered by providers external to the organization (Gibelman & Furman, 2008). Providers may include universities or commercial and professional associations offering programs to help update professional skills. Professional development activities are a method thought to be beneficial to employee morale, productivity, and longevity on the job. Supporting employees to attend or present at their professional conferences is an example of professional development. Many employees who hold professional licenses or certifications will have annual requirements for continuing education credits (CEUs). Budgeting for conference tuition, allowing associated travel, and granting time away from work are ways to support employees in their professional development activities.

One approach to professional development for human services administrators is being pioneered at the University of Texas at Arlington's Center for Advocacy, Nonprofit and Donor Organizations (CAN-DO) with its Triple A Project. The Triple A Project assesses and augments the administrative skills of individuals within community agencies who seek to become higher level administrators, managers, and leaders (http://www.uta.edu/ssw/research/can-do.php). Many universities provide continuing education opportunities and professional development opportunities that can be invaluable to human services administrators in meeting their obligations for providing training and development activities for their organization and for themselves.

PERFORMANCE MANAGEMENT

Many employees do not look forward to the dreaded "annual review." Even if the employee is confident she is doing a good job, there is something unpleasant about being put under the microscope. Part of it may be that it reminds us that there is a power differential between the employee and supervisor, or it may raise old issues of being unfairly evaluated by others in the past. The other side of the equation is that many people who do the annual evaluation don't like doing them any more than the employees like being subjected to them. However unpleasant, performance management is an important component of human services administration (Weinbach & Taylor, 2011). The ability to effectively manage the performances of employees is a major responsibility of human services managers and establishing and implementing a complete performance improvement process is an essential skill. Designing your performance review process, maintaining it, and effectively monitoring its implementation are challenging tasks. The purpose of employee appraisal is to determine to what extent employees are achieving the requirements of their jobs. For the evaluation to be effective, it must be based on realistic and measurable criteria that are clear, realistic, and achievable (Kadushin & Harkness, 2002; Pecora & Wagner, 2000, as cited in Gibelman & Furman, 2008).

In regard to the use of performance assessments, the Council on Accreditation (2013) states,

The performance review process assesses job performance, recognizes accomplishments, provides constructive feedback, and emphasizes self-development and professional growth, in relation to:

a. specific expectations defined in the job description;
b. organization-wide expectations for personnel;
c. objectives established in the most recent review, accomplishments and challenges since the last review period, and objectives for future performance;
d. developmental and professional objectives;
e. recommendations for further training, skill building, and other resources that may contribute to improved job performance; and
f. knowledge and competence related to the characteristics and needs of service recipients, if applicable.

Ideally, the performance evaluation allows you to tell employees that they are doing a great job and to support them in their work. From the strength-based perspective, you want to highlight and build on the positive contributions being made by the organization's employees. Unfortunately, it will sometimes be your responsibility as a human services administrator to take corrective action because of the behavior of an employee or because he is not fulfilling the requirements of the job. This is a part of the job responsibility that you accept when you become a human services administrator, and like other skills, you must be able to perform the required function. Brody (2005) outlines several steps necessary when taking corrective action with an employee. First, you will need to document specific, concrete behaviors that reflect the unacceptable work performance or behavior. Once these have been well documented, you will need to discuss the unacceptable behavior as soon as possible after it occurs. This discussion should be conducted in private. The focus of the discussion is on changing behavior and is not about personalities or issues unrelated to the workplace. You should provide the employee with explicit expectations for behavior and performance. If the problem continues, you would begin a series of corrective actions starting with a verbal warning. If there is not improvement, the next step is to issue a written warning indicating that if the employee does not correct the problem, it will result in suspension or termination. If the problem continues, follow through with the stated consequence of suspension or termination.

As stated at the beginning of this chapter, dealing with employee issues is one of the most difficult challenges of the administrator.

A human service administrator was meeting with the chair of the agency board of directors to discuss an employee issue. The employee, an agency secretary, was unhappy with a decision the administrator had made and was threatening to file a lawsuit or go to the media with her complaints. The administrator was meeting with the board chair to keep him informed and to seek his advice since he was an attorney. After listening to the administrator briefing on the situation, the boar chair lawyer said, "You know, as I think back over my years of law practice and the problems I have had—it isn't the clients, it isn't the other lawyers or the judges—it's the secretaries!"

The effective human services administrator must have a working knowledge of the many laws that govern the administration of employee relationships. From the time you begin to recruit employees until the time employees leave the agency, there are laws and regulations that must be taken into account. Human service administrators need to know when they need to consult an attorney or human resources professional. The best protection for you and your organization is to have clear policies that are followed consistently. The annual review process should be taken seriously. If there are performance problems, but they are not documented in the review process, this can become a major problem for you and the organization. There is always the possibility of employment complaints or lawsuits related to employment practices. The way to minimize this risk is by operating fairly and just communicating openly and candidly. Documentation is key in employment issues. Your motto should be, "Document, document, and document!"

SUPERVISION

Supervision of staff and volunteers is critical at all levels of the organization. In all but very small nonprofit organizations, the human services administrator will provide supervision of the executive team or the heads of the major components of the organization. Supervision tasks generally fall into three categories: administrative, educational, and supportive functions (Kadushi & Harkness, 2002). Administrative tasks include assigning employees to work units and developing procedures to increase productivity. The responsibility to complete performance evaluations and make recommendations for compensation, promotion, or discipline falls within the realm of administrative supervision. The educational tasks are teaching, orienting new employees, modeling professional behaviors, and helping employees access needed information. Supportive activities include providing emotional support, motivating, empowering, and mediating disputes (Kadushi & Harkness, 2002; Lauffer, 2011).

Lewis, Packard, and Lewis (2011) identify the following as the supervisory process:

THE SUPERVISORY PROCESS

1. Providing encouragement and support for the supervisee

2. Building motivation

3. Increasing the mutuality of individual and organizational goals

4. Enhancing the supervisee's competence in service delivery

5. Carrying out ongoing assessments on the supervisee's success in fulfilling his or her responsibilities

6. Providing prompt and objective feedback designed to enhance the supervisee's professional development

DIVERSITY IN THE WORKPLACE

Having a diverse workforce is essential for the health and well-being of a human services organization. Diversity is not something that the human services administrator needs to "handle" but rather is something that needs to be developed, celebrated, and cherished. The staffing of the organization should, at a minimum, reflect the demographics of the community served by the organization. When clients come to the organization for services, they need to see people that look like them and that speak their preferred language. Diversity should be one of the "guiding principles" of a nonprofit organization. Mor Barak (1999, as cited in Golensky, 2011) calls for an expanded definition of diversity that recognizes observable or readily detectable attributes such as race, gender, or age, and less visible or invisible attributes such as religion, education, tenure with the organization, or sexual orientation.

SUMMARY

This chapter has presented a brief overview of human resource management—one of the most challenging responsibilities of a human services administrator. We have discussed topics of hiring, employment law, compensation, training and development, performance management, supervision, and diversity. Human resource management can be one of the most difficult tasks of the administrator but can also be one of the greatest joys. To find employees who share your passion for the services you provide and see people grow and develop in their professional career is a rare opportunity.

REFERENCES

Bernardin. (n.d.). Compensation: Base pay and fringe benefits. *McGraw Hill Answers*. Retrieved from http://answers.mheducation.com/management/human-resource-management/compensation-base-pay-and-fringe-benefits#fringe-benefits

Brody, R. (2005). *Effectively managing human services organizations* (3rd ed.). Thousand Oaks, CA: Sage.

Council on Accreditation. (2013). *PA-HR 6: Performance review*. Retrieved from http://www.coanet.org/standard/pa-hr/6

Gibelman, M., & Furman, R. (2008). *Navigating human service organizations* (2nd ed.). Chicago: Lyceum Books.

Glisson, C. (2000). Organizational climate and culture. In R. Patti (Ed.), *The handbook of social welfare management* (pp. 195–218). Thousand Oaks, CA: Sage.

Glisson, C., & Hemmelgarn, A. (1998). The effects of organizational climate and interoganizational coordination on the quality and outcomes of children's service systems. *Child Abuse and Neglect, 22(5)*, 401–421.

Golensky, M. (2011). *Strategic leadership and management in nonprofit organizations: Theory and practice*. Chicago: Lyceum Books.

Grobman, G. M. (2011). *An introduction to the nonprofit sector: A practical approach for the 21st century* (3rd ed.). Harrisburg, PA: White Hat Communications.

Jones, A. P., & James, L. R. (1979). Psychological climate: Dimensions and relationships of individual and aggregated work environment perceptions. *Organizational Behavior and Human Performance, 23*, 201–250.

Kadushin, A., & Harkness, D. (2002). *Supervision is social work* (4th ed.) New York: Columbia University Press.

Lauffer, A. (2011). *Understanding your social agency* (3rd ed.). Thousand Oaks, CA: Sage.

Lewis, J. A., Packard, T. R., & Lewis, M. D. (2011). *Management of human service programs* (5th ed.). Belmont, CA: Brooks/Cole.

Montana, P. J., & Charnov, B. H. (1993). *Management*. Hauppauge. NY: Barrons Business Review Series..

Mor Barak, M. E. (1999). Beyond affirmative action: Toward a model of diversity and organizational inclusion. *Administration in Social Work, 23*(3–4), 47–68.

O'Reilly, C. F., & Chatman, J. A. (1996). Culture as social control: Corporations cults, and commitment. *Research in Organizational Behavior, 18*, 157–2000.

Ouchi, W. G. (1981). *Theory Z*. Reading, MA: Addison-Wesley.

Pecora, P. J., & Wagner, M. (2000). *Managing personnel*. In R. J. Patti (Ed.), *The handbook of social welfare management* (pp.395–423). Thousand Oaks, CA. Sage.

Van Wart, M. (1998). Organizational investment in employee development. In S. Condrey (Ed.), *Handbook of human resources management in government* (pp. 276–297). San Francisco: Jossey-Bass.

Weinbach, R. W., & Taylor, L. M. (2011) *The social worker as manager: A practical guide to success.* Boston: Allyn & Bacon.

Wiener, Y. (1988). Forms of value systems: A focus on organizational effectiveness and cultural change and maintenance. *Academy of Management Review, 13*(4), 534–545.

World Health Organization. (2005). *Task analysis: The basis for development of training in management of tuberculosis.* Geneva: Author.

HELPFUL TERMS

Employee appraisal—an evaluation to determine to what extent employees are achieving the requirements of their jobs.

Organizational culture—the shared values, beliefs, and behavioral norms in an organization.

Professional development—activities beneficial to employee morale, productivity, and longevity on the job.

Psychological climate—an employee's perception of the psychological impact of the work environment on her/his well-being.

Staff training—most often the "in-house" method for improving staff functioning of specific tasks and functions within the organization.

EXERCISES

1. In-Basket Exercise

Directions

Review the following memo and write a response explaining your decision on this matter.

Memo

Date: September 1, 20XX

To: Administrator

From: Director of Social Services

Subject: Request to offer employment

As you know, we have been interviewing candidates to fill the open caseworker position in our department. I have identified two finalists for the position. Here is a description of the two applicants.

Applicant 1. This applicant holds a master's degree in social work. She comes highly recommended to us. She has about one year of relevant experience.

Applicant 2. This applicant will complete her bachelor's in social work next month. She has excellent references and has over seven years of experience working with the population we serve.

We advertised the position as requiring a bachelor's degree, but, in my opinion, Applicant 2's experience will be extremely valuable to us, and she will have the degree soon. In choosing between the two applicants, I think experience is more valuable to us than a master's degree. I would like to have your approval to move forward and offer the position to Applicant 2. Please advise.

2. Interview Questions

You have been recruiting to hire a new director of professional services for your organization. After screening the applicant, you are now ready for the interview. Because this is such an important position in the organization, you have asked other key administrators and a board member to help with the interview process. You want all of the candidates to be asked the same questions, so you have decided to write a list of questions that will be asked of each candidate. Keeping in mind the laws regarding what you can and cannot ask in an interview, develop 10 standard questions that you and the others will ask of the candidates during the interview process.

3. Nine Motivating Factors

Review Montana and Charnov's (1993) nine motivating factors. Assume that you are putting together a packet of information about your agency to send to potential employees. Write a one-page description of the working conditions at your organization that describe how your organization addresses these nine factors.

ASSIGNMENTS

1. As the manager of several human services units providing services to low-income families and seniors, you have received notification that one of the larger grants that has funded these services will not be renewed. This will most likely result in layoffs and the termination of services to clients. Prepare a memo to announce this issue to the staff and develop an approach to plan for the changes that must be made.

2. One of your supervisors has approached you indicating a concern about possible substance abuse by an employee. The supervisor is requesting guidance on how to deal with the problem. Prepare written guidelines for the supervisor to follow in dealing with this issue.

3. Go online and look for employee evaluation forms that are available for public use. Find three different forms and compare them. How are they similar and different? Which of the forms, if any, would you want to use to evaluate the employees of your organization?

Boards

10

In this chapter, we will examine the duties and responsibilities of the board of directors and how those duties relate to the duties of the administrator. We will also review some of the techniques to build a strong and well-informed board of directors.

One of the unique aspects of nonprofit organizations is that they are governed by volunteer boards of directors. The board does not own the nonprofit organization but has the responsibility to be caretakers of the public trust, and, therefore, sometimes the board of directors is referred to as the *board of trustees*. In some ways, *trustees* more accurately describes the function of the board in protecting the organization that belongs to the public. This chapter focuses on working with nonprofit boards of directors, but much of the material is applicable to working with advisory boards in public agencies or boards in the private sector.

Board members and administrators have a responsibility to work together and to share the responsibility for the organization's success. The working relationship between the administrator and the board of directors is key to the effective operation of the organization. In fact, one of the key responsibilities of the board is to hire, and sometimes fire, the administrator. For this reason alone, it is important for the administrator to foster an effective working relationship with the board of directors.

> "There should be only one agenda item for a board of trustees: Should we fire the executive director or not? If the answer is 'no,' we should go home." This is a quote for the chairman of the board of a nonprofit organization. Few would agree totally with this assessment, but it does make the point that one of the most important roles for a board of trustees is to select and sometimes dismiss the executive director of an organization.

WHY DO NONPROFITS HAVE BOARDS?

Nonprofits are corporations and, as such, they are legal entities. Boards of directors have legal and ethical responsibilities that cannot be delegated. The board's responsibilities fall into four major categories:

- *Legal and fiduciary.* The board is responsible for ensuring that the organization meets legal requirements and that it is operating in accordance with its mission and for the purpose for which it was granted tax exemption. As guardians of the public trust, board members are responsible for protecting the organization's assets.

- *Oversight.* The board is responsible for ensuring that the organization is well run. The board is responsible to hire and fire the administrator or chief executive.
- *Fundraising.* The board is responsible to see that the organization has the money it needs.
- *Representation of constituencies and viewpoints.* Often, board members are chosen so that they can bring to the board the experience or perspective of a particular group or segment of the organization's constituency (Ingram, 2009).

RESPONSIBILITIES OF NONPROFIT BOARDS

In *Ten Basic Responsibilities of Nonprofit Boards*, Richard T. Ingram (2009) outlines the 10 major responsibilities of nonprofit boards of directors.

1. Determine the organization's mission and purpose. It is the board's responsibility to create and review a Statement of Mission and Purpose that articulates the organization's goals, means, and primary constituents served.

2. Select the chief executive. Boards must reach consensus on the chief executive's responsibilities and undertake a careful search to find the most qualified individual for the position.

3. Provide proper financial oversight. The board must assist in developing the annual budget and ensuring that proper financial controls are in place.

4. Ensure adequate resources. One of the board's foremost responsibilities is to provide adequate resources for the organization to fulfill its mission.

5. Ensure legal and ethical integrity and maintain accountability. The board is ultimately responsible for ensuring adherence to legal standards and ethical norms.

6. Ensure effective organizational planning. Boards must actively participate in an overall planning process and assist in implementing and monitoring the plan's goals.

7. Recruit and orient new board members and assess board performance. All boards have a responsibility to articulate prerequisites for candidates, orient new members, and periodically and comprehensively evaluate its own performance.

8. Enhance the organization's public standing. The board should clearly articulate the organization's mission, accomplishments, and goals to the public and garner support from the community.

9. Determine, monitor, and strengthen the organization's programs and services. The board's responsibility is to determine which programs are consistent with the organization's mission and to monitor their effectiveness.

10. Support the chief executive and assess his or her performance. The board should ensure that the chief executive has the moral and professional support he or she needs to further the goals of the organization. (p. 9)

Look at this list again. As you can see, these functions describe the "trustee" functions of the board of trustees. Next, we turn to the issue of structuring the board to carry out their important function as trustee.

HOW SHOULD THE BOARD BE STRUCTURED?

The size of the board, the officers of the board, how often they meet, and how members are elected are all defined in the legal documents of the nonprofit. The articles of incorporation outline the purpose of the organization, and the bylaws determine how the board will function. The bylaws also determine the size of the board and the committee structures.

Size

Boards of directors come in all sizes. Some are very small (five members or less), while others are very large (50 members are more). Many factors come into play in determining the size of the board. The size and complexity of the agency will often dictate the size of the board. It takes more than a few members to deal with a complex organization with many programs, a multi-program budget, and a large staff. The major determination is whether or not there are enough people involved to do the jobs necessary for the board to function productively. In most cases, the real work of the board is done in committees.

Officers

The officers of the nonprofit corporation are determined by the bylaws. The core offices are the board chair, secretary, and treasurer. Oftentimes, there is also a vice-chair or a chair-elect to provide continuity in board leadership when the chair's term is completed. Another variation on this theme is to have an immediate past chair. Sometimes, the chairs of each committee are considered officers of the board.

TYPICAL OFFICERS OF THE BOARD OF TRUSTEES

Board chair—responsible to conduct board meetings and work with the executive director to develop the board meeting agenda.

Vice-chair—conducts board meeting if the board chair is absent. Often the vice-chair will become the board chair after the term of the chair is expired

Secretary—the secretary is responsible to record the minutes of official actions of the board of trustees. Staff members often take minutes of the meeting, but it is the responsibility of the secretary of the board to verify the accuracy of the minutes and to present the minutes to the board for approval. Approval of the minutes is a standard agenda item on the board meeting agenda.

Treasurer—the treasurer is responsible to report the financial status of the organization to the full board. The monthly financial statements are typically prepared by staff or the organization's accountant, but it is the responsibility of the treasurer to present the financial reports to the board.

Board Committees

We have said that the work of the board is to perform a trustee function for the organization and to determine the policy. The committee structure of the board mirrors the many responsibilities of the administrator. Think about the major areas of responsibility for the administrator: program development and oversight, personnel management, budgeting and financial management, maintaining a positive work environment (physical plant), public relations, and fundraising. Each of these areas requires policy decisions by the board of trustees. There are many configurations of committees. The following list is only one possibility but will give you the idea of a typical structure. The committees we will consider here are standing committees of the board. These are the committees required in the bylaws.

TYPICAL BOARD COMMITTEES

Executive committee—acts on behalf of the board between the times of regularly scheduled board meetings.

Program committee—considers recommendations from the administrator when there is a proposal to begin a new program or to discontinue a program.

Personnel committee—is responsible for personnel policies.

Finance committee—is responsible to monitor the financial performance of the organization.

Development committee—is responsible to oversee the fundraising and public relations activities of the organization.

Physical plant committee—is responsible to provide a safe and comfortable environment for staff and clients.

In addition to the standing committees, the board chairman may appoint ad hoc committees from time to time. For example, unless there is a standing committee for nominations, the board chair may appoint a committee to bring nominations for new board members. Another example of an ad hoc committee is a search committee. If the administrator's position becomes vacant, the board chair may choose to appoint a search committee to look for a new administrator and to bring candidates to the full board for their consideration.

Executive committee—Many boards choose to have an executive committee that can act on behalf of the board between the times of regularly scheduled board meetings. A typical configuration is for the officers and, perhaps, standing committee chairs to act as the executive committee. While this arrangement can be very beneficial to smooth operations of the board, it can be problematic unless there are clear lines of responsibility between the full board and the executive committee.

Program committee—The program committee is responsible to study policy issues related to the organization's programs and to make recommendations to the full board. The program committee considers recommendations from the administrator when there is a proposal to begin a new program or to discontinue a program. The committee is also responsible to set program admission criteria, set fees, and determine the policies of each of the organization's programs. The program committee is also responsible to assess the effectiveness of the program services provided. It is the administrator's responsibility to have a program evaluation process in place, but it is the responsibility of the program committee to receive and evaluate this information.

Personnel committee—The organization's personnel policies are the responsibility of the personnel committee. Hiring and firing decisions are the prerogative of the administrator, but personnel actions must be taken within the structure of the organization's personnel policies. It is the responsibility of the committee to see that there is fairness in hiring, promotion, and firing decisions. The personnel committee is also responsible to assure equity in compensation for staff. Are employees treated equitably in their salaries and are similar jobs compensated at the same rate? Defining the benefits package of the organization is a policy decision for the board. What will be the policy for vacation and sick leave? What insurance and pension benefits will be provided by the organization?

Finance committee—The finance committee is responsible to work with the administrator in developing the organization's annual budget. The preparation of the budget is, in most cases, a staff function, but the finance committee is responsible to review the budget, recommend changes, and, finally, recommend the budget to the full board for approval. The committee must examine the budget to see that it is realistic by comparing the proposed budget to the current year's operation. It is also the responsibility of the finance committee to review the monthly (or sometimes quarterly) financial statements. The finance committee must also fulfill its trustee responsibility by closely monitoring the financial performance of the organization. The finance committee must also monitor contract compliance. Is the organization performing to the levels required by the contracting agency's expectation, and is the contract financially advantageous to the organization? The finance committee must review the annual independent audit. This is the annual audit of the financial statement by a certified public accountant. The finance committee will typically meet with the independent auditor before the auditor presents the audit to the full board. It should be noted that the audit is presented to the board, not to the administrator. This is one of the checks and balances of the nonprofit board and administrator relationship.

Physical plant committee—This committee may go by other names such as the *work environment committee*, but the function is to provide a safe and comfortable environment for staff and clients. At the most basic level, it must assure that health and safety standards are maintained. This committee deals with the issues of office space, program space, and the equipment needed by the organization to carry out its functions. The technology needs of the organization may be within the responsibility of this committee. If the organization maintains a large physical plant, this committee may have a major role to play in the functioning of the board. However, if the organization does not have or need a large space, then the functions of this committee may be handled by the finance committee.

Development committee—The development committee is concerned with the fundraising and public relations activities of the organization. Its members are first responsible to review and approve the communication vehicles used by the organization. The website, program brochures, and advertising are all items that the development committee should review and on which they should make recommendations to the administrator. This committee also makes recommendations to the board on the fundraising activities to be carried out by the organization. Proposed special events should be reviewed and approved by the committee. The committee should also be involved and help involve all the board in such activities. An overall fundraising plan is the responsibility of the administrator, and this plan should be approved by the committee and taken to the full board for approval. If there is the need for a major fundraising effort, such as a capital campaign to raise funds for a new building or other major undertaking, it is the responsibility of the development committee to bring this need to the board.

WHOSE JOB IS IT?

If the administrator is responsible for all the functions outlined above and the board also has responsibility in each of these areas, how is it determined who is responsible for which function? Board committees are supposed to help get the board's job done, not to help with the staff's job (Carver, 1990). It is often said that the job of the board of trustees is to set policy, and the role of the administrator is to carry out those policies in the day-to-day operation of the organization. This concept dates back to the 1800s and comes from a theory known as the *politics/administration dichotomy* (Goodnow, 1900; Wilson, 1887/1941). The idea is that elected officials define policy, and the administrator implements the policy. In this view, there is a clear division of responsibility between the officials (in our case, the elected board of directors) and the administrator. In the 1920s, charitable organizations that had been managed by boards began to hire professionals to serve as professional administrators. During this time, agency administrators promoted the idea that the function of the board of directors was to establish policy, and the administrator was to have full responsibility for day-to-day operations (Kirschner, 1986).

In general terms, it is true that boards establish policy and the administrator is responsible for day-to-day operations, but the reality is very different. Most boards of trustees rely heavily on the administrator to assist them in making policy decisions. It is the administrator who is intimately familiar with the day-to-day operations of the organization. It is ultimately the board of director's responsibility to set policy for the organization, but the administrator is in most cases a key player in the development of those policies. It is critical for administrators and their board of directors to have excellent communication and a strong working relationship.

> The executive director of an agency was proposing a major change in the service delivery method of one of the agency's programs. The board of trustees was not convinced that this was the best move for the agency to make, and some board members were personally opposed to this method of service. During the board meeting, when the change was being debated, the executive director stated that this was really a program issue and was her decision to make. At that point, the board chair stated, "It may be your decision to make but as a board it is our decision whether or not to raise money for the program." The executive director quickly saw the error of her thinking.

It is not the board's responsibility to be involved in the day-to-day operations of the organization—that is the role of the administrator. When conflicts arise between board members and administrators, it can often be related to the question of "whose responsibility is it?" It is vitally important for the administrator to develop clear channels of communication with the board. We will now turn to some of the methods of communication.

WORKING WITH THE BOARD

Working with boards has been described as doing the tango: You have to know when to lead and when to follow, while keeping your balance (Robinson, 2001). To successfully dance this tango, there must be strong respect between the board and the administrator.

Remember that your board members are volunteers. While the agency consumes a large part of your time and attention, board members have jobs, business interests, and other nonprofits that put demands on their time. The effective administrator will respect the board members for their contribution of their time and talent to the organization and view the board as a valuable asset to help achieve the organization's goals. The administrator must respect the board members' time by providing clear and concise information to help them perform their board function. What are some of the methods used to provide such information?

Sharing Information

Your board should never be surprised. Anything they hear in the community about the organization, either positive or negative, should be news they have already heard from you. It has been said that if you don't like the news you need to share with the board, you will like it less later. In other words, the administrator needs to get information to the board as soon as possible. If there is a bad situation, it will only be worse if the board members hear it from another source. On the positive side, board members need to have the good news of the organization so they can help spread the good word and also so they will be knowledgeable when approached in the community about the organization. The following are some types of information you will have to share with your board.

The insider newsletter—Of course, your board members will receive your organization's newsletter, but your board members will need much more information. Administrators often find it helpful to develop an informational newsletter to go to insiders, such as board members and leadership staff, on a regular basis. The frequency of this communication device depends on the needs of the organization. It may need to be produced weekly, but in most cases, it is produced on a monthly basis. The frequency of board meetings will also influence your decision on how often to send the insider newsletter.

The board meeting materials—At least two weeks before the board meeting, you will mail the board materials to be used at the board meeting. These materials will include the agenda, minutes of the previous meeting, committee reports, and financial reports. These materials, if done well, can take a great amount of your time and energy.

> One of the most horrifying sounds to an administrator is the sound of board members opening their board packets at the beginning of the board meeting!
>
> The board chair can help avoid this situation by starting each meeting with a statement such as "We will assume everyone has reviewed the board materials" and then move to the business at hand. This will set the expectation that the materials you developed will be read before the meeting begins.

The administrator and the board chair work together to develop the agenda for the board meeting. The administrator may also put out a call to the board membership and ask for any board agenda items they may have. The board meeting agenda will include reports, action items, and discussion items. It is important to identify action items on the agenda so board members can read the supporting materials, develop any questions they may have, and think about how they will vote on the issue. Each of the program areas may have action items. For instance, the finance committee may suggest a revision to the approved budget, or the program committee may recommend a change in the admission criteria for a program. These are policy issues that the board must decide. The board materials are provided to give the board members the information they need to make a decision.

Below is the skeleton of a board agenda. A real agenda would be much more detailed and would include the action items to be decided under each of the report items. The board agenda becomes the basis for the minutes of the board of trustees meeting and, therefore, the official document of the decisions of the board of trustees. The agenda and minutes of the board meetings are critical because they are the source of information when there is a question about the decisions of a board. The minutes also become an important part of the history of an organization. The minutes tell the story of the organization. The approval of the minutes is usually the first agenda item, when the board confirms, by their vote, that the minutes are a true and accurate representation of their actions at the last meeting.

AGENDA

  I. Approval of the Minutes

 II. Review of the Agenda

III. Reports

    Administrator's Report

    Program Committee Report

    Personnel Committee Report

    Finance Committee Report

    Development Committee Report

    Physical Plant/Work Environment Committee Report

IV. Other

 V. Adjourn

In addition to the agenda, the board package should include the reports from the administrator and each of the committees. These reports will provide detailed information from each committee but, more importantly, will provide the information that board members will need to make decisions on the action items related to each committee report. Special attention should be paid to the materials related to the finance report. The finance committee should deal with the detailed financial report for the organization, but few members of the full board will want to study page after page of financial information. There should be a simplified, easy to understand summary of the financial report for the entire board. Of course, the full financial report is made available to individual board members, if they wish, but a simplified version will be more useful to most board members and will help the board meeting go more smoothly.

Barry S. Bader (1985), a consultant and author specializing in hospital governance, identifies seven guidelines for developing effective board information:

1. Concise—Is the information communicated as quickly or as briefly as possible?

2. Meaningful—Is the information presented in relationship to a significant factor, such as a goal set by the board, past performance, or comparative data?

3. Timely—Is the information relevant to the current agenda?

4. Relevant to responsibilities—Does the information help the board or board committee discharge its responsibilities?

5. Best available—Is the information the best available indicator of the situation or condition being described? Can better information be provided?

6. Context—Is it clear why this information is important?

7. Graphic presentation—Could the information be presented better graphically than in words?

SUMMARY

Board members and human services administrators have a responsibility to work together and to share the responsibility for the organization's success. The working relationship between the administrator and the board of directors is key to the effective operation of the organization. Nonprofits are legal entities, and boards of directors have legal and ethical responsibilities that cannot be delegated. The board's responsibilities fall into four major categories: (1) legal and fiduciary, (2) oversight, (3) fundraising, and (4) representation of constituencies and viewpoints. Working with boards of trustees is a critical administrative skill. Human service administrators must have excellent communication skills and develop strong working relationships with the members of the board.

REFERENCES

Bader, B. S. (1985). Keys to better hospital governance through better information. In R. D. Herman (Ed.), *Nonprofit boards of directors: Analyses and applications* (pp. 118–132). New Brunswick, NJ: Transaction.

Carver, J. (1990). *Boards that make a difference.* San Francisco: Jossey-Bass.

Goodnow, F. J. (1900). *Politics and administration: A study in government.* New York: Russell & Russell.

Ingram, R. T. (2009). *Ten basic responsibilities of nonprofit boards* (2nd ed.). Washington, DC: BoardSource.

Kirschner, D. S. (1986). *The paradox of professionalism: Reform and public service in urban America 1900–1940.* New York: Greenwood.

Robinson, M. K. (2001). *Nonprofit boards that work: The end of one-size-fits-all governance.* New York: John Wiley.

Wilson, W. (1941). The study of public administration. *Political Science Quarterly, 56*(4), 197–222. (Original work published 1887)

EXERCISES

1. In-Basket Exercise

Directions

Read the following memos from your in-basket. For each memo, draft a reply outlining your decision or the action you plan to take.

Memo

Date: November 9, 20XX

To: Administrator

From: Board Chair

Subject: Committee Structure

As the new board chair, I have been giving some thought to our board structure. I do not really understand the need for a program committee. We have excellent program directors in each of our program areas. Since they are the experts, it seems redundant to have a program committee looking over their shoulders. Therefore, my recommendation to the board will be that we disband the program committee and reassign its members to more important committees. Please give me your thoughts on this.

2. In-Basket Exercise

Memo

Date: March 17, 20XX

To: Administrator

From: Program Director

Subject: Sick Leave

We continue to have problems with staff in my area abusing our sick leave policy. Some employees use their sick days as soon as they are accumulated. I would like to change our policy from a sick leave system to a well days system. We could lower our current number of sick leave days from 12 days per year to six days per year and simply add this number of days to our vacation days. Employees could use all of the days if they wished and would be entitled to the days whether or not they were sick. How can this change be made? Do I have your OK?

3. In-Basket Exercise

Directions

Structure your agenda using the committee structure outlined in this chapter.

Memo

Date: August 22, 20XX

To: Administrator

From: Board Chair

Subject: Board Meeting Agenda

As the new board chair, I want to be involved with you in developing the agenda for each board meeting. Please develop a draft agenda and send it to me. I want the agenda to include the items you think require the attention of each committee. Thank you.

ASSIGNMENTS

1. Attend a meeting of the board of trustees of a local nonprofit organization. Write a three- to four-page summary of your experience. Relate the material in this chapter to your experience in observing the board meeting.

2. Find a peer-reviewed journal article on the functioning of boards of directors. Write a review/critique of the article.

3. You have been assigned the task of developing a half-day orientation for new board members of your organization. Develop an outline of the major topics you will present to new board members. Choose the topics that you think are the most important for new board members to understand about their role and function as a board member.

Fund Development

11

This chapter will present the basics of fundraising, including the annual campaign, direct mail, special events, major gifts, and planned gifts. The concept of moving donors from annual giving to major gifts and planned gifts will be presented. This chapter will also explore donor motivation and present a fundraising strategy based on the concept of providing donors with opportunities rather than approaching fundraising as a "begging" activity.

Begging is not a strategy to raise funds. The alternative to begging for funds is to have a well-developed fundraising program. Even if the organization employs a professional fundraiser, the administrator is still the chief fundraising officer and, as such, will develop professional fundraising skills or risk becoming the chief beggar for the organization. Securing resources for the organization is ultimately the responsibility of the board of directors, but it is the administrator's responsibility to develop and oversee a well-developed fundraising program.

Effective fundraisers work from a strategic fundraising plan that is long term, has specific goals, and uses a variety of fundraising methods and techniques. The organization's financial strength can be developed and maintained only through a fundraising strategy that is diversified by using many different fundraising approaches appropriate for their various categories of donors. Fundraising must be approached as any other major project in that it requires the administrator to develop a plan. The planning process for fundraising includes the same steps as any other planning process. As the administrator, you must set goals, allocate resources, develop action steps and timelines. and then evaluate the process.

There are many "truisms" in fundraising, but the one most important to remember is that "people give to people, not to organizations." This is another way to say that fundraising is really "friend-raising." The people that will give money to your organization are those who share a passion for the mission of the organization and who trust that their money will be used wisely. It is the responsibility of the administrator to develop and nurture relationships that will financially sustain the organization.

Another truism is that people will not give anything to meet your agency needs, but they will give when presented with the opportunity to invest in an organization that will make a difference in the lives of others. People will give when they think they can make a positive difference in something they care about. At whatever level of fundraising activity, your approach should be to present opportunities that will make a positive impact in the lives of the people your organization serves and not to present the "needs" of the agency.

> You may need funds to hire a new counselor, but the fundraising approach should be to secure funds to serve more clients. You must tell the potential donor why the clients need this service and what difference it will make in their lives if the services are provided. The approach should NOT be that your organization needs a new counselor.

Remember that people want to give to successful causes. You want to give the donor not only the opportunity to give but also a reason to contribute to a cause that will support success. Your appeal is not that your organization has great needs, but that it is successful in meeting the needs of your clients.

Before we explore the many levels of activities in a fundraising program, we will look at the factors that motivate people to give.

DONOR MOTIVATION

Why do people give? Often, you will hear that most people give a donation because they will get a tax break. It is very seldom that tax donations are the major reason for making a donation.

> A new executive director was excited to learn that an elderly couple had decided to leave their 1,000-acre ranch to the organization in their will. The executive went to visit the couple and raised the possibility that they could use a planned giving vehicle to go ahead and make their gift to the agency and at the same time enjoy a tremendous tax advantage, plus increase their income for the rest of their lives. In fact, through this gift, the couple could be rich. After listening politely, the elderly woman said, "Young man, I don't want to be rich. I want to go to our ranch and hunt birds!" It is important to know what motivates a donor. In this case, it was certainly not a tax break or more income.

So why do people give?

In a review of over 500 articles on charitable giving, Bekkers and Wiepking (2011) found eight mechanisms as the most important forces that determine a person's decision to give. These are (1) awareness of need, (2) solicitation, (3) costs and benefits, (4) altruism, (5) reputation, (6) psychological benefits, (7) values, and (8) efficacy.

People will give only when they are interested and involved in your cause. Of course, there are different levels of giving. The new donor, responding to a direct mail piece, will be very different from a board member donor with years of experience with the organization. People will respond to different kinds of appeals because they have different reasons. So, why do they give? Giving behavior is just as complex as any other behavior.

In his book *Tested Ways to Successful Fund Raising*, George A. Brakeley, Jr. (as cited in "8 Rules of Thumb," 2012) wrote that virtually every fundraising campaign and development program depends on nine factors in motivating donors to support their organization:

> 1. The right person or persons ask them, at the right time, and in the right circumstances.
>
> 2. People have a sincere desire to help other people.

3. People wish to belong or be identified with a group or organization they admire.

4. Recognition of how vital their gifts can be satisfies a need for a sense of personal power in many people.

5. People have received benefits—often, personal enjoyment—from the services of the organization and wish to support it.

6. They "get something" out of giving.

7. People receive income and estate tax benefits from giving.

8. People may need to give; that is, altruism might not be an option but a "love or perish" necessity for many people.

Source: 8 rules of thumb when soliciting prospects. (2012, May 23). *The NonProfit Times.* Retrieved from http://www .thenonprofittimes.com. © 2012 The NonProfit Times Publishing Group, Inc.

Whatever their other motivations, people will give only when they are interested and involved, and when they are asked. To determine how to ask for a gift, we must know where our donors fit on the "donor pyramid."

THE DONOR PYRAMID

Fundraising professionals often use the donor pyramid as a way to conceptualize the fundraising program (see Figure 11.1). Each level in the pyramid builds on the level beneath it. For example, direct mail solicitation is appropriate to attract new donors to your organization, but once they have responded with even a small gift, your goal is to move them up to the next level of the pyramid. You want your new direct mail donors to become major givers. Of course, some donors will always be small givers or even stop giving to your organization, but most of your future major gift donors of tomorrow are your small gift givers today. Also, remember that all those small gifts add up and are very important to your overall fundraising plan.

The Association of Fundraising Professionals (AFP) *Fundraising Dictionary* (2004) describes the donor pyramid as:

A diagrammatic description of the hierarchy of donors by size of gifts. The diagram reflects that: as the size of donations increases, the number of donations decreases; as the number of years a donor is asked to renew increases, the number of donors decreases; as campaign sophistication progresses from annual giving to planned giving, the number of donors decreases; as donor involvement increases, the size of the donor's contribution increases and the response to campaign sophistication increases.

As you work through this chapter, refer back to the donor pyramid. In a sophisticated fundraising program, donors will be treated differently depending on where they are on the donor pyramid. Donors will move up the donor pyramid through involvement with the organization and through receiving personal attention from the board and staff of the organization. Notice that, as you move up in the pyramid, the fundraising techniques become increasingly more personalized.

What seems to be a simple and obvious truism is, "No one gives at any level unless they are asked!" As uncomfortable as it may be at times, eventually someone has to ask for the gift, but, if you and your board believe in your mission and truly believe you are giving others the opportunity to participate in your important work, then the "ask" will be less difficult.

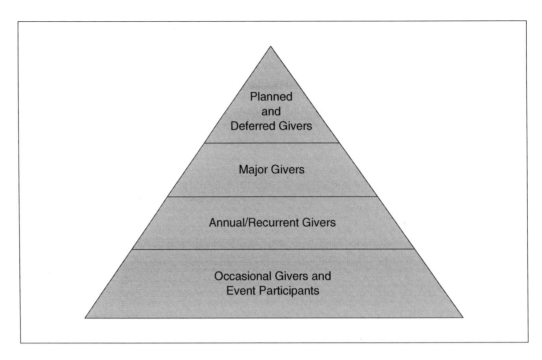

Figure 11.1 Sample Giving Pyramid

WHERE'S THE MONEY?

There is a lot of charitable gift money out there. American individuals, estates, foundations, and corporations gave an estimated $298.42 billion to charitable causes in 2011, according to Giving USA (Hoffman, 2011). Why do individuals, foundations, and corporations give so much? What motivates a person to give?

> "People are motivated to give because they value the cause, whether it is religion, education, health care, or international relief," said Henry (Hank) Goldstein, chair of Giving USA Foundation. "Charitable giving above 2 percent of gross domestic product is one demonstration of our nation's renewed commitment to the good works done by charities and congregations."
>
> —AAFRC Trust for Philanthropy/Giving USA, 2004 (Hoffman, 2011)

Notice in the charts below that 73% of donations come from individual donors. While corporate, foundation, and planned giving are all important elements of a fundraising program, it is the individual donor that gives the most every years. It is critical to bring new individual donors into your organization.

Look at Figure 11.3, which shows types of recipients. Only about 12% of the funds donated go to human services activities. It important for you to know what other types of organizations are competing for the charitable dollars available.

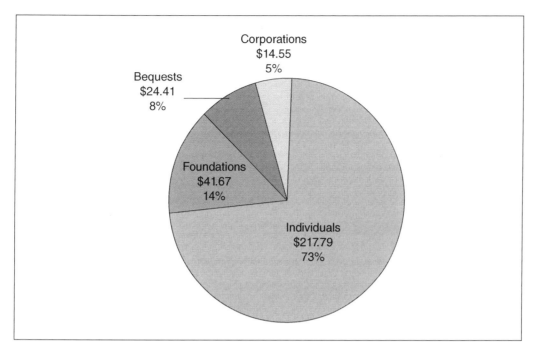

Figure 11.2   2011 Contributions: $298.42 Billion by Source of Contributions (in billions of dollars—all figures are rounded)

Source: © 2012 Giving USA Foundation.

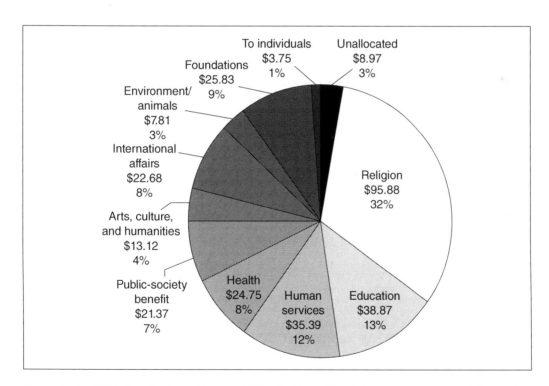

Figure 11.3   2011 Contributions: $298.42 Billion by Type of Recipient Organization (in billions of dollars—all figures are rounded)

Source: © 2012 Giving USA Foundation.

THE BASICS OF FUNDRAISING

Annual Campaign

The annual campaign consists of the fundraising activities that are conducted for the purpose of supporting the organization's annual operating budget. Even though these funds will be used for the organization's operating budget, your approach will focus on the services to be provided, not on the need for things like staff raises or paying the electric bill. The operating expenses support the services your organization provides. Ask your donors to help serve your clients. Generally, the largest number of donors will be giving to the annual campaign. Some organizations may not think of their many and diverse fundraising activities as an "annual campaign," but whether it is thought of in these terms or not, it is in effect the annual campaign for the organization. The approaches used in the annual campaign may include direct mail, phonathons, or special events such as golf tournaments or galas.

The defining feature of annual fund activities is that they are activities intended to raise gift income, *every year*. It is expected that you will approach the same donors every year and, sometimes, several times within the same year. Funds donated to the annual campaign are intended to support operational costs such as salaries, supplies, utilities, and client needs. The purpose is to support any part of the organization's operation that requires continuous and regular support.

Most donors will come into your organization through the annual campaign. It is rare that a person's first gift to the organization will be a major gift. More likely, those who become major donors are those who have been consistent annual campaign donors.

Direct Mail

You probably know about direct mail fundraising from your personal experience. Direct bulk mail is used to ask millions of people for money, and most people receive solicitations in their mail on a regular basis. What rate of return should you expect for your direct mail campaign? Typically, the response is somewhere in the range of 1%. Even though the return is small, it is an economical way to get your message before thousands of potential donors and a key strategy in bringing new people into the bottom of your pyramid. The typical direct mail package includes the carrier (outside), the letter, a reply device, and a return envelope.

The carrier or outside envelope should be designed with one objective in mind: to get the recipient to open it. If the piece goes into the trash, your chance of getting a donation is zero. The goal is to make the pieces look as much as possible like a personal letter and to make it look different from other solicitations in the mail box that day. Ideally, the envelope could be hand addressed, but since direct mail is a strategy of large numbers, this is rarely possible. Pre-cancelled bulk mail stamps give a more personal look than the standard postal indicia used on most bulk mail. The other strategy is to use an envelope other than the standard "number 10" business envelope that many fundraisers refer to as "the number 10 ugly." Choose an envelope that is smaller, larger, or a different shape. You may also want to consider using color or a see-through window to peak your potential donor's interest.

Once you get the potential donors to open the letter, your task is to capture their attention long enough to consider making a gift to your cause. The task here is not to write a scholarly piece or to impress anyone with your vocabulary. The letter should strike an informal tone and be easy to ready and understand. Kim Klein (2000) proposes a set of principles to remember as you develop your letter:

1. **People have a very short attention span.** Sentences should be short and take no more than six to fifteen seconds to read.

2. **People love to read about themselves.** The letter should refer to the reader at least twice as often and up to four times as often as it refers to the organization sending it. For example, "You may have read . . . " or "If you are like me, you care deeply about . . . "

3. **People must find the letter easy to look at.** The page should contain a lot of white space and wide margins, and be in a clear and simple font. Paragraphs should be short, no more than two or three sentences. You should feel free to use contractions (won't, you're, can't, we're) as this will add a more informal tone to your letter.

4. **People read the letter in a certain order.** First, they read the salutation and the opening paragraph, but then, no matter how long the letter is, they read the closing paragraph and then the postscript. Only a small number of people will read the entire letter.

The opening paragraph of your letter is critical. It must capture the attention of your readers and make them want to read on. Remember the truism that people will not give anything to meet your agency needs, but they will give when they have an opportunity to invest in a service that is of interest to them. Your letter must be about the people you serve, not the needs of your organization. Also, people do not relate well when you talk about the thousands of people you serve. Your letter should tell the story of one person helped by your organization and how this potential donor can make a difference in the life of someone else.

How long the letter should be is always a debate. Our natural instincts tell us that the letter should be short and to the point, but many fundraising consultants counsel that long letters are better and claim that a two-page letter will get a better response than a one-page letter, and that even three- and four-page letters will often outperform a shorter letter. There are many theories about why you should consider writing a longer letter. Some will say that it gives the impression that your organization has a lot to say, while others believe that more pieces of paper and longer letters give an opportunity for the potential donor to feel more involved with your organization.

In the closing paragraph, you ask for the money. Tell the reader what you want them to do. They have read your letter, now what do you want them to do about it? For example, say, "Send your gift of $25, $50 or $100 today." It needs to be direct and specific. No one gives unless they are asked.

The postscript is that small P.S. at the end of the letter. The reader will read the P.S. if they do not read anything else in the letter. This is your final opportunity to ask for the gift. Examples are, " Send your check today" or "Johnny needs your help."

Finally, the reply device is a small card that gives the potential donor the opportunity to respond. It will typically have a box to check that says something like, "Yes! I'll help" and then gives several options of giving—$10, $25, $50, $100, or more. The donor completes the card, encloses the check, and returns it in the enclosed return envelope. With that, your campaign is a success—at least with this donor.

Special Events

Special events are limited only by your imagination. The events may be galas, golf tournaments, walk-a-thons, performances—the possibilities are endless. Many times, special events do not raise large sums of money for the first few years but, over time, grow into major events that raise large amounts of money. When planning a special event, there are considerations other than the amount of money to be raised. The special event may be the activity that will raise the visibility of your organization in the community and an opportunity to involve more volunteers in your work. Special events are by their nature very labor intensive and can take a great deal of your time and staff time. Before deciding on a special event, it is important to consider the volunteer and staff resources necessary for a successful event. Any special event will require a major investment of time in planning, marketing, and execution.

Major Gifts

Major gifts are the larger gifts that you will solicit for your cause. These gifts will typically come from those individuals, foundations, and corporations with whom you have developed a long-term ongoing relationship. Many times, major gifts are solicited within the framework of a "capital campaign" for the purpose of capital improvement, such as building a new building or, in some cases, to develop or strengthen the endowment of an organization. An organization will often contract with a consulting firm to conduct a capital campaign. You, your board, and your staff will still have to solicit the gifts, but a good consultant can help structure and focus a successful campaign.

Major gifts require personal solicitation and the preparation of a proposal. A foundation may require a fully developed proposal, but an individual donor may prefer a short, well-developed statement of the purpose of the proposed donation. These donors are higher on the "pyramid" and, in most cases, know about your organization, believe in your work, and are willing to make a major contribution. When seeking a foundation or corporate gift, it is important to research the previous gifts and areas of interest of the foundation or corporation. As in all fundraising, finding a personal connection between your organization and the foundation or corporation is a great asset in your attempt to secure a gift.

Planned Gifts

Planned giving is a complex area. The bequest is the simplest form of planned giving. This means that someone has named your organization in a will and that, on passing away, a portion or sometimes all of that person's estate will come to your organization. As the administrator, you have an awesome responsibility to see that a person's life work is used for the intended purposes.

Other planned giving arrangements include charitable gift annuities, revocable and non-revocable trusts, and other financial vehicles to transfer funds from the donor to the organization. These gifts have tax implications for the donor and are in many cases a part of the estate planning process. Any gift of this type will involve an attorney or certified public accountant. The role of the administrator is to see that the organization has the structure and the advisors necessary to accept gifts of this nature.

Say Thank You!

It is impossible to say thank you too much to your donors. The acknowledgement or "thank you" is a vital part of your fundraising system. Donors should be thanked in writing as quickly as possible for their gift, and, whenever possible, donors should be thanked with a telephone call. For large donations, you as the administrator or your board chairman should make a phone call or a visit to thank donors for their gifts. Since successful fundraising is based on relationships, it is important to nurture and sustain relationships by showing gratitude to those who invest in the mission of your organization.

SUMMARY

Effective fundraisers work from a strategic fundraising plan that is long term, has specific goals, and uses a variety of fundraising methods and techniques. The organization's financial strength can be developed and maintained only through a fundraising strategy that is diversified by using many different fundraising approaches appropriate for their various categories of donors. Fundraising must be approached as any other major project in that it requires the administrator to set goals, allocate resources, develop action steps and timelines, and then evaluate the process.

REFERENCES

Bekkers, R., & Wiepking, P. (2011). A literature review of empirical studies of philanthropy: Eight mechanisms that drive charitable giving. *Nonprofit and Voluntary Sector Quarterly, 40*(5), 924–973.

8 rules of thumb when soliciting prospects. (2012, May 23). *The NonProfit Times.* Retrieved from http://www.thenonprofittimes.com/management-tips/8-rules-of-thumb-when-soliciting-prospects

Hoffman, M. (2011). Americans give $241 billion to charity in 2003. *Foundation for the Carolinas.* Retrieved from http://fftc.pgdc.com/pgdc/americans-give-241-billion-charity-2003

Klein, K. (2000) *Fundraising for social change* (4th ed.). Oakland, CA: Chardon Press.

HELPFUL TERMS

Annual campaign—the fundraising activities that are conducted for the purpose of supporting the organization's annual operating budget.

Direct mail—a fundraising approach using bulk mail to reach potential donors. The typical direct mail package includes the carrier (outside), the letter, a reply device, and a return envelope.

Donor pyramid—a diagrammatic description of the hierarchy of donors by size of gifts. The diagram reflects that: as the size of donations increases, the number of donations decreases; as the number of years a donor is asked to renew increases, the number of donors decreases; as campaign sophistication progresses from annual giving to planned giving, the number of donors decreases; as donor involvement increases, the size of the donor's contribution increases, and the response to campaign sophistication increases.

Major gifts—the larger gifts that typically come from individuals, foundations, and corporations with whom the organization has developed a long-term, ongoing relationship. Some major gifts are solicited within the framework of a "capital campaign" for the purpose of capital improvement, such as building a new building or, in some cases, to develop or strengthen the endowment of an organization.

Planned gifts—The bequest is the simplest form of planned giving. Other planned giving arrangements include charitable gift annuities, revocable and non-revocable trusts, and other financial vehicles to transfer funds from the donor to the organization. These gifts have tax implications for the donor and are, in many cases, a part of their estate planning process.

Special events—events such as galas, golf tournaments, walk-a-thons, performances, and so on; very labor-intensive activities that have the advantage of increased volunteer participation and the opportunity to increase the visibility of the sponsoring organization.

ADDITIONAL RESOURCES

The Association of Fundraising Professionals (AFP) represents 26,000 members in 174 chapters throughout the United States, Canada, Mexico, and China working to advance philanthropy through advocacy, research, education, and certification programs. Visit the AFP website at http://www.afpnet.org.

EXERCISES

1. In-Basket Exercise

Directions

Read the following memos from your in-basket. For each memo, draft a reply outlining your decision or the action you plan to take.

Memo

Date: May 3, 20XX

To: Administrator

From: Director of Development

Subject: Phone Call ref. Possible Bequest

I received a phone call today from Mr. Jim Wilson, one of our long-time supporters. Mr. Wilson stated that he is revising his will and is considering leaving his ranch to our agency. I was planning to send him our new brochure. Is there anything else I need to do? Please advise.

2. In-Basket Exercise

Memo

Date: June 14, 20XX

To: Administrator

From: Program Service Supervisor

Subject: Golf Tournament for the Agency

My husband played in a golf tournament for the ABC Children's Home last weekend. He was told that they raised over $10,000 in just one day! I've been talking with the social workers and secretaries in my unit, and we would like to organize a golf tournament for the agency to benefit our unit. We think it would be great fun and raise a lot of money. Do we have your permission to proceed? Please advise.

3. In-Basket Exercise

Memo

Date: September 18, 20XX

To: Administrator

From: Director of Development

Subject: Fundraising Letter

You mentioned to me that you would like to personally write the fundraising letter for our holiday season appeal. I will need this to be to the printers in the next few weeks. Please send me your letter as soon as you can, and I will start working on the printing and production. Thank you.

Directions: Use the following "fact sheet" to develop your mail fundraising letter and response card.

FACT SHEET

Cornerstone Community Services

Our Mission—To assist youth in becoming independent self-sufficient adults who make a contribution to our society.

History—Cornerstone Community Services was established in 1895 by Rev. Joseph P. Wilson, a Protestant minister. At the turn of the century, Rev. Wilson became very concerned about the number of orphan boys who were unsupervised and becoming juvenile delinquents. In response to this, he worked with other ministers and established the Cornerstone Home and Training School for Boys. Rev. Wilson became the first superintendent of the school and served faithfully for over 25 years. The Home for Boys started in a small frame house near downtown. The Boys Home continued to grow, and in 1942 a beautiful 30-acre location was donated to the institution for a new campus. In 1968, a major fundraising campaign was conducted to build most of the buildings as they exist today. Through the years, the need for "orphanages" decreased, and the CCS Board of Trustees developed new programs to meet the changing needs of society.

Today, CCS has evolved to a multi-service organization with four major programs, including residential treatment services, therapeutic foster care, maternity and adoption services, and independent living services for youth with physical disabilities. Both residential and community based services are provided. CCS has a $4 million annual budget and 85 employees. Funding sources include the Department of Protective Services, the Rehabilitation Commission, MH-MR, United Way, foundations, and fundraising.

ASSIGNMENTS

1. Find direct mail fundraising letters from three organizations. Evaluate the strengths and weaknesses of each of the letters in a four- to five-page paper.

2. Examine the website of a large, medium, and small nonprofit organization. How is each organization using the website for its fund-development efforts?

3. Find three peer-reviewed journal articles on fund development that have been written in the past three years. Give a brief summary of each article.

Marketing

12

> The monthly all staff meeting included an agenda item called "marketing our services."
> The CEO talked about the need to increase the number of client referrals to the agency
> and the need to become better known in the community. She called on everyone to be a
> marketer for the organization and gave examples of how everyone could play a part in
> marketing the organization's services. A hand went up in the back of the room. One of the
> caseworkers asked, "Isn't it enough that we provide excellent service? People will come to
> us if we provide excellent services, right?" "No," answered the CEO. "Sadly, we will go broke
> providing excellent services if we are unwilling to market our organization."

This exchange demonstrates the distaste that many human services organization employees
have for the concepts of marketing human services. The caseworker in the scenario above was
reflecting a *product mindset* that assumes if you "build a better mousetrap, customers will
beat a pathway to your door." The CEO, however, was coming from the perspective of the
sales mindset that an organization must convince customers to choose their services rather
than those of a competitor (Andreasen & Kotler, 2003, p. 40, as cited in Worth, 2009, p. 211).
In some ways, both the caseworker and the CEO were wrong in their approach. Providing
excellent services is not enough to assure organizational success, but neither is convincing
potential clients and referral sources to use the organization's services. Both the product mindset and the sales mindset come from an inward-looking focus. More modern approaches to
marketing begin by looking from the outside from the perspective of the *customer mindset*
that "systematically studies customers' needs, wants, perceptions, preferences, and satisfaction, using surveys, focus groups, and other means . . . and constantly acts on this information
to improve its offerings and to meet its customers' needs better" (Andreasen & Kotler, 2003,
p. 42, as cited in Worth, 2009, p. 211). Of course, a human services administrator must view
marketing activities within the context of the mission and goals of the organization. It is
important to understand not only the preferences of the clients, funders, and donors, but also
how these preferences fit within the mission of the organization.

> According to Andreasen and Kotler (2003), "Marketing is . . . a means to achieve the orga-
> nization's goal. It is a tool—really a process and set of tools wrapped in a philosophy—for
> helping the organization do what it wants to do. Using marketing and being customer-
> oriented should never be thought of as goals: they are ways to achieve goals" (p. 57, as
> cited in Worth, 2009, p. 212).

Marketing has become recognized as an important component of human service agency functioning (Lauffer, 2009; Lewis, Packard, & Lewis, 2011) and, therefore, an important task for human service administrators. Hardcastle and Powers (2004) review the business literature on marketing and find several sources that refer to the "Ps" of marketing (Andreasen & Kotler, 2003; Fine, 1992; Winston, 1986). While there are several versions of the Ps of marketing, the most common four are *products*, *price*, *place*, and *promotions*. Lauffer (2009) adds a fifth P for *publics* to represent the stakeholders in human service organizations.

THE 5 Ps OF MARKETING

Publics—Lauffer (2009) adds *publics* as the fifth P of marketing to recognize the unique character of nonprofit organizations. This characteristic applies as well to human service organizations regardless of their sector. While businesses are concerned with the consumers of their products, human services have other stakeholders that must be taken into account. Many times, it is not the client who is paying for the services provided, but the services are paid for by a third party through a contract; or, in the case of nonprofit organizations, the services may be paid for through donated funds. Therefore, it is not only the client (consumer) that must be taken into account in a marketing plan but other stakeholders as well, such as donors, funders, volunteers, and the community at large.

Products—Products may be tangible goods such as food or services such as counseling or case management. The product may even be something as intangible as conservation or social justice. Regardless of the product offered by the organization, the expectation is that there will be an exchange of resources from the consumer (or a third party) for the organization to have the capacity to offer the products (Hardcastle & Powers, 2004). Often, the product that is promised to the funder or to the community is a change in the conditions in the community. For example, if the desired impact is a reduction in childhood obesity or a reduction in teenage pregnancy, then it is an important marketing strategy to be able to demonstrate that the products provided are effective in producing the desired change. This is one reason why program evaluation is a critical component of agency functioning (see Chapter 7).

Price—Price has to do with the cost of providing the services in comparison to other providers of similar services. The human services administrator must have knowledge of the fees of other organizations providing similar services and of the unit costs (see Chapter 8). There is also the question of the reasonableness of the price of providing services. As government agencies and third-party insurance payers seek out contractors, they seek to find the best services they can find at the lowest cost. Part of a marketing plan is to make the case that the services provided are quality services at a reasonable and competitive price.

Place—What is the geographic location of the agency and what is the geographic area served? There are several issues related to "place." Government contracts are restricted to the area of their governmental jurisdiction. Similarly, many corporations are interested in supporting organizations in the area where they have their headquarters or where their consumers are located. For example, think about utility companies that will provide grants in the states where they provide services. In some cases, foundations, donors, or even government agencies will restrict their gifts to an area that they perceive as having the greatest need.

There is also a practical and political dimension to where the human service organization is located. Is the agency or branch located in an area that is convenient for the population that it seeks to serve? Is there public transportation available so that the services are accessible?

The administrator of a human services organization was being interviewed on local TV about the agency's new office location. The reporter made the point that the new office building was located in a very affluent part of town, but that its mission was to serve poor people. When the reporter asked the administrator why that location was selected, he said, "Because most of our employees live in this area"—not a good marketing strategy.

Think about "place" as aligning the needs of the clients served and the resources that can be attracted based on the geographic location of the agency and geographic area served by the agency. Think about the possibilities that exist within that common space.

Promotion—Promotion is the communication between the agency and its various publics. Promotion takes many forms. It is the agency newsletter, the website, the fundraising letters, and the funding proposals. It is public speaking, participation in community activities, special events, and TV interviews. Promotion is about building relationships—with board members, with donors, with funding sources, and with the community. In the last chapter, we talked about the concept of "friend-raising." It is the same concept in marketing. Promotion is the art and the tools of persuasive communications to interpret the mission of your organization to others and to gain their support of your efforts. Promotion is about motivation and inspiration. As a human services administrator, it is the power of your conviction for the services that you provide and your commitment to those you serve that will inspire others to join you in your life's work.

MARKET SEGMENTATION

To develop an effective marketing plan for an organization, it is first necessary to identify the *target markets*. Because of the many "publics" of a human services organization, this can be a complex task. Think first about the clients served by your organization. If you serve only one very specific population, then the task of segmenting the client market would not be that difficult, but many organizations provide multiple program services for a variety of populations. The first task then is to identify each of the segments of the client market.

Clients are not the only public that requires you to think about market segmentation. What are the demographics of your donor population? Do you think it might require a different approach for your donors under 30 years old as opposed to your donors over 60? Is there a difference in your donors who have donated to your organization for many years and those who have made their first gift? Will you approach them any differently? Segmentation is required unless you can determine that all of the people in the target market are likely to respond in the same way (Hardcastle & Powers, 2004). The first task is to identify each category in your target market and then to further refine these categories into subsets as appropriate.

COMPONENTS OF NONPROFIT MARKETING PLANS

Marketing plans for nonprofit organizations should specify how the organization plans to reach each target audience group identified in the segmentation exercise. Typically, nonprofit marketing plans include the following elements for each target population:

1. Mission and Goal Statement: This portion of your marketing plan should express what it is that your organization hopes to accomplish for the clients you serve. Your mission and goal statement should clearly define the overall purpose of your organization. The marketing plan should tie specifically to accomplishing the mission and goal.

2. Set Outcome Objectives: Define specific, measurable outcome objectives for each target audience (see Chapter 6). What do you want the results to be of your marketing activities? How many clients do you want to serve in the coming year? What kinds of results do you expect to see with the organization's stakeholders? How much money do you need to raise this year? How many volunteer hours do you hope to log?

3. Develop Strategies Through Process Objectives: What steps can you take to accomplish your outcome objectives? For example, if you want to increase the number of clients served by 250 next year, what will you need to do to accomplish this result? If you want to attract 50 new major donors, what steps will you take to reach this outcome objective?

4. Action Plan: How will your organization go about implementing the defined marketing strategies identified in the process objectives? Who is responsible for each component of the plan? What is the timeline for each activity to be implemented? The action plan should be written in a manner that makes it easy to determine who is to do what by when.

5. Budget: How is the marketing plan built into the organization's budget? What resources will be allocated to the marketing plan?

6. Monitoring: How will you evaluate your progress and make any necessary adjustments to the plan? What is the system for evaluation of both outcome and process objectives? Who is responsible to see that reporting and review procedures are followed? How will progress be measured? (White, 2013).

SUMMARY

Human service administrators must be aggressive marketers of their organizations. The organization is in competition for clients, for funding, for volunteers, for staff, and for the overall support of the community. Marketing is not advertising or sales, but it is understanding the needs of clients and other stakeholders. Like all functions of administration, there is a need to be systematic and to have a well-developed plan for marketing the organization. Understanding the interplay of publics, products, price, place, and promotion are keys to marketing the organization and its services. A clear understanding of the organization's market share and the segmentation of that market guide the administrator toward a well developed and effective marketing program for the organization.

REFERENCES

Andreasen, A. R., & Kotler, P. (2003). *Strategic marketing for nonprofit organizations* (6th ed.). Upper Saddle River, NJ: Prentice Hall.

Fine, S. H. (1992). *Marketing the public sector: Promoting the causes of public and nonprofit agencies.* New Brunswick, NJ: Transaction.

Hardcastle, D. A., & Powers, P. R. (2004). *Community practice: Theories and skills for social workers* (2nd ed.). New York: Oxford University Press.

Lauffer, A. (2009). *Confronting fundraising challenges.* In R. Patti (Ed.), *The handbook of human services management* (2nd ed., pp. 351–372). Thousand Oaks, CA: Sage.

Lewis, J. A., Packard, T. R., & Lewis, M. D. (2011). *Management of human service programs* (5th ed.). Belmont, CA: Brooks/Cole.

White, M. (2013). *Nonprofit marketing plans.* Retrieved from http://charity.lovetoknow.com/charitable-organizations/nonprofit-marketing-plans

Winston, W. J. (1986). Basic marketing principles for mental health professionals. *Journal of Marketing for Mental Health, 1,* 9–20.

Worth, M. J. (2009). *Nonprofit management.* Thousand Oaks, CA: Sage.

Market segmentation—the process of identifying each category of the organization's target market and then further refining the categories into subsets as appropriate. For example, the clients and subsets of clients and the donors divided into subsets such as age, interest, or motivation.

Marketing—a means to achieve the organization's goal. It is a tool—really a process and set of tools wrapped in a philosophy—for helping the organization do what it wants to do. Using marketing and being customer oriented should never be thought of as goals: They are ways to achieve goals (Andreasen & Kotler, 2003, p. 57, as cited in Worth, 2009, p. 212).

Marketing mindsets—

product mindset assumes if you "build a better mousetrap, customers will beat a pathway to your door."

sales mindset assumes that an organization must convince customers to choose their services rather than those of a competitor.

customer mindset "systematically studies customers' needs, wants, perceptions, preferences, and satisfaction, using surveys, focus groups, and other means . . . and constantly acts on this information to improve its offerings and to meet its customers' needs better" (Andreasen & Kotler, 2003, p. 42, as cited in Worth, 2009, p. 211).

Ps of marketing—Several authors refer to the Ps of marketing as products, price, place, and promotions. Lauffer (2009) adds a fifth P for publics to represent the stakeholders in human service organizations.

EXERCISES

1. In-Basket Exercise

Directions

Review the following memo and write a response explaining your decision on this matter.

Memo

Date: May 16, 20XX
To: Administrator, Sheltering Arms, Inc.
From: Board Chair, Sheltering Arms, Inc.
Subject: Marketing Plan and Segmentation

I am looking forward to your board retreat next month to develop our much-needed marketing plan for Sheltering Arms. I know from our meeting with our marketing consultant that one of our tasks will be to identify our target markets and to do a market segment analysis. Frankly, I'm a little stuck in trying to think about how to approach this issue. It seems to me that our only market is the homeless population in our community. I want to be prepared for the meeting and to provide appropriate leadership, but I need your help in thinking this through. I understand that we are to break the major market groups into subgroups. Please prepare a list of those groups and subgroups that you think of as our "markets." Thanks for your help.

2. Isn't It Enough . . . ?

Assume that you are leading an all staff meeting and the topic is how to market the organization and its services. If an employee says, "Isn't it enough that we provide excellent service? People will come to us if we provide excellent services, right?" How would you respond? With your small groups, develop a response based on the content of this chapter. You will read your response to the class and ask for their feedback.

3. The Five Ps

Review the section of this chapter on the 5 Ps. Working within your group, think of an agency with which you are familiar. Define each of the Ps for that organization and report your work to the class.

4. Distaste for Marketing

This chapter starts with a statement that many human services organization employees have a distaste for the concepts of marketing human services. Do you think this is true? If so, why do you think it is true? If not, why not? Discuss this issue in your small group.

ASSIGNMENTS

1. *International Journal of Nonprofit and Voluntary Sector Marketing* provides an international forum for peer-reviewed papers and case studies on the latest techniques, thinking, and best practice in marketing for the not-for-profit sector. Find an article written in the journal within the past three years and write a two-page summary and review of the article.

2. Write a five-page "executive summary" of a marketing plan for a nonprofit organization. Cover each of the six components of a marketing plan as outlined in this chapter.

3. You have been asked to be on a panel discussion concerning marketing of nonprofit organizations. You are to make a five-minute introductory statement of the use of social media in marketing. Research this topic and write a two-page statement to be included in the handout materials for the panel presentation.

Persuasion

13

The ability to persuade others is a vital skill for managers and leaders. Persuasion involves getting people to do something because they want to, not because they must. With subordinates, you might believe you can just issue commands and people will obey. This seldom works well, however, as most people do not like to be ordered around. People may comply at one level, but may also undermine directives given in this manner.

Another reason to become an effective persuader, not relying on command or coercion, is that nonprofit managers very often work with peers and people in the community, such as donors (or potential donors), elected officials, client group representatives, and other stakeholders who have their own viewpoints and positions. These people are not your subordinates and must be convinced to follow your lead of their own will. In addition, there are many opportunities within nonprofit organizations to be influential before you assume the organization's top spot, and it is important to practice your persuasion skills long before you apply for such positions. You will find that being able to persuade others is essential to being a successful manager and leader.

Research on persuasion usually treats it as a goal-oriented behavior (Wilson, 2002). Persuasion is in many ways more powerful than coercion or negotiation. If you command someone to do something, and you have the power needed to ensure compliance, you may very well lose the willingness of your subordinate to implement the order well, or in the spirit of making the organization operate optimally. With negotiation, you and the other party make a series of concessions. This implies that neither side gets what it really wants. In persuasion, however, you are able to get the other party to accept what you want. In persuasion, one party gets all or nearly all of what it wants, and the other side, by now agreeing to a new position, also receives what it wants. Research tells us a great deal about how to be persuasive. In every persuasion attempt, four variables are important: the context, the message, the sender, and the receiver.

THE CONTEXT

The context of the persuasion attempt determines most of the content used. How the situation is viewed by the actors establishes, to a large extent, their reaction to it. Framing is the process of getting a particular viewpoint accepted as the "right" way to see a situation. According to Rhoads (1997), "A frame is a psychological device that offers a perspective and manipulates salience in order to influence subsequent judgment." A frame thus provides a certain standpoint on how the facts should be seen, emphasizing some facts and minimizing others, to get the target to act a certain way. Framing is a skill often used by direct practice social workers and occurs in many other situations as well. The ability to frame an issue advantageously is often enough to be very persuasive.

Some frames hurt an idea's chances of being adopted, while other frames make an idea more likely to be chosen. When you are persuading someone, you will want to connect a particular frame with the idea in question. Here are some typical frames used to guide the way a situation is viewed (Hoefer, 2012; Rosenthal, 1993). The first five are useful when you want to work against an idea. The last four can be used to persuade people in favor of a proposal.

It isn't fair. Proposals are often tagged "unfair" to one group or another. Almost any proposal an advocate comes up with, from helping one client more than others to economic policy that affects global trading, can be called unfair. Because people like to be "fair," this frame can keep an idea from being adopted.

It won't work. An alternative frame to argue against a proposal is that whatever goal is set won't be reached. If a proposal is seen as unworkable, it is easy to keep it from being tried.

It can be done in other ways. This is similar to the previous frame, although it presents an alternative to what it attacks. The persuader substitutes a new idea in place of the one initially under discussion.

It costs too much. An idea that is seen as too expensive is unlikely to be adopted.

It will hurt clients. This frame can be used at any level, but is often used in intra-agency debates by arguing that a new idea will do harm to the organization's clients. It is difficult for people in human service organizations to adopt ideas that they see will hurt clients.

It will help consumers/clients. At the agency level, many advocates focus on the benefits of their suggestions for clients. If a plan is seen as being beneficial to clients, it is often difficult to derail it in a human service organization.

The benefits outweigh the costs. While the idea is not perfect, on the whole, there are more pluses than minuses. If people think that there are more benefits, then it is easy to support the idea. Talking about the difference between short-term and long-term thinking and accounting often takes place in this frame.

If it saves the life of one child, it will all be worth it. This frame unashamedly pulls at heartstrings. It says that costs might be high, but it challenges anyone to say that life, particularly an innocent child's life, is less precious than gold. Obviously, this frame can be extended to other "worthy" populations as well.

After what they've gone through, they deserve it. The argument here acknowledges that the outcomes of the idea might not be fair in some sense because some people will get more than others. Yet, there is an element of fairness involved because the people who are getting more (money, services, opportunities) have also earned it by what they have gone through. Programs for veterans or the elderly are often talked about in this way.

The importance of framing in persuasion cannot be overstated. As an agency leader or manager, thinking carefully about the frame you want to use will make it much easier to persuade others to accept your ideas. On the other hand, you must not uncritically accept someone else's view of a situation. Make sure to understand what frame is being used when listening to what is being stated and proposed.

THE MESSAGE

The message that is sent from the persuader to the target is the information that is designed to be persuasive. Here, we look at characteristics of the message, rather than the content of the message. Six general principles of persuasive messages are discussed in this section: intent, organization, sidedness, repetition and redundancy, rhetorical questions, and fear appeals. This discussion is based largely on Booth-Butterfield (1996), although the examples are original.

Intent. In most cases, it is counterproductive to announce that you are going to try to influence someone. The moment the target hears your intent, defensive walls start going up. It is better to begin the persuasion effort without forewarning the person whose mind you want to change. There are two important exceptions to this general guideline, however. The first is when you only want to ask for small changes, knowing that the message receivers already agree with most of what you are about to say. Thus, by saying that you want to ask only for small changes, resistance is lowered. The target feels safer, knowing that you are not wanting to shake things up too much. The second exception is when your target already expects you to attempt persuasion. Thus, in many situations, it doesn't hurt to say you are going to try to influence the target's opinion because everyone knows that is why you are communicating.

Organization. Well-organized messages are more persuasive than are poorly organized ones. There is always a temptation to neglect the preparation and organizing phase of developing your message. It is important to take the time to make your key points more salient and to ensure a logical consistency in the material.

Sidedness. Research shows that two-sided messages (those that present the position advocated and also the opposing view) can be extremely persuasive if they do two things. They must both defend the desired position and attack the other position. If the other position is mentioned but not attacked, then there is no advantage for the two-sided presentation compared to a one-sided presentation (Cialdini, 2000). The reasons for these results are that a two-sided message appears more balanced. Since most people don't think deeply about most issues, presenting the "other side" makes the presenter seem more credible. The attack on the other position and the defense of your own ideas can leave a lasting impression of having explored the issue completely.

Repetition and redundancy. Repetition and redundancy are different, though closely related. *Repetition* refers to communicating the same thing over and over. *Redundancy*, on the other hand, refers to having multiple ways of communicating similar information. A redundant message repeats the major theme of other messages, but does it in a different way.

Rhetorical questions. The use of rhetorical questions is very effective, isn't it? Leaders who understand the science of persuasion achieve more results, don't they? Rhetorical questions are disguised statements—they stake out a position without appearing to and can be backed away from if opposition emerges. Research shows that the use of rhetorical questions can change how people think (Cialdini, 2000).

Fear appeals. A fear appeal is a message that focuses on the bad things that will happen if you do or don't do something. The message indicates that you should do whatever it is that the persuader is suggesting to avoid some sort of catastrophe. When a situation is described in a way that increases fear, a natural reaction is to want to take action to protect oneself against that threat. To work, however, not only must a person feel a realistic and personal fear of negative consequences, but the appeal must also provide information about a feasible way to avoid those consequences. In other words, you can't just scare people into action. You must also guide them to safety.

INFORMATION

When you think about persuading someone on a topic, you must decide what type of information you need to present. As a nonprofit leader, your information may be as simple as stories about how an agency policy is affecting clients or as complex as a community needs assessment.

The information that you present, to be useful, can be of two types: substantive and contextual. *Substantive information* is the set of facts on which you base your arguments. *Contextual information* relates to how the situation appears to interested (or potentially interested) others—political information, if you will.

Substantive Information

Substantive information relates to what most people would call "the facts of the case." Substantive information can range from singular anecdotes that are compelling and (hopefully) representative of the issue, to the results of rigorous empirical research. In-between levels of quality can be found from official documents, statistical data (such as from the Census Bureau), testimony from individuals, newspapers and popular magazines, television and radio, and public meetings (Richan, 1996). We can rate the quality of these different sources of information in a conventional way, but for our purposes, the best information is the information that is most persuasive to the target. Thus, stories of individuals (particularly if they tell their own stories) are often the most persuasive sort of information because they carry a considerable emotional impact.

Contextual Information

Information about the context of a decision can be important to a target. A colleague of yours, for example, may not be persuaded of the validity of your assertions until it is pointed out that your information came from the agency's chief financial officer. Even if that one bit of information is not enough to be convincing, it will give your statements credibility. Other contextual information in an agency setting may relate to the way other staff members view the situation, or how the issue is being discussed "around the water cooler."

PRESENTING THE INFORMATION

Once the information is gathered, you must decide how to present it to the identified target. This decision has two key elements. The first relates to the manner of delivering the information, and the second to the format of the presentation.

Manner

The important elements when considering the manner of presentation are accuracy, time, message style, content, and clarity.

Accuracy

Your information must be carefully checked and fully reliable. Be sure to document the source(s) for each fact you present.

Time

The second important element is that brevity is usually beneficial. Five minutes of your target's full attention may be all you are going to get, whether you are meeting in person, making a phone call, or having your written information read. Make the most of it.

Message Style

The choice of message style should be made after analyzing the receiver(s) you will be working with. Many different message styles may be appropriate in one setting to reach people where they are, particularly in a large group setting. Three are discussed here: positive vs. negative, private vs. public, and collaborative vs. confrontational.

Positive vs. negative. You should decide if you are going to emphasize positive or negative appeals. In this context, a positive message means to stress the good things that will result from taking the action you are suggesting. A negative message means to call attention to the bad things that will ensue if the desired action is *not* done. Some research suggests that people are more likely to want to protect themselves from negative events than to push for more positive outcomes (Cialdini, 2000). Thus, negative appeals based on what bad things will happen are more persuasive than are positive appeals describing the good things that will happen.

Private vs. public. Information can be delivered in private (individual conversations or via written material such as letters or briefing papers) or small-group meetings or communications, or it can be presented via larger group settings, such as staff meetings or in public venues. Research indicates that having a relationship with decision makers that is personal and private (an individually oriented strategy) is more effective than working in public settings (Hoefer, 2001). Still, each situation requires a separate decision to be made because the circumstances are different.

Collaborative vs. confrontational. Persuasion is often part of a collaborative, rather than confrontational, process. If persuasion efforts do not achieve your goals, you may, in fact, turn to confrontational tactics, but doing so too often can burn bridges to decision makers whose support you need to achieve your goals. Remember that confrontation exists on a continuum, with gentle confrontation being a possibility as well as more forceful confrontation.

Content

A general template for any persuasive message has two elements:

- Describe the problem (including how serious the problem is)
- Tell what can be done to solve the problem

The content of the message should, of course, be in line with the message style that was chosen. Try different frames to determine which evokes the best response. Be ready to switch to another message style and use different content if one effort begins to lose its punch. Try, however, to keep the same frame—reframing an issue is a long-term process that needs consistency over time to be effective.

Clarity

The sad truth is that communications are often unclear. For a message to be communicated clearly, the information must first be delivered using language the target can understand, and second, after receiving the message, the target must know what you want done because you have provided a clear call to action. Your audience may not agree with you or comply with your wishes, but communication has not occurred effectively if the decision maker doesn't know what you said or what you want done.

Format

The decision relating to the format of how information is presented has three main options. It can be presented in person (such as at a one-on-one meeting with the target, a small group meeting with the target, or testifying at a public hearing), via a telephone call, or in a written form through a letter, fax, or e-mail. Each of these options has advantages and disadvantages. The choice should be made on the basis of which approach is most convincing to the target as well as what is practical for you. Still, within each format, more effective and less effective ways of presenting the information exist.

In Person

The in-person format is generally considered the most powerful. This is because there is an immediacy and power in personal communication where feedback can be seen and heard instantaneously, even if such feedback is nonverbal. An in-person persuasion effort also shows the most commitment, because it is the most trouble to do.

In many cases, presentations might be accompanied by a computer-based set of slides, using a program such as PowerPoint or Prezi. These programs are ideal when used to help structure the information visually, when data or other information can be presented using charts, graphs, and animation, and as a way to appeal to people with visual learning styles.

Telephone Call or Online Video Conference

A telephone or online video conference call (such as Skype) may also carry considerable weight with people you are trying to persuade, particularly if it would be very difficult for you to make an in-person visit. Online video conferencing is much like being with someone in person, in terms of being able to see and send nonverbal information (intentionally or not). A normal telephone call can also convey much nonverbal information, including the intensity of your beliefs, the degree of confidence you have in yourself, and the depth of your knowledge, but does not convey as much information as a video-enhanced call.

Written (Letters, Faxes, E-Mail, Websites, and Other Documents)

The written document is also a powerful tool for persuaders. Information on paper, such as a letter or fax, often takes on more weight simply because it is connected with a material object. Use your leanest writing style, stating plainly what the situation is and what you would like to see happen in the first or second paragraph. Many busy people find themselves looking for the meat of the document immediately. Help them out by being as clear and concise as possible.

Faxes have perhaps become less used now that e-mail has become almost universally available, but they still have their own advantages. Because a fax is essentially a letter transmitted over a phone line, anything that could be in a letter can be in a fax. The main difficulty with faxes is that you must be able to connect one phone line to another, and fax machine phone lines may frequently be in use.

Despite the ease in sending e-mail, any e-mail that is sent should be as carefully composed as a letter or prepared presentation. E-mail is now frequently read on mobile communication devices such as tablets and smartphones so they can be read nearly anywhere cell phone service is available. Text messages, while short, may be effective in communicating key points.

Websites

Increasingly, web pages are used to provide information and persuasive arguments. Websites can provide these to both internal and external audiences. Staff members can be kept aware of change efforts and their benefits, while outsiders can view an organization's reasons for changing (or not changing) positions and views. Reporters and others in the media may turn to such sites for background.

In the end, the format chosen depends greatly on the way that the target is most easily persuaded. Each format, however, has advantages and disadvantages, and so, if not all are used, the format must be chosen only after careful thought.

This section has covered ways to shape your message so that it is more persuasive. There are also principles that apply to the message's senders themselves.

THE SENDER

No matter how you shape your message, a considerable amount of your ability to be persuasive is dependent on how you are perceived by your audience. This section emphasizes the role of credibility. To be persuasive, you must be believable. Without it, you are not going to persuade anyone. Credibility, however, is a multi-dimensional concept comprising three factors: expertise, trustworthiness, and likeability.

Expertise. Expertise in an area is important to be persuasive but is not enough, by itself. In fact, if your target already has a strong position on an issue or is distracted from paying attention to what you are saying, all the expertise in the world will do no good. If you are an agency leader, you may not need to do much to establish your expertise within your own organization, but you may need to establish your expert status in meetings with external stakeholders.

Trustworthiness. The difference between expertise and trustworthiness is important. Both are vital to being an effective advocate. Whereas expertise indicates that you know what you are talking about, trustworthiness indicates that you are honest and lack bias (Rhoads & Cialdini, 2002). Because of its central role in establishing credibility, leaders must be seen as trustworthy in the eyes of their targets. The best advice for establishing a reputation for trustworthiness is to be trustworthy: Do what you promise, don't promise what you can't or won't do, and admit when you don't know something.

Likeability. The quality of likeability, while perhaps not as important as expertise and trustworthiness, nonetheless has an influence on how persuasive you are. According to Roger Ailes, who has advised U.S. presidents on how to present their messages most successfully,

> If you could master one element of personal communications that is more powerful than anything we've discussed, it is the quality of being likeable. I call it the magic bullet, because if your audience likes you, they'll forgive just about everything else you do wrong. If they don't like you, you can hit every rule right on target and it doesn't matter. (as cited in Mills, 2000, p. 269)

In summary, the most important attribute you must have to be persuasive is credibility. Credibility is composed of several components: expertise, trustworthiness, and likeability. Each of these can be altered to at least some degree and is important to your ability to be persuasive.

THE RECEIVER

The receiver is the last of the four main variables in determining the approach and level of success of any persuasion effort. Successful persuasion requires different approaches to different types of audiences. The bottom line of persuasion is a bit counter-intuitive, however—you, the advocate, don't change the target's mind. The only way targets can be convinced to adopt a view or take an action is if they convince themselves. Your job as a leader is to understand your targets well enough that you assist in this process. The only true way of getting what you want from people is convincing them that it is in their best interest to agree. As Bedell (2000) states, "People will do what you ask only if they believe they'll fulfill their own personal needs by doing so" (p. 22).

SUMMARY

This chapter has covered a great deal of ground. The basics of persuasion have been described, along with implications for their practical use by nonprofit leaders working at all levels. Armed with this knowledge, you can persuade others to work for important organizational goals.

REFERENCES

Bedell, G. (2000). *Three steps to yes: The gentle art of getting your way.* New York: Crown Business.

Booth-Butterfield, S. (1996). *Dual process persuasion.* Retrieved on June 28, 2004, from West Virginia University website: http://www.as.wvu.edu/~sbb/comm221/chapters/dual.htm

Cialdini, R. (2000). *Influence: Science and practice* (4th ed.). Boston: Pearson, Allyn & Bacon.

Hoefer, R. (2001). Highly effective human services interest groups: Seven key practices. *Journal of Community Practice, 9*(2), 1–14.

Hoefer, R. (2012). *Advocacy for social justice* (2nd ed.). Chicago: Lyceum.

Mills, H. (2000). *Artful persuasion: The new psychology of influence.* New York: AMACOM.

Rhoads, K. (1997). What's in a frame? *Working Psychology.* Retrieved from www.workingpsychology.com/whatfram.html

Rhoads, K., & Cialdini, R. (2002). The business of influence: Principles that lead to success in commercial settings. In J. Dillard & M. Pfau (Eds.), *The persuasion handbook* (pp. 513–542). Thousand Oaks, CA: Sage.

Richan, W. (1996). *Lobbying for social change* (2nd ed.). New York: Haworth Press.

Rosenthal, A. (1993). *The third house: Lobbyists and lobbying in the states.* Washington, DC: CQ Press.

Wilson, S. (2002). *Seeking and resisting compliance: Why people say what they do when trying to influence others.* Thousand Oaks, CA: Sage.

HELPFUL TERMS

Call to action—an element of your persuasive measure that identifies the action you want your target to take.

Contextual information—information provided to your target about the validity or source of the substantive information in your persuasive message. Providing contextual information can strengthen your target's acceptance of your substantive information and your persuasive effort. (See also *Substantive information.*)

Credibility—the amount that your target believes what you have to say. Credibility resides in the target, not in you—it is a judgment about you by the target.

Fear appeal—a way to deliver your message that focuses on what negatives will occur should you not do as the persuader suggests.

Framing—the process of getting a particular viewpoint accepted as the "right" way to see a situation.

Intent—a declaration to your targets that you are attempting to persuade them. Usually, declaring your intent is counter-productive but can sometimes be acceptable.

Manner of presentation—Persuaders can choose the way they deliver their information. Elements regarding manner are accuracy, time used, message style, content, and clarity.

Message style—Persuaders should choose a particular message style depending on the way the target is most likely to be influenced. Three different approaches are positive vs. negative, private vs. public, and collaborative vs. confrontational.

Redundancy—A redundant message is one that is similar to, but not exactly the same as, previous persuasive messages. It may have the same call to action, but the words and images used are different.

Repetition—Messages may be repeated in the same way to ensure that the target is aware of the message being sent.

Substantive information—information provided to your target that is directly related to the persuasive message—the facts of your argument. (See also *Contextual information*.)

EXERCISES

1. In-Basket Exercise

Directions

Use the information in this chapter to respond to the following memo.

Memo

Date:	August 8, 20XX
To:	Roberta Danzell, Chief Financial Officer
From:	Beverly Johnson, CEO
Subject:	Community/Business Partners Advisory Council Meeting

As we have discussed, we have a meeting scheduled between ourselves and our community/business partners advisory council at the end of September, in about seven weeks.

One of the major items that I want to place on the agenda for the meeting is to try to bring the advisory council (AC) members to accept an increased expectation that every council member should be willing to donate financially to our organization, conduct fundraising on our behalf, and advocate on our behalf with political leaders to increase government funding to support our clients, if not us directly.

Research indicates that this type of support is extremely advantageous to nonprofits like us and the clients we serve. I have also investigated whether this type and level of commitment is unusual among our set of comparable agencies. My findings are that almost all other organizations have these expectations for their boards of directors, but not advisory councils. Still, given the challenging situation we face financially, I would like to instigate this change, although we first will need board approval. My impression is that the board will not welcome such a change in our rules unless the AC approves it first.

What I would like from you, given your authoritative position as chief financial officer (CFO) is a three- to five-page document outlining a persuasion campaign that we can use to convince the advisory council to enthusiastically adopt this idea at the next AC meeting.

Please include, at a minimum, the following:

a. Frame
b. Message content: Should I present all the results of my research or just the part that supports my idea? Should I appeal to their hopes and dreams for the agency and clients, or should I stress what may happen if we don't raise additional funds?
c. I'd like to hear some ideas on how adopting this new policy is in the AC's best interests
d. Three salient points that are the most powerful talking points I have
e. Anything else you think is important regarding how I can be very persuasive

I don't have to tell you just how important it is for us to bring in additional funding in the next three months. Government grants are drying up, foundations are hurting, and we risk running out of money to pay staff early next year if the situation doesn't turn around quickly.

2. Name That Frame!

Read the following sentences. Which persuasion frame (listed in this chapter or not) is being used in each one?

a. Oh, come on—it'll be fun!
b. We went to the movie you wanted to see last time, so I think it is my turn to choose.
c. If you can't pay me more, I'll have no choice but to find another job.
d. I've done research on this, and the proper course of action is to do as I suggest.
e. You've done a great job on this report! And I agree with all your recommendations except the third one. It's just a small thing I'm asking for, but could we delete that one?
f. Don't you see—if we don't act on this quickly, the best candidates will already be hired by someone else!
g. Haven't you noticed that other nonprofit leaders in town are all attending the Social Venture Partnership Council's meetings? Wouldn't it be a good idea for you to go, too?

Variation: Develop your own statements using one or more elements of persuasion and negotiation to use in class or in a small group. Turn it into a competition, with the person or group having the most correct answers winning a small prize.

3. Persuasion Practice

Working on your own or in a small group, write a short essay to try to persuade your instructor to change some element of the course (be sure it is something that your instructor could actually change) or your supervisor to change something at your job (again, be realistic). Then, imagine it as a one-on-one conversation. How might you change the wording or other elements of the effort between written submission and conversational delivery? (If you are in a classroom, be prepared to present this as a formal address to the class. Have several such presentations, and have everyone in the class vote on the idea that was best presented.)

4. Influencing Your World: What Works and What Doesn't?

Use the ideas presented in this book and in class for a week or two in your internship, job, and personal life. Keep a log, detailing what decisions you tried to influence, the principles you incorporated in your efforts, and what the results were. Reflect in writing or discuss in class what worked, what didn't work as well, what the circumstances were for either outcome, and what you've learned as a result.

ASSIGNMENTS

1. Look at television or radio ads through the prism of what you've read. Choose two advertisements to describe and critique using the concepts in this chapter. What elements of persuasion are being used? What's the frame? What information is presented to persuade you? What emotions are being targeted?

2. Choose a position on an issue of controversy within the field of nonprofit administration (your instructor may assist you in this). Write an essay on what the controversy is and what the two (or more) sides of the controversy are, and end with an explanation of why you believe one position is correct. Do your best to persuade your reader that you have chosen the better position using information from this book and other sources.

3. Choose a position on a controversial issue taking place in society at large. Create a short presentation to support that position. Make a video of yourself delivering this presentation. Post the video where your instructor can watch it (and possibly other students or the general public). Analyze your delivery and presentation, either in a separate video or in a written format.

Advocacy

14

This chapter builds directly on the previous chapter, which dealt with persuasion. Advocacy is a special case of persuasion, in that you are working to negotiate and persuade people in elected or appointed offices, rather than staff within your organization, board members, clients, peers at other organizations, and other important people who are in your environment. Everything covered in Chapter 13 applies directly to advocacy, though we should consider advocacy a process that extends both before and after the persuasion effort.

THE ROLE OF ADVOCACY FOR NONPROFIT ORGANIZATIONS

In an insightful analysis of the role of nonprofit organizations in welfare states, Ralph Kramer (1981) indicated that being change agents "comes close to being a unique organizational competence of the voluntary agency" (p. 231). According to the Commission on Private Philanthropy and Public Needs (1975), also known as the Filer Commission, an ambitious examination of the role of nonprofit organizations in the United States, "the monitoring and influencing of government may be emerging as one of the single most important and effective functions of the private nonprofit sector" (p. 45). These statements from nearly 40 years ago may not have come entirely true, partially because nonprofit managers have not been taught a systematic approach to advocacy that fits in with other skills they have had the opportunities to develop. Yet, advocacy remains an important function of the nonprofit sector. Ruggiano and Taliaferro (2012) support this view, arguing that lobbying is important for nonprofits to gain the resources they need to serve the public good.

In addition to this view of nonprofit organizations being needed to voice important viewpoints, advocacy by individuals is considered an ethical responsibility by some organizations' codes of ethics. The National Association of Social Workers (2008), for example, states this explicitly:

> Social workers should engage in social and political action that seeks to ensure that all people have equal access to the resources, employment, services, and opportunities they require to meet their basic human needs and to develop fully. Social workers should be aware of the impact of the political arena on practice and should advocate for changes in policy and legislation to improve social conditions in order to meet basic human needs and promote social justice. (Section 6.04a)

THE SIX STAGES OF ADVOCACY PRACTICE

Hoefer (2012) defines *advocacy practice* as taking "action in a systematic and purposeful way to defend, represent, or otherwise advance the cause of one or more clients at the individual, group, organizational, or community level in order to promote social justice" (p. 3). He describes the advocacy process as a form of the general problem-solving method used in social work and other professions. Specifically, Hoefer describes six distinct stages in his unified model of advocacy practice. Each will be covered briefly.

Stage 1: Getting involved. The idea of getting involved is simple: Are you going to put some of your life into trying to make a difference in a particular area, or are you not? Large numbers of Americans are not involved in political efforts at all (not even voting), much less a more difficult and time-consuming activity such as political advocacy.

Seven variables are seen as affecting the likelihood that a person will get involved with advocacy (Hoefer, 2012). These are the person's educational level, values, sense of professional responsibility, interest, skills, level of participation in other organizations, and amount of free time. No matter your current level on all of these variables, you can increase them to some extent by consciously shaping your own environment to support growth on each variable.

METHODS NONPROFITS CAN USE TO AFFECT "GETTING INVOLVED" VARIABLES

Education: Get CEUs or other training relating to political advocacy.

Values: Shape organizational norms by hiring people with an activist orientation.

Sense of professional responsibility: Hire professional social workers.

Interest: Expose staff members to results of political decisions on clients.

Skills: Provide advocacy mentors to selected staff members.

Participation in other organizations: Assign staff members to work with coalitions.

Time: Allow flextime to assist staff members to attend meetings.

Stage 2: Understanding the issue. Inexperienced advocates or people new to a specific policy arena often want to move forward quickly without taking the time to understand fully the issue(s) at hand. In particular, there is a temptation to try to understand the issue from only your own side without trying to research and appraise any other approach or perspective. Moving forward without truly understanding the issue from at least two perspectives is a mistake and may doom your advocacy effort from the start.

Hoefer (2012) lists five steps in understanding an issue. First, advocates must define the issue so that they can talk confidently within a particular frame of reference about the impacts of a problem on a particular group of people (see Chapter 13 for the discussion on persuasion frames, such as "it isn't fair" or "after what they've been through, they deserve this"). Without completing this step, there is a danger you will adopt the frame someone else has set forth rather than developing a clear sense of how you view the situation.

The second step is to decide who is affected by the issue, and how. If there is a problem, then the issue is hurting someone or a larger group of people. But it is also vital to understand who is being helped by the current situation—is it helping someone make money, or does it support the current emotional needs of a powerful person or group of people? Is the situation just "tradition" that has not been examined for some time? The third step is to decide what the main causes of the issue are. It may be impossible to determine what the ultimate cause is, but if you can determine what is causing the issue, at least at the proximate (immediate) level, it is far easier to solve the issue.

Fourth, you need to generate solutions to the issue, at least to the immediate problem. It is tempting to take the first plausible solution you come up with, but you should generate (at least) several potential solutions to have a wider variety of choices, some of which may be easier to adopt than others. You can look to other cities, states, and countries for ideas, or generate additional potential solutions on your own through techniques such as brainstorming.

METHODS FOR DEVELOPING ALTERNATIVE SOLUTIONS

Brainstorming: A process of generating ideas without evaluating them right away. Save evaluation until after a set time period for idea generation is completed.

George Costanza approach: Think of how things are done now, and imagine what "doing the opposite" would be. What benefits might ensue from doing things "oppositely"?

Win-win approach: Create an alternative policy that restructures the current situation. A set of prompts and questions can be used to generate ideas.

Source: Hoefer (2012, pp. 73–75).

The fifth step in understanding the issue is to review all of the proposed solutions to estimate their impact on the problem and on social justice more broadly. Each advocacy effort requires a thoughtful decision about which solution or solutions to pursue. The ones you choose may be of different priorities, and you may trade off achieving one for having a better one enacted. Sometimes you may have to accept an easy-to-pass bill when you'd rather have a law that has a greater chance of impacting the problem.

Stage 3: Planning. Just as it is easy to want to try to solve a problem without taking the time to understand it fully, it is also easy to want to jump into action before planning adequately. Hoefer (2012) uses the analogy of using a map of getting from one place to another to planning in advocacy, which is laying out how to get from here (the current state of affairs) to there (a different and better state of affairs). Advocates can use various methods to lay out the steps in their plan, but it is important to relate the actions you take to the outcomes you want to achieve. You need to choose the precise goals and objectives of your advocacy. You also want to select an appropriate target—if you try to change Medicaid funding formulas at the local level, for example, you'll find your concerns can't be addressed at that level—it is a problem for the federal and state governments to address. Before you can advocate with your targets, you need to know who they are. Getting information about legislators and their staff members is not difficult. Elected officials almost all have websites where you can learn what their interests and positions are on issues. You can also discover their contact information such as office address, phone number, and e-mail address.

Your advocacy plan should also include a timeline for action, perhaps tied to other stakeholders' schedules. For example, if you wait until after the legislative session is over to advocate, you may seriously delay achieving the policy change you want. Planning does not take place on its own—all the steps up to now must be completed, and the information must then be used in the planning stage. Good planning takes the information from before it and makes it possible to apply a clear set of feasible steps in the future.

Stage 4: Advocating. This is the stage where you actually contact decision makers. Using your skills in persuading (as discussed in Chapter 13), you make your best efforts to have your target adopt (to the greatest extent possible) the ideas, plans, and positions that you put forward. You have your desire to be involved and you have your plan, based on your understanding of the issue. Advocating is simply the stage to put your plan into action. You may not have considered everything that you could have, and your plan may not be working as well as you thought it would. Then, of course, you may need to adapt your plan to better fit the changing realities before you. It is much better to adjust your advocacy plan and tactics than to abandon your values and goals.

Stage 5: Evaluating. Once your advocacy effort is completed, it is time to take stock of the results you achieved, and the costs that you paid to achieve those results. It is rare when you achieve everything you started out wanting. Other participants in the policy process will want their views adopted, and your persuasion efforts may not have been fully effective. It becomes vital to judge exactly what you achieved compared to what you planned to accomplish—is it close to three-fourths of what you wanted? More like half? Even less than half? This is an important part of your evaluation but not the entire evaluation. (This should sound similar to the material in Chapter 7 relating to outcome evaluation.)

You also need to compare what you did with what you planned to do—were you (or your group) able to meet as often as you desired with key decision makers? Were you able to round up the number of volunteers needed to make calls or write letters? If the answers are no, you'll want to examine the reasons why you weren't able to do so. If the answers are yes, you'll want to document what you did so that you'll also be able to do it again in the next advocacy effort. (In Chapter 7, we covered the idea of fidelity assessment, which is important in advocacy evaluation as well.)

The final element of the evaluation is to link your actions and your achievements. It may be you didn't do as many of your actions as you thought you would need to. If this is so, then you likely didn't achieve as much as you thought you would. But it may be that you did everything you planned to do and still didn't achieve all that you desired. In your evaluation, you'll want to analyze what happened and why you weren't as successful as you thought you would be. What lessons can you develop to improve the results from future advocacy?

Beyond the immediate results of your advocacy effort, you will want to examine the context of the policy debate. It may be you didn't get the exact policy you were working for, but you may be changing the terms of the debate (the frame used to discuss the issue). If you find key actors starting to use the same language you use when describing the problem, the population affected, or the policy options, you are winning many small victories that should be celebrated, remembered, and built on for the next time the issue is raised.

Stage 6: Monitoring. The final stage of advocacy practice is that of ongoing monitoring. You need to pay attention to the way any programs you supported are actually being run. Regulations determine much of what program staff members can do, so you will want to pay attention to the way these are written. You may find that you lose much of the gains you believed you had won if others control the way the rules are written. You also need to attend to the budgeting process to ensure that any new provisions you supported have enough resources to do what they are supposed to do. A program that is not given sufficient funds to run itself will be crippled and ineffective, thus leading to charges in the future that it should be eliminated.

Monitoring by advocates almost always takes place within the executive branch, not the legislative branch. The executive branch operates in significantly different ways than does the legislative, and skilled advocates will need to be aware that this is true. Legislators, for example, are used to being lobbied by constituents and interest groups. This is less true of people working in the executive branch who are selected primarily for their specialist expertise and are not lobbied often in the same way that lawmakers are. Another important difference is that legislators and their staff members are well known to advocates because they have chosen to be in the spotlight. Executive branch employees, however, are much more likely to be fairly anonymous, working far from the public eye. It may be more difficult just to find out who to contact.

RECENT EMPIRICAL RESEARCH

Recent years have brought a number of research studies that provide nonprofit managers with empirical information to be better advocates. The research indicates that policy-relevant information and research results are important when lobbying. Giesler, Parris, Weaver, Hall, and Sullivan (2012) studied how local level policy makers are influenced in their decision making. Decision makers at this level use "social service agency reports, social service agency staff consultation, and other [decision-makers'] opinions" (p. 236). At the state level, in Texas, research was seen as very important to legislators when voting on human service issues (Cochran, Montgomery, & Rubin, 2010). This insight regarding research is strengthened by a study examining conservative think tanks at the national level, even if the "research" is of poor quality and ideologically biased (Miller-Cribbs, Cagle, Natale, & Cummings, 2010).

Two state-level comparative policy studies have very similar results as to what variables shape particular policies. Lee and Donlan (2009) found that Democratic political party control leads to higher expenditures for Medicaid; Hoefer, Black, and Salehin's (2012) results show that Democratic Party control is the primary determinant of strong teen dating violence prevention policy. This indicates that advocates in favor of stronger human service legislation may wish to help ensure that candidates from the Democratic Party are elected. Conversely, people who have another viewpoint may wish to work to elect Republican Party officials.

SUMMARY

While this is only a quick overview of the advocacy process that nonprofit leaders can use, you can see how the steps of this approach fit in well with the general problem-solving approach that emphasizes assessment, planning, intervention, and evaluation of intervention. In addition, you must decide to get involved to begin with and you must keep monitoring the situation to determine if the problem is improving, getting worse, or staying the same once some new proposal is adopted, or if nothing is done. Additional information regarding empirically supported ways to be effective in your advocacy efforts is also presented to provide more specifics for new and experienced advocates. Persuasive techniques (information covered in Chapter 13) need to be recalled as you plan and conduct your advocacy efforts.

REFERENCES

Cochran, G., Montgomery, K., & Rubin, A. (2010). Does evidence-based practice influence state legislators' decision-making process? An exploratory process. *Journal of Policy Practice, 9*(3–4), 263–283.

Commission on Private Philanthropy and Public Needs. (1975). *Giving in America: Toward a stronger voluntary sector.* Washington, DC: Author.

Giesler, F., Parris, A., Weaver, L., Hall, L., & Sullivan, Q. (2012). Sources of information that influence social service public policy decisions. *Journal of Policy Practice, 11*(4), 236–254.

Hoefer, R. (2012). *Advocacy practice for social justice* (2nd ed.). Chicago: Lyceum Press.

Hoefer, R., Black, B., & Salehin, M. (2012). Making the grade: Correlates of dating violence policies. *Journal of Sociology and Social Welfare, 39*(4), 9–24.

Kramer, R. (1981). *Voluntary agencies in the welfare state.* Berkeley: University of California Press.

Lee, J., & Donlan, W. (2009). Cultural, social and political influences on state-level indigent health care policy formation. *Journal of Policy Practice, 8*(2), 129–146.

Miller-Cribbs, J., Cagle, B., Natale, A., & Cummings, Z. (2010). Thinking about think tanks: Strategies for progressive social work. *Journal of Policy Practice, 9*(3–4), 284–307.

National Association of Social Workers. (2008). *Code of ethics.* Washington, DC. Author. Retrieved from http://www.socialworkers.org/pubs/code/default.asp

Ruggiano, N., & Taliaferro, J. D. (2012). Resource dependency and agent theories: A framework for exploring nonprofit leaders' resistance to lobbying. *Journal of Policy Practice, 11*(4), 219–235.

HELPFUL TERMS

Advocacy practice—taking action in a systematic and purposeful way to defend, represent, or otherwise advance the cause of one or more clients at the individual, group, organizational, or community level in order to promote social justice.

Executive branch—The executive branch interprets and implements the laws developed by the legislative branch. This is true at the national, state, and local levels. (See also *Legislative branch*.)

Legislative branch—The legislative branch passes bills that may then be signed into law by the chief executive. These are then interpreted and implemented by the executive branch. This is true at the national and state levels. Local governments also have legislative bodies, although chief executives at that level operate somewhat differently than at the national and state levels. (See also *Executive branch*.)

Proximate cause (of a problem)—the immediate identifiable cause of a current problem. Focusing on the proximate cause can give advocates something to work on, even if it isn't the "true" cause in some philosophical sense. (See also *Ultimate cause*.)

Target—the individual or group that can make the authoritative decision that you desire.

Ultimate cause (of a problem)—the root cause of a current problem that may extend back in time and across political boundaries. It is the "true" cause of the problem but may be intractable and impossible to impact. Focusing on ultimate causes can quickly lead to demoralization. (See also *Proximate cause*.)

EXERCISES

1. In-Basket Exercise

Directions

For this in-basket exercise, personalize your response by finding legislators for your location. Use any human services agency you desire for Question 2c and Question 3. Be as realistic as possible when considering who should be the targets of your advocacy.

Memo

Date: September 6, 20XX

From: Kenyonne Hightower, Chair of Board

To: Samantha Velasquez, Advocacy Volunteer Coordinator

Subject: Beginning Steps for New Advocacy Efforts

It is becoming clear to us on the board that we need to become involved in the realm of educating our legislators about our organization's needs. Unfortunately, we have very little idea about how to begin. This is where your expertise comes in.

    We believe that the first step is to get to know more about our legislators. We would like you to write up the following information:

1. Search for information on the following four people: our U.S. senator, our U.S. house representative, our state senator, and our state house representative.

2. For each of these four elected officials, get this information:

   a. The committees they serve on
   b. Their office location, phone number to speak to an aide, and an e-mail address to communicate with them
   c. Their position on one issue related to our agency's mission

3. Of these four legislators, which one do you think is the one we should start building a relationship with first? Why?

2. What's in a Name?

Discuss with one or two other people what your perceptions of lobbying and advocacy are. Would you want to tell new acquaintances that you are a "lobbyist"? Would it sound better if you indicated your job is to influence elected officials? Why or why not? How would you like talking about your position if it were called "social justice champion"?

3. Social Media and Advocacy

While this chapter doesn't address the ways to use social media in an advocacy campaign, brainstorm with colleagues how you could use Facebook, Twitter, Reddit, Pinterest, or other social media outlets in an advocacy effort.

4. Give It a Try

Search the web for an advocacy organization or interest group that has views you agree with. Look on its website for information about advocacy and how you can be involved in their issue. Select one of their suggestions (don't choose "donate money"!) and tell your colleagues or classmates which one you have chosen to do. Within one week, complete this self-chosen task. Discuss what you did and how you feel about your effort with the colleagues or classmates you declared your intentions to.

ASSIGNMENTS

1. The seven variables related to getting involved with advocacy are the person's educational level, values, sense of professional responsibility, interest, skills, level of participation in other organizations, and amount of free time (Hoefer, 2012). Give yourself a grade from A to F on each variable. Discuss why you think this is so. Create a plan to improve each area where you have a grade of B or less.

2. Choose a human services issue that is of interest to you. Write a one- to two-page letter that you can send to a legislator that presents your ideas on this issue. Review your letter in light of the information on persuasion discussed in an earlier chapter. Send it.

3. Select an existing human services program. Find information on how its budget has changed over the past five years. Relate this to the change in need for the program. Write a short paper (two to three pages) summarizing the information and whether you believe the budget has been adequate or not. If you feel particularly passionate about this topic (or for extra credit, if your instructor agrees), schedule an appointment with an appropriate target to explain why you believe the budget needs to be increased, decreased, or remain the same.

Conclusion

Putting the Pieces Together

In the previous chapters, we have looked at many aspects of human services administration. Figure C.1 replicates Figure 4.1 to remind us of the breadth of topics addressed so far. In Part I, we began by looking at the context of human services and the values and theories that underlie our work in this sector. We further examined the tasks of leadership and the importance of communication skills in Part II. Beginning in Part III, we began to look in more detail at the four quadrants of human service administration functions. In Quadrant 1, we examined functions that are task oriented and internal to the organization. The specific topics covered were planning, evaluation, and budgeting. Quadrant 2 functions

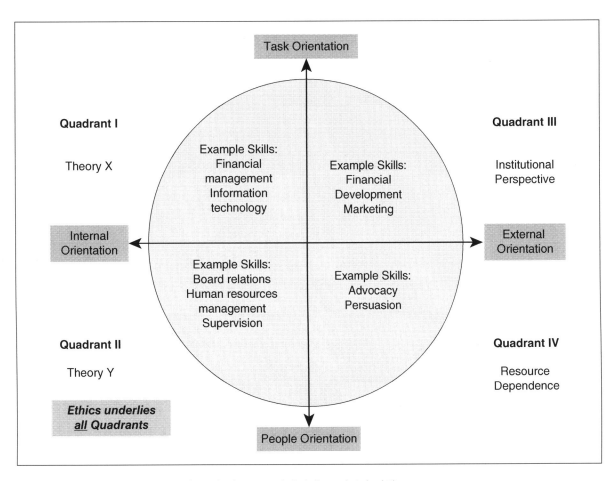

Figure C.1   A 4-Quadrant View of Leadership, Needed Skills and Linked Theory

are those that are internal but more people oriented. In this section, we examined issues of human resources and board relationships. As we moved to more externally oriented tasks, we explored issues of fund development and marketing in Quadrant 3. Finally, in Quadrant 4, we moved to people-oriented and externally focused functions to explore advocacy and persuasion skills. As you look back across the topics covered, you will find that a common denominator in almost all the functions of human services administration is the ability to form and maintain relationships.

BUILDING RELATIONSHIPS

Human service administration is about forming relationships at all levels. Relationships are key dealings with funding sources, regulatory agencies, the general public, boards and commissions, referral sources, staff, clients, and all other stakeholder groups related to the organization. *Relationship* is a term of great historical significance in the social work literature (Johnson & Yanka, 2010) and in other disciplines, as well. While it is often used in relation to the direct service worker/client dyad, it is of equal importance in administrative practice. Perlman (1979) describes relationship as "a catalyst, an enabling dynamism in the support, nurture and freeing of people's energies and motivation toward problem solving" (p. 2). This definition well describes the tasks of human services administrators.

The importance of administrative relationships is documented in a study of 37 companies from 11 parts of the world in which Kanter (1994) found that relationships between companies grow or fail, much like relationships between people. She reports that when relationships between organizations were built on creating new values together, rather than on a mere exchange arrangement, both partners considered their alliance a success. True partners valued the skills that each brings to the relationship. The same can be said for all levels of human service administration. Human services administrators understand intuitively the importance of relationships. Relationships are key to our professional identity.

Hoefer (2009) identified 37 skills, attitudes, and knowledge areas needed for human service administration and then condensed them to four categories: people skills, attitudes and experiences, substantive knowledge, and management skills. People skills were found to be the most important, and management skills were the least important. While it is important for human services administrators to have the management skills necessary to be technically competent administrators, these management competencies are not a substitute for the core values and interpersonal skills. Denhardt (2004) advised public administrators not to define their role or gauge their actions based solely on business values and market-based approaches but, rather, on democratic ideals such as citizenship, community, and participation in decision making.

Human service administrators must find the balance between business- and market-driven approaches and foundational principles such as fairness and social justice. Efficiency and effectiveness are not enough. They must be coupled with principles of participation, trust, fairness, honesty, and reciprocity. Building and maintaining relationships within the organization and in the external environment will be key to your success as a human services administrator.

THE JOY OF ADMINISTRATION

One of the assignments that we give to the students in our nonprofit administration class is for them to go into the community and interview an agency executive director. During a class discussion of the student's interview experience, one of the students made a very interesting comment. She said that she was fascinated when the administrator she was interviewing began to talk about the joys of being a human services administrator. During the next class after the interview, the student said, "You teach us about the challenges and the tasks of administration, but we don't hear about the joys of being an administrator." This comment led to a modification of the assignment and the beginning of a research project to explore the "joys of human service administration." The early results of this exploration with 20 executive director interviews have revealed several themes.

Making a Difference in People's Lives

Without exception, the human services administrators said that the greatest joy of their job was knowing that their agency was making a difference in people's lives. If an administrator has true passion and a heart for the people served by the organization, she will find joy in her work. As you consider where you will expend your time and your energies in your career, be sure that you have passion for the people served and a belief in the mission of the organization.

Mentoring Staff

The second most common source of joy identified by the human services administrators was helping their staff to grow and to advance in their careers. Several talked about people who had been mentors in their lives, and they now found joy in helping others to reach their career and professional goals. As you advance in your career, remember those who have served as your role models and mentors. Remember your responsibility to be a mentor and to help others to meet their professional goals.

Finding Meaning in Work

Some of the administrators had come to the human services field by way of the business world. In their interviews, they talked about the differences in the setting and what that difference meant to them. One said, "At my other job, we were concerned about money. Here we are concerned about helping autistic children learn to speak."

Being an Advocate

Other administrators said they found joy in advocating for their clients who could not advocate for themselves. In most cases, they spoke of being an advocate at the community level and seeing that services were available for their client populations. Many who had come from direct services spoke of feeling they could help more people as an administrator than they could as a direct service provider. Many saw their work in the community of human services as a function of advocating for the people served by their organizations.

You Can See It in Their Eyes

Several students commented that when they asked the question, "What brings you the most joy in your work?" they could see a physical change in the administrator's facial expression. "Their face lit up" or "I could see the passion in their eyes" was a common observation made by the students. Find a position that will be so important and meaningful to you that others can see it in your face when you talk about your work.

SUMMARY

As a human services administrator, you will want to master each of the areas discussed in this book. While the tasks and skills are important to your success, much of your success will be related to your ability of form and maintain relationships with the stakeholders of the organization. You will be the face of the organization in the community you serve. Serving as a human service administrator will, no doubt, bring great challenges, but it can also be a fascinating and rewarding career that will bring you great joy.

REFERENCES

Denhardt, R. B. (2004). *Theories of public organization.* Belmont, CA: Thomson Wadsworth.

Hoefer, R. (2009). Preparing managers for the human services. In R. J. Patti (Ed.), *The handbook of human services management* (pp. 483–501).Thousand Oaks, CA: Sage.

Johnson, L. C., & Yanca, S. J. (2010). *Social work practice: A generalist approach.* Boston: Allyn & Bacon.

Kanter, R. M. (1994). Collaborative advantage: The art of alliances. *Harvard Business Review, 27,* 96–109.

Perlman, H. H. (1979). *Relationship: the heart of helping people.* Chicago: University of Chicago Press.

Index

About the Authors

Larry D. Watson is an assistant professor at the University of Texas at Arlington (UTA) School of Social Work. He publishes and teaches in the area on nonprofit administration and social policy. He is a member of the National Association of Social Workers (NASW), the Council on Social Work Education (CSWE), the Association for Research on Nonprofit and Voluntary Action (ARNOVA), and the International Society for Third Sector Research (ISTR). He is the president of the Texas Chapter of NASW. Prior to joining the faculty of the UTA School of Social Work, he served as the president/CEO of Methodist Mission Home in San Antonio, Texas, and was executive director of Catholic Family Services in Amarillo, Texas. He is a faculty associate of the Center for Advocacy, Nonprofit and Donor Organizations (CAN-DO) at the University of Texas at Arlington School of Social Work.

Richard (Rick) A. Hoefer is the Roy E. Dulak Professor for Community Practice Research at the University of Texas at Arlington, School of Social Work. He has published frequently on nonprofit administration, advocacy, social policy, and program evaluation, and teaches in those areas at the BSW, MSW and PhD levels. He is also the director of the Center for Advocacy, Nonprofit and Donor Organizations (CAN-DO), which assists local nonprofits with consulting on administrative skills development, board relations, strategic planning initiatives, and other aspects of nonprofit organization life. Dr. Hoefer is the founding and continuing editor of the *Journal of Policy Practice*, an award-winning teacher, and recipient of NASW Tarrant County Social Worker of the Year award. He is a member of the National Association of Social Workers (NASW), the Council on Social Work Education (CSWE), the Association for Research on Nonprofit and Voluntary Action (ARNOVA), the International Society for Third Sector Research (ISTR), and the American Evaluation Association (AEA).

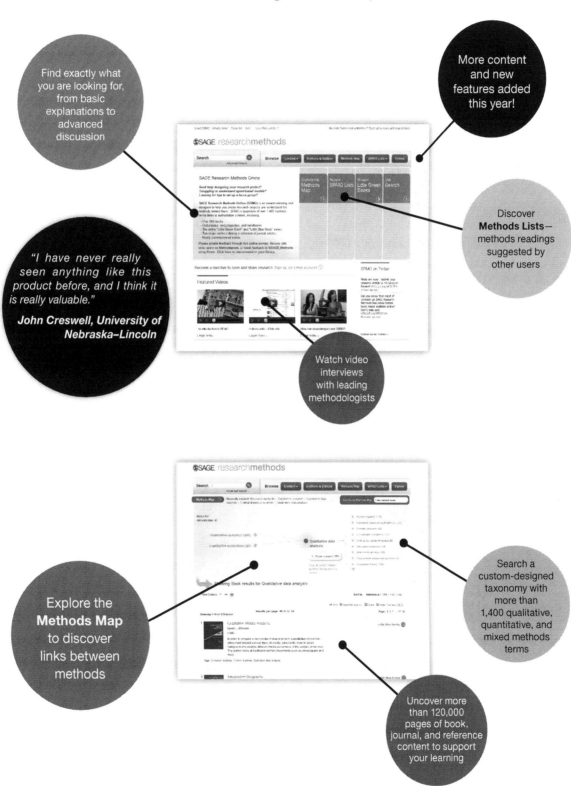